Frommer's®

Melbourne day BY day™

1st Edition

by Lee Mylne

Wiley Publishing Australia Pty Ltd

Contents

Published by:

John Wiley & Sons Australia, Ltd

42 McDougall Street, Milton Qld 4064
Office also in Melbourne

National Library of Australia Cataloguing-in-Publication Data:

Author:	Mylne, Lee.
Title:	Melbourne day by day / Lee Mylne.
ISBN:	978-0-7314-0981-5
Notes:	Includes index.
Subjects:	Melbourne (Vic.)—Guidebooks.
	Melbourne (Vic.)—Description and travel.
	Melbourne (Vic.)—Maps, Tourist.
Dewey Number:	919.451047

Cartographer: Tim Lohnes

Printed in China by Printplus Limited

10 9 8 7 6 5 4 3 2 1

A Note from the Editorial Director

Organising your time. That's what this guide is all about.

Other guides give you long lists of things to see and do and then expect you to fit the pieces together. The Day by Day guides are different. These guides tell you the best of everything, and then they show you how to see it in the smartest, most time-efficient way. Our authors have designed detailed itineraries organised by time, neighbourhood or special interest. And each tour comes with a bulleted map that takes you from stop to stop.

Hoping to wander Melbourne's hidden laneways and arcades in search of the best bars and boutiques? Planning to visit Melbourne's world-class museums and art galleries, or cheer along with the locals at a footy game? Whatever your interest or schedule, the Day by Days give you the smartest routes to follow. Not only do we take you to the top attractions, hotels and restaurants, but we also help you access those special moments that locals get to experience—those 'finds' that turn tourists into travellers.

The Day by Days are also your top choice if you're looking for one complete guide for all your travel needs. The best hotels and restaurants for every budget, the greatest shopping value, the wildest nightlife—it's all here.

Why should you trust our judgment? Because our authors personally visit each place they write about. They're an independent lot who say what they think and would never include places they wouldn't recommend to their best friends. They're also open to suggestions from readers. If you'd like to contact them, please send your comments our way at feedback@frommers.com, and we'll pass them on.

Enjoy your Day by Day guide—the most helpful travel companion you can buy. And have the trip of a lifetime.

Warm regards,

Kelly Regan

Kelly Regan,
Editorial Director
Frommer's Travel Guides

About the Author

Lee Mylne first lived in Melbourne for a couple of years in the early 1980s and although a lot of other places got in the way in the intervening years, found her way back in 2004 and has lived here ever since. She has spent almost all her working life as a journalist and author and has travelled to more than 40 countries. Born and raised in New Zealand, Lee has been a resident of Australia since 1986. She is a co-author of *Frommer's Australia* and *Australia for Dummies*, the author of *Frommer's Portable Australia's Great Barrier Reef* and a contributor to *Frommer's Dream Vacations*. She is also the co-editor and a contributor to the anthology *Best Foot Forward, 30 Years of Australian Travel Writing*, and is a Life Member and past president of the Australian Society of Travel Writers.

Acknowledgements

Many people helped and accompanied me on my discovery and re-discovery of this fantastic city and its surrounds. Thanks in particular to Rosalind Smallwood, Ewen Bell, Melissa Mac Court, Mara Rados, Katarina Smolcic, and Zeljka Pokrajcic for being my companions on dining and bar research; to my mother, Val Pierce, for spending at least some of her holiday helping me check out attractions and restaurants; to Liz Cooper for lacing up her walking shoes and pounding pavements with me; to Betsy Pie for introducing me to the delights of the Macedon Ranges; to Jeremy Vincent for his wide-ranging and invaluable advice on the Melbourne arts scene in general and The Arts Centre in particular; to 'Uncle' Len Tregonning at the Koorie Heritage Trust for his guiding and insights into Aboriginal culture; to Laura Cavallo, Karen Strahan and Anna Hendriksen at Tourism Victoria for their suggestions, advice and general help. Thanks also to Lee Atkinson for always being at the end of the phone, and to Brooke Lyons and Katherine Drew at Wiley for their guidance and patience. Finally, thank you to all those Melbournians over the years who have, for reasons both professional and personal, opened their doors to share ideas, knowledge and observations with me.

An Additional Note

Please be advised that travel information is subject to change at any time—and this is especially true of prices. We therefore suggest that you write or call ahead for confirmation when making your travel plans. The author, editors and publisher cannot be held responsible for the experiences of readers while travelling. Your safety is important to us, however, so we encourage you to stay alert and be aware of your surroundings.

Star Ratings, Icons & Abbreviations

Every hotel, restaurant and attraction listing in this guide has been ranked for quality, value, service, amenities and special features using a **star-rating system**. Hotels, restaurants, attractions, shopping and nightlife are rated on a scale of zero stars (recommended) to three stars (exceptional).

In addition to the star-rating system, we also use a **kids** icon to point out the best bets for families. Within each tour, we recommend cafes, bars or restaurants where you can take a break. Each of these stops appears in a shaded box marked with a coffee-cup-shaped bullet.

The following **abbreviations** are used for credit cards:

AE	American Express	DC	Diners Club
MC	MasterCard	V	Visa

Frommers.com

Now that you have this guidebook to help you plan a great trip, visit our website at **www.frommers.com** for additional travel information on more than 4000 destinations. We update features regularly to give you instant access to the most current trip-planning information available. At Frommers.com, you'll find scoops on the best airfares, accommodation rates and car rental bargains. You can even book your travel online through our reliable travel booking partners. Other popular features include:

- Online updates of our most popular guidebooks
- Vacation sweepstakes and contest giveaways
- Newsletters highlighting the hottest travel trends
- Podcasts, interactive maps and up-to-the-minute events listings
- Opinionated blog entries by Arthur Frommer himself
- Online travel message boards with featured travel discussions.

A Note on Prices

In the Take a Break and Best Bets sections of this book, we have used a system of dollar signs to show a range of costs for one night in a hotel (the price of a double-occupancy room) or the cost of a main meal at a restaurant. Use the following table to decipher the dollar signs:

Cost	Hotels	Restaurants
$	under $150	under $20
$$	$150–$250	$20–$30
$$$	$250–$350	$30–$40
$$$$	$350–$450	$40–$50
$$$$$	over $450	over $50

An Invitation to the Reader

In researching this book, we discovered many wonderful places—hotels, restaurants, shops and more. We're sure you'll find others. Please tell us about them, so we can share the information with your fellow travellers in upcoming editions. If you were disappointed with a recommendation, we'd love to know that, too. Please write to:

Frommer's Melbourne Day by Day, 1st Edition

John Wiley & Sons • 42 McDougall Street • Milton Qld Australia 4064

SBS

16 Favourite **Moments**

16 Favourite **Moments**

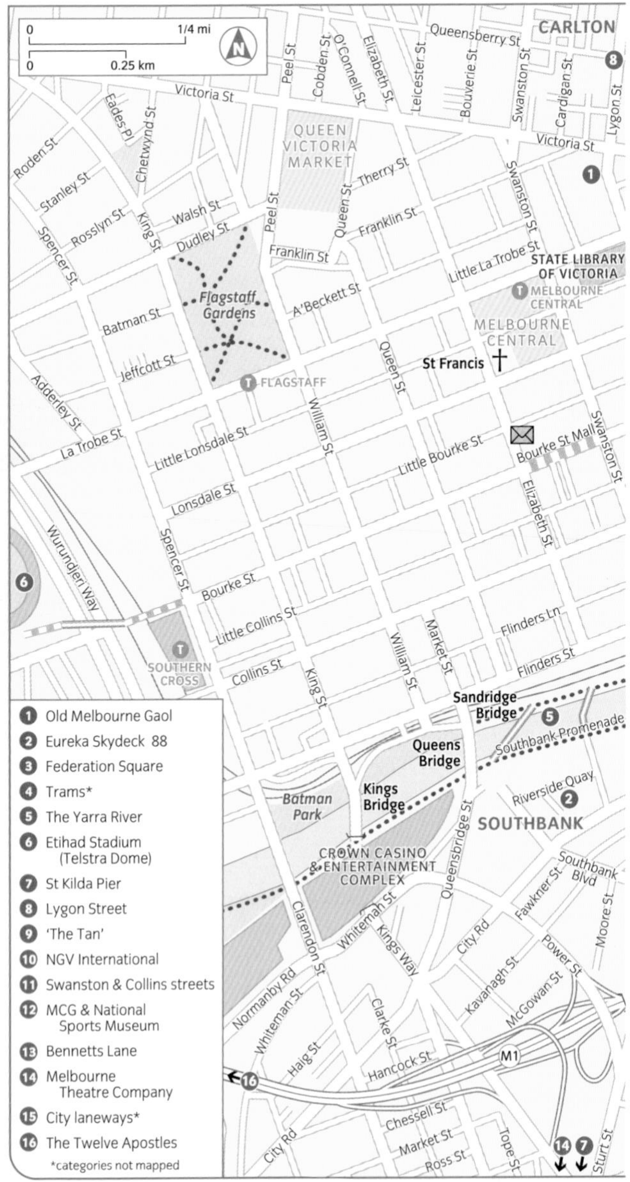

Previous page: Love it or hate it, Fed Square is a talking point.

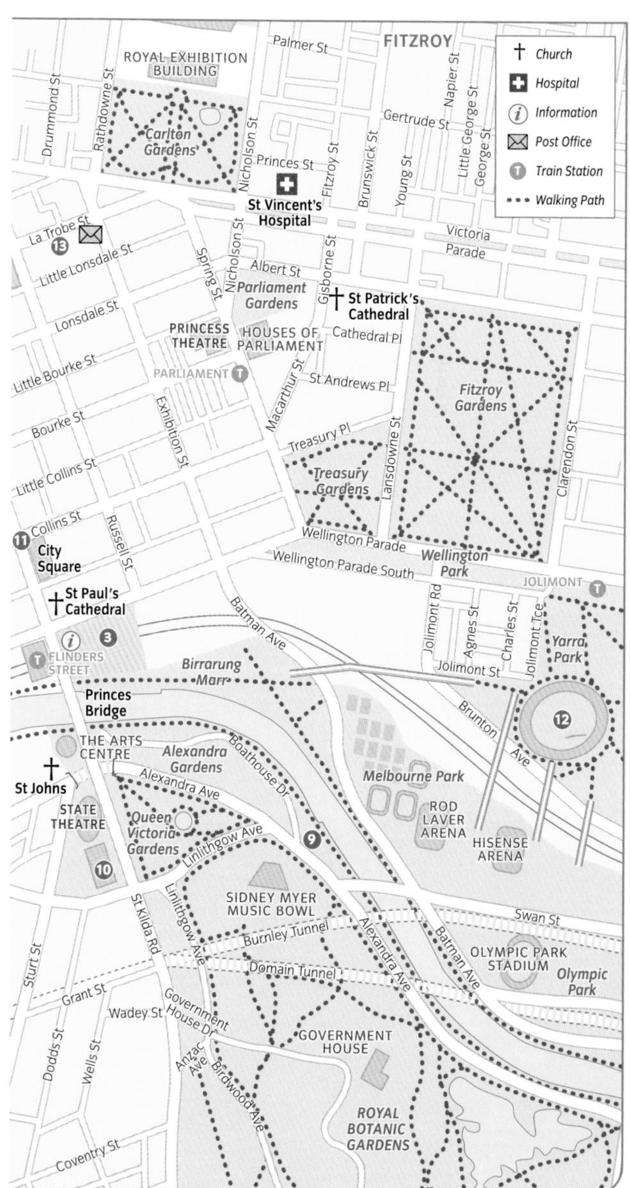

FITZROY
ROYAL EXHIBITION BUILDING
Carlton Gardens
Palmer St
Gertrude St
Princes St
St Vincent's Hospital
Victoria Parade
Albert St
Parliament Gardens
St Patrick's Cathedral
PRINCESS THEATRE
HOUSES OF PARLIAMENT
Cathedral Pl
PARLIAMENT
St Andrews Pl
Fitzroy Gardens
Treasury Pl
Treasury Gardens
Wellington Parade
Wellington Park
Wellington Parade South
JOLIMONT
City Square
St Paul's Cathedral
FLINDERS STREET
Birrarung Marr
Princes Bridge
THE ARTS CENTRE
Alexandra Gardens
St Johns
STATE THEATRE
Queen Victoria Gardens
Melbourne Park
ROD LAVER ARENA
HISENSE ARENA
Yarra Park
SIDNEY MYER MUSIC BOWL
Burnley Tunnel
Domain Tunnel
OLYMPIC PARK STADIUM
Olympic Park
GOVERNMENT HOUSE
ROYAL BOTANIC GARDENS
Church
Hospital
Information
Post Office
Train Station
Walking Path

Melbourne: enigmatic, elegant and invigorating. Once you arrive and absorb its infectious energy, you'll understand why Melbournians love their city with such passion. There's so much to delight in this southern metropolis, whether you're a foodie, a design buff, an art lover, a nightclubber or on a family holiday. Here are some of my favourite things to do.

1 **Experience the Old Melbourne Gaol.** Death masks, a gallows, clanging cell doors…what's not to love about this spookiest of buildings? It's top of my list of places to bring visitors. This is where infamous bushranger Ned Kelly was hanged (one of 135 people over the gaol's working life). Why not get locked up in the former City Watch House next door, or take part in a mock court in the old Magistrates' Court? *See p. 11.*

2 **Step out on the Eureka Skydeck 88.** Got a head for heights? I hope so, because one of the best views in town isn't for scaredy-cats. From 285 m above ground (that's 88 storeys) you get a 360-degree view of the city. If you want to pump a bit more adrenaline, step into The Edge, a huge moving glass cube that will carry you out over the tower's east side, complete with creaks and groans. *See p. 9.*

3 **Space out in Federation Square.** No other piece of Melbourne architecture polarises opinion quite like 'Fed Square': people either love it or hate it. I love it. Wander around for a while to get the full effect of its angles and edges, slopes and stairs. Despite the debate over its aesthetics, it's an effective gathering point, and thousands turn out if there's a big event on. *See p. 10.*

4 **Ride a rattling tram.** Whether it's one of the classic old green rattlers that have been trundling through Melbourne's streets since the 1930s or a slick, advertising-laden new model, a tram is the best way of seeing Melbourne. Rub shoulders with commuters, kids, shoppers and tourists, just as Melbournians have been doing since the 1880s. *See p. 10.*

Get a 360-degree view of Melbourne in the Eureka Skydeck's The Edge.

Don a team scarf and roar with the crowd at the MCG.

5 Stroll the banks of the Yarra. The lower reaches of the Yarra River run through the city to the sea, lined with trees, cafes, buskers and public barbecues. Crisscross a few of the many bridges that link the city and Southbank—my favourite is the Sandridge Bridge, with its 10 enormous steel sculptures, The Travellers, telling the story of Melbourne's cultural diversity. *See p. 9.*

6 Cheer at an AFL game. You may need help to decipher the rules of this uniquely Australian football code, but the atmosphere at the MCG or Etihad Stadium (Telstra Dome) will leave you in no doubt about where the supporters' hearts are. Melbournians are passionate about their footy, so the best plan is to adopt a team quick smart. *See p. 42.*

7 Enjoy the view from St Kilda Pier. Fishermen drop lazy lines over its side, lovers stroll hand-in-hand down it and kids race by. Buy an ice-cream on a hot day or rug up against the wind on a cold one, and walk the length of this historic pier, admiring the kite-surfers and sailboarders skimming across the water. Before you turn around, stop for a drink or a bite at the pier's kiosk, rebuilt exactly as it was before fire destroyed it in 2003. *See p. 49.*

8 Eat pasta on Lygon Street. This stretch of Victorian terraces crammed with restaurants is the birthplace of Melbourne's cafe culture and the heart of its Italian community. Since the 1950s, pizza, pasta and gelato have ruled here. Today, the street may be full of tourists (and sometimes pushy waiters vying for business), but it's still a 'must' for first-time visitors. *See p. 58.*

9 Walk or jog 'The Tan'. Lace up your shoes and hit the track around Melbourne's Royal Botanic Gardens. 'The Tan' is a 3.8km path looping around the perimeter of the gardens, and a popular haunt for joggers, dog-walkers, sports professionals, parents with strollers and anyone who wants to stretch their legs. *See p. 76.*

⑩ **Admire the NGV's stained glass ceiling.** Don't hesitate to join those prone bodies on the floor of the Great Hall at the National Gallery of Victoria (NGV International) on St Kilda Road. Lying flat on your back is the way to get the best view of the wonderful stained-glass ceiling, created by Melbourne artist Leonard French. *See p. 13.*

⑪ **Shop for Australian fashion.** Melbourne is the place to find innovative and distinctly Australian designs. Hit the CBD (Swanston and Collins streets and Flinders Lane) for local designers and some fantastic retro stores in the arcades, or head to Chapel Street in Prahran, the queen of high streets, or to Bridge Road, Richmond, for outlets galore. *See p. 65.*

⑫ **Tour the MCG and National Sports Museum.** All the great names of Australian sport are represented in this new museum inside the Melbourne Cricket Ground. Whether you love cricket, basketball, boxing or golf—or anything else—true fans will be in heaven. You can also tour the MCG itself. *See p. 42.*

⑬ **Listen to jazz at Bennetts Lane.** Great jazz is hard to beat, and great jazz clubs harder to find. But once you slip into Bennetts Lane, tucked down a cobbled backstreet in the CBD, you know the search is over. Often exceptional and always varied, Australia's best jazz club offers a great night out. Get there early if you want a table. *See p. 100.*

⑭ **Catch a play at the MTC.** See some of Australia's finest actors tread the boards in one of the Melbourne Theatre Company's productions. The MTC is one of Australia's oldest, largest and most respected theatre companies, housed in one of its newest, most extraordinary buildings. Whatever your taste in theatre, prepare to be entertained and stimulated. *See p. 111.*

⑮ **Wander the city's laneways.** Getting lost was never so much fun. Melbourne's lanes and arcades seem made for secrets—every new venture into them results in new discoveries. Narrow cobbled alleys and dead-end streets hide graffiti and street art, galleries, small gems of boutiques and quiet cafes and bars perfect for a tryst, as well as those designed for noisy groups. And there's a sense that it just might be different the next time you wander past. *See p. 30.*

⑯ **See the Twelve Apostles.** For this, you have to leave the city... but it's a quintessential part of a visit to Victoria. Stand on a headland, feeling the wind tug at your coat and hair, breathe in the salty sea air and marvel at how the forces of nature have sculpted these sandstone pillars reaching up out of the sea. Only eight of the Twelve Apostles are now left, but they've lost none of their drama. *See p. 146.* ●

Hidden, cafe-lined laneways abound in this coffee-loving city.

1 The Best **Full-Day Tours**

The Best in One Day

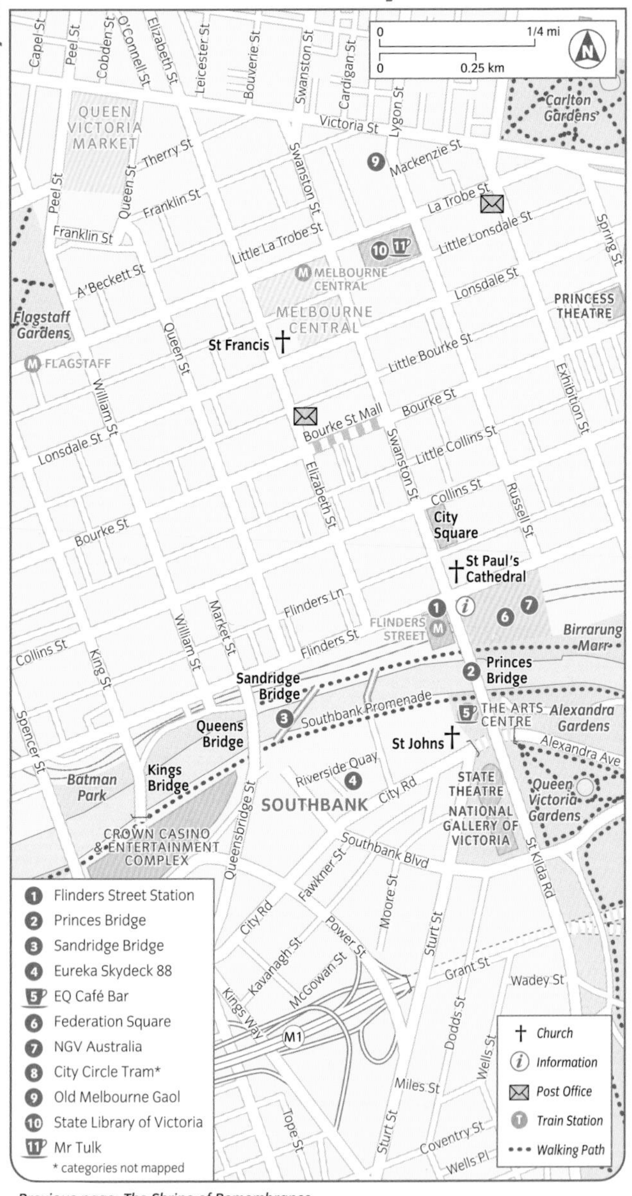

Previous page: The Shrine of Remembrance.

Many of Melbourne's main attractions are within walking distance of each other in the city centre or close by. If you don't want to walk, there are trams rattling by every few minutes, and the burgundy-coloured City Circle tram is free. There's also a free tourist shuttle bus. On your first day, I recommend visiting some of the places that reveal Melbourne's history—plus a new thrill ride just for fun!

START: **Flinders Street Station.**

Melbourne icon Flinders Street Station.

1 ★★ Flinders Street Station. Generations of Melbournians have met loved ones, friends and strangers 'under the clocks' at Flinders Street Station. Built between 1900 and 1910, the station is arguably Melbourne's most famous landmark. *10 min. 201–361 Flinders St. Train: Flinders St.*

2 Princes Bridge. This lovely bluestone bridge, built in 1888 to link bustling St Kilda Road with Swanston Street, gives a great view of the Yarra in both directions. After you've enjoyed the panorama, turn back towards Flinders Street Station to the end of the bridge, take the stairs down to the river bank and turn right along Flinders Walk. *10 min. Train: Flinders St.*

3 ★★★ The Travellers on Sandridge Bridge. Ten 7.5m-high silver sculptures stud this pedestrian bridge, depicting the arrival of Melbourne's migrants and Indigenous people. Spanning the bridge under the sculptures are 128 glass panels in A-to-Z order, telling the stories of the migrants from each country. Sandridge Bridge was built in 1853 for Melbourne's first railway line, and was the route many migrants took when they arrived in the city for the first time. *20 min. Train: Flinders St.*

4 ★★ kids Eureka Skydeck 88. This ear-popping, jaw-dropping observation deck, on the lucky 88th floor of the gold-topped Eureka Tower, offers one of Melbourne's best views. If a 360-degree outlook on the city isn't enough for you, add an extra dimension and enter The Edge, a glass cube that moves from inside to outside the walls of the skydeck, carrying up to 12 passengers for four minutes of between-your-feet views hanging off the tower's east side. Not as scary as it sounds. *45 min. 7 Riverside Qy, Southbank. ☎ (03) 9685 0188. www.eurekatower.com.au. Tickets $17 adults, $9 children 4–16, $39 family of 4. The Edge costs an extra $12 adults, $8 children & $29 families. Daily 10am–10pm (last entry 9.30pm). Train: Flinders St.*

The Smartvisit Card

The See Melbourne & Beyond Smartvisit Card provides unlimited public transport and free entry to many of the city's major attractions, as well as to a range of Victoria's best regional sights such as the Phillip Island Penguin Parade and Ballarat's Sovereign Hill. Cards can be purchased for one, two, three or seven consecutive days, starting from $69 for adults and $49 for children aged four to 15 for one day. A seven-day card costs $205 for adults, $135 for children. Contact ☎ 1300 661 711; www.seemelbournecard.com.

5 **Southbank Promenade.** For such an ideal spot to linger, there's a dearth of truly good outdoor coffee shops along the riverfront between Queensbridge Square and St Kilda Road. The best option is **EQ Café Bar**, overlooking the Yarra. *100 St Kilda Rd. ☎ (03) 9645 0644. $–$$.*

6 ★★ kids **Federation Square.** Controversial for its daring design, 'Fed Square' is a hub for many of Melbourne's attractions. Walk into the square's cobbled heart and the ground seems to fall away from you in all directions. On weekends, this is the spot for events of all kinds—concerts, festivals, exhibitions, charity events ... you never know what you'll find. Pop into the Australian Centre for the Moving Image (p. 109), Champions—Australian Racing Museum & Hall of Fame (p. 38), and the Melbourne Visitor Centre. *Swanston & Flinders sts. ☎ (03) 9645 5188. www.federationsquare.com.au. Train: Flinders St.*

7 ★★★ **The Ian Potter Centre: NGV Australia.** Dedicated purely to Australian art, these 20 galleries come under the umbrella of the National Gallery of Victoria. The centre has the largest collection of Australian art in the country, showcasing works from colonial times through to the present day, as well as Indigenous art. Names to watch out for include Sidney Nolan, Russell Drysdale, Tom Roberts and Aboriginal artist Emily Kngwarray. *1½ hr. Federation Square. ☎ (03) 8620 2222. www.ngv.vic.gov.au. Admission free, except to some special exhibitions. Daily 10am–5pm & until 9pm Thurs. Closed Mon, except public holidays. Free 30 min tours Tues–Fri 10.30am–2pm; Sat & Sun 11am & 2pm. Train: Flinders St.*

8 ★ **City Circle tram.** Jump on the free burgundy-coloured City Circle tram in Flinders Street and do a loop of the city centre. The route runs along Flinders, Spring and La Trobe streets to the

Fed Square's bold design is a talking point.

The ornate ceiling of the State Library's La Trobe Reading Room.

Docklands precinct, which takes around 45 minutes if you don't get off. There's a short commentary on places of interest near each stop, and the driver will announce each stop in advance so you have time to decide whether to jump off. *45 min. Free. Daily, every 12 min 10am–6pm (except Christmas Day & Good Friday). During summer, it runs until 9pm Thurs–Sat.*

9 ★★★ kids **Old Melbourne Gaol Experience.** Top of my list, always! A wander around Melbourne's historic gaol, scene of many hangings and harrowing stories, is great for all ages. Start off at the historic old prison, with its tiny cells and spooky collection of death masks—including one of bushranger Ned Kelly—then move next door for a guided tour and (sometimes confronting) role play at the former City Watch House. On Wednesdays and Sundays at 12.30pm you can also visit the adjacent former Magistrates' Court and take part in a 90-minute re-enactment of a real-life court case: the trial of Elizabeth Scott, the first woman hanged in Victoria. Chilling candlelight tours of the gaol run Monday, Wednesday, Friday and Saturday nights, guided by a 'hangman'. Not for the fainthearted or children under 12. *2–4 hr. Russell St (between La Trobe & Victoria sts). ☎ (03) 9663 7228. www.oldmelbournegaol.com.au. Admission $18 adults, $10 children, $44 families of 6. Daily 9.30am–5pm (except Good Friday & Christmas Day). On Saturdays, free performances of 'The Real Ned Kelly Story—Such a Life' are held at 12.30pm & 2pm. Tickets for candlelight tours $30 adults, $23 children under 15. Tram: City Circle to corner of Russell & La Trobe sts.*

10 ★★ **State Library of Victoria.** Wander the halls of this magnificent 19th-century building for sheer joy in its beauty. Most lovely are the Queen's Hall, the Redmond Barry Reading Room and the domed La Trobe Reading Room. The best perspectives are from the Dome Galleries and a public viewing platform on Level 6. On Level 5, the permanent exhibition 'The Changing Face of Victoria' traces the social and cultural history of the state. *2 hr. 328 Swanston St. ☎ (03) 8664 70004. www.slv.vic.gov.au. Admission free. Mon–Thu 10am–9pm, Fri–Sun 10am–6pm. Train: Melbourne Central.*

11 **Mr Tulk.** Named for the State Library's first chief librarian, Augustus Tulk, this delightful cafe is just the thing for a quick baguette or risotto (or a glass of wine). If you're alone, take a seat at the communal table and browse the newspapers and magazines while you choose from sandwiches, soups and more hearty daily specials. Tulk Junior, down the hallway, also does takeaway. *State Library of Victoria, 328 Swanston Street. ☎ (03) 8660 5700. $.*

The City Circle tram.

The Best in Two Days

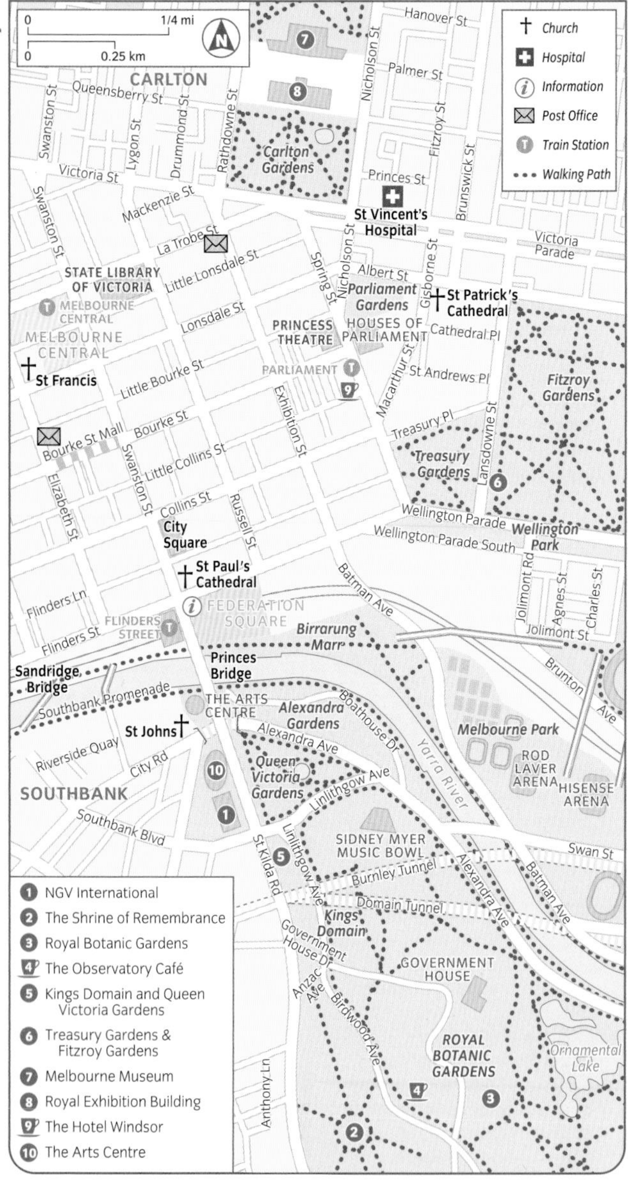

Once you've seen what I think are the not-to-be-missed parts of central Melbourne on your first day, lace up your walking shoes and explore some of Melbourne's wonderful parks, gardens and heritage buildings. START: **Flinders Street Station, then walk across Princes Bridge and along St Kilda Road.**

1 ★★ NGV International. Now you've visited the NGV Australia collection, it's time to cross the road and check out the international big names of art. Here you'll find works by Gainsborough, Constable, van Dyck, El Greco, Monet, Manet, Magritte, Rembrandt and more. Wander through four levels, discovering European, Asian, Oceanic and American art; the collection holds more than 70 000 works, including sculpture, ceramics, photography, costume and design pieces. The building, too, is a masterpiece, with high ceilings, fabulous lighting and great open spaces. *2 hr. 180 St Kilda Rd. ☎ (03) 8620 2222. www.ngv.vic.gov.au. Admission free to general collection; fees for some temporary exhibitions. Wed–Mon 10am–5pm. Closed Tues, Good Friday, Dec 25, & until 1pm on Apr 25. Tram: 1, 3, 5, 6, 8, 16, 22, 25, 64, 67 or 72 from Swanston St. Train: Flinders St.*

2 ★★ The Shrine of Remembrance. A memorial to the servicemen and women lost in Australia's wars, the Shrine is designed so that at 11am on Remembrance Day (November 11), a beam of sunlight hits the Stone of Remembrance in the Inner Shrine. This event is recreated, using an artificial beam of light, every day for visitors. An eternal flame burns in the forecourt of the Shrine. Guided tours run at 11am and 2pm daily, leaving from the visitor centre, and services of Remembrance are held

An exhibition at the NGV International.

The Royal Botanic Gardens' Children's Garden is a favourite with youngsters.

every half hour from 10.30am in the sanctuary. This is a place which is often emotional for Australians to visit, and it's not uncommon for tears to flow. It's also the setting for annual Anzac Day services on April 25 in remembrance of those who served and died in war. Huge crowds turn out for dawn and morning services on Anzac Day. From time to time during the year you might also chance upon smaller commemorative services and wreath-laying ceremonies to mark particular battles or losses. The Shrine Reserve covers 13ha, and has many memorials. Among the most famous is The Man with the Donkey, showing a medic transporting a wounded soldier to the casualty hospital. The most recent addition to the reserve is a statue entitled 'Cobbers', unveiled in 2008, in the Southern Shrine Reserve, which commemorates the battle of Fromelles. The cast of the original is located in France and has been reproduced for the Shrine Reserve. The Visitor Centre has two rooms which host changing exhibitions. 🕘 *30 min. Birdwood Ave, South Yarra.* ☎ *(03) 9661 8100. www.shrine.org.au. Admission free. Daily 10am–5pm (except Christmas Day & Good Friday). Tram: 3, 5, 6, 8, 16, 22, 25, 64, 67, or 72 from St Kilda Rd.*

3 ★★ Royal Botanic Gardens. From the Shrine, you can see the Observatory buildings at the 40-ha Royal Botanic Gardens. These are among the best gardens in Australia, home to about 12 000 plant species from all over the world, and well worth a few hours of wandering. Don't miss the oldest part of the garden, the Tennyson Lawn, with its 120-year-old English elms. Other special corners include the Fern Gully, camellia gardens featuring over 600 varieties of these beautiful shrubs, the Australian Forest Walk, the Children's Garden and the Ornamental Lake. You're also likely to find an interesting array of birdlife. To explore the Indigenous history and spiritual links with this part of Melbourne, take a guided Aboriginal Heritage Walk through the gardens. The gardens also has a gift shop, which is worth exploring for great botanical and Australiana souvenirs, and two cafes when you need to rest. 🕘 *2–4 hr. Birdwood Ave, South Yarra.* ☎ *(03) 9252 2429. www.rbg.vic.gov.au. Admission free. Daily from 7.30am, closing at 8.30pm Nov–Mar, 6pm Apr & Sept–Oct; 5.30pm May–Aug. Tropical Display Glasshouse open daily 10am–4pm. Tram: 1, 3, 5, 6, 8, 16, 22, 25, 64, 67, or 72 from Swanston St.*

4 The Observatory Café. Snacks and sandwiches, cakes and coffee are all served in this open, glass-fronted cafe which also has seating under umbrellas outside. Great for kids and the sparrows love it too! *Birdwood Ave (cnr Observatory Drive). ☎ (03) 9650 9600. $–$$*

5 Kings Domain and Queen Victoria Gardens. Stroll back into the CBD via these two pleasant gardens. In the King's Domain, take a look at Victoria's first Government House, Latrobe's Cottage, built in England and transported to Australia brick by brick in 1836. Look out for the Pioneer Women's Memorial Garden and the Stapley Pavilion. The King's Domain is also home to the Sidney Myer Music Bowl, an amphitheatre used for concerts and other events. The fern gully, with steps leading down to a small pool, is also a popular feature of these gardens. Nearer Further towards the city, a statue of Queen Victoria surveys the gardens that bear her name. The gardens were named and the memorial erected after Victoria's death in 1901. Other historic and contemporary sculptures and memorials are scattered around the gardens, and include a statue of Australian war hero Sir Edward 'Weary' Dunlop. But the most famous of its features is the floral clock that faces the NGV International on St Kilda Rd. *1 hr. St Kilda Rd & Linlithgow Ave. Tram: 1, 3, 5, 6, 8, 16, 22, 25, 64, 67, or 72 from Swanston St. Train: Flinders St.*

6 ★★ kids Treasury Gardens and Fitzroy Gardens. On the southeast corner of the city, these two gardens are home to tributes to two men from very different worlds and different times. In Fitzroy Gardens is Cook's Cottage, built by the parents of explorer Captain James Cook and moved to Melbourne from England in 1934, and the intriguing Fairies Tree, carved by Melbourne sculptor Ola Cohn in the 1930s and still a source of interest for young and old visitors. In the neighbouring Treasury Gardens, look for the small memorial to former US president John F Kennedy

The floral clock in Queen Victoria Gardens.

Melbourne City Tourist Shuttle

The free Melbourne City Tourist Shuttle stops at the major places of interest around the city, including the Melbourne Museum, the Arts Centre, the Royal Botanic Gardens and the Shrine of Remembrance (and all the attractions in this chapter). The shuttle runs every 15–20 minutes between 10am and 4pm daily, and the complete trip takes around 50 minutes. There's a helpful commentary, and you can hop on and off at any of the 15 stops. Pick up a map of the route from the Visitor Centre in Federation Square to help you plan, as the bus only runs in one direction. The easiest stops to pick it up from are The Arts Centre or Federation Square, and the bus then runs up Exhibition Street (good for Chinatown) and then to the Melbourne Museum and Carlton Gardens before heading down Lygon St. You can hop on or off at the University of Melbourne or Queen Victoria Markets, or continue on along William Street, close to many attractions, and on to Southbank, the casino and the Eureka Skydeck. Later stops include Melbourne's sports and entertainment precinct, the Shrine and the Royal Botanic Gardens.

beside the lake in the centre of the gardens. The larger of the two gardens—Fitzroy—is a popular spot for picnics, impromptu games of football, or just wandering—and there's plenty of room for all pastimes! ⌚ *1 hr. Wellington Parade.*

High tea at The Hotel Windsor is an occasion to be savoured.

☎ *(03) 9419 4677 (Cook's Cottage). Admission free to gardens; $4.50 adults, $2.20 children 5–15, $12 for a family for Cook's Cottage. Daily 9am–5pm. Tram: 75 from Flinders St.*

7 ★★ kids **Melbourne Museum.** This is Australia's largest museum, and one of its most interesting. Among the highlights are a blue whale's skeleton, an indoor rainforest, a brilliant insect collection with lots of live exhibits—including cockroaches, ant colonies, and huge spiders—and Bunjilaka, the award-winning Aboriginal and Torres Strait Islander Centre. And don't miss the Melbourne Gallery, home to the taxidermied remains of Australia's most famous and best-loved racehorse, Phar Lap. ⌚ *2 hr. 11 Nicholson St, Carlton.* ☎ *131 102. www.museumvictoria.com.au. Admission $6 adults, free for children under 16. Daily 10am–5pm. Closed Good Friday & Christmas Day. Tram: 86, 96 or City Circle.*

8 ★★★ **Royal Exhibition Building.** Next door to the museum is this spectacular monument, which was given top billing when it became—together with its Carlton Gardens surroundings—Australia's first UNESCO World Heritage–listed building. Built in 1878 for the Melbourne International Exhibition of 1880–81, this was once the largest building in Australia and the tallest in the city. The only way to view its beautifully restored interior is on the guided tour that leaves from the Melbourne Museum at 2pm every day—unless, of course, there's an exhibition on! Your guide will fill in the human stories of the many uses the building has been put to, including as a wartime barracks for servicemen. You can wander the expansive galleries under the soaring dome and marvel at the frescoed ceilings. *1 hr. Nicholson St, Carlton. ☎ 131 102. www.museum.vic.gov.au/reb. Tours daily 2pm. Admission $5. Tram: 86, 96 or City Circle. Train: Parliament.*

9 ★★★ **The Hotel Windsor.** High Tea has been served at The Windsor, Australia's only surviving 'grand' hotel, every afternoon for more than a century. Indulge in a little tradition and some scrumptious cakes, finger sandwiches and other elegant fare. Expensive, but a wonderful experience. *103 Spring St. ☎ 1800 033 100. $$$$–$$$$$.*

10 ★★ **The Arts Centre.** End your day with a night out at a show at Melbourne's premiere arts venue. There'll be a performance or concert to suit most tastes in one of the venues collected under the floodlit spire of this unusual building. Set for a multimillion-dollar staged revamp, starting in 2010, the Arts Centre houses several theatres and is the place you'll find ballet, opera, theatre, concerts and musicals. *100 St Kilda Rd. ☎ (03) 9281 8000. www.theartscentre.com.au Ticket prices vary. Train: Flinders St.*

The colourful exterior of Melbourne Museum.

The Best in Three Days

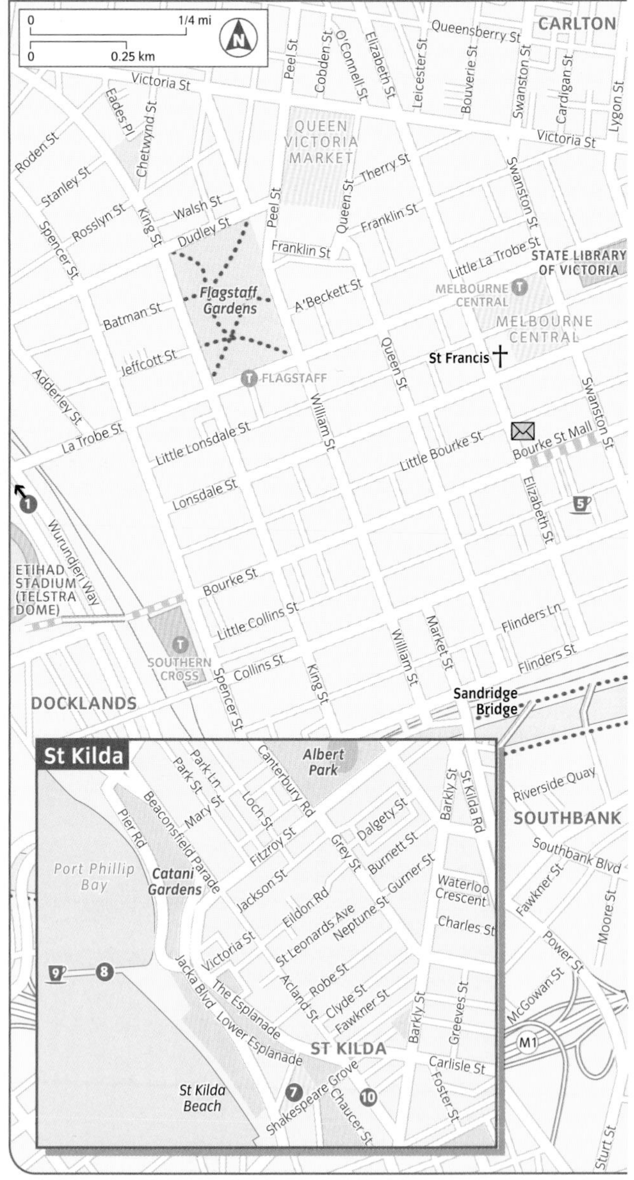

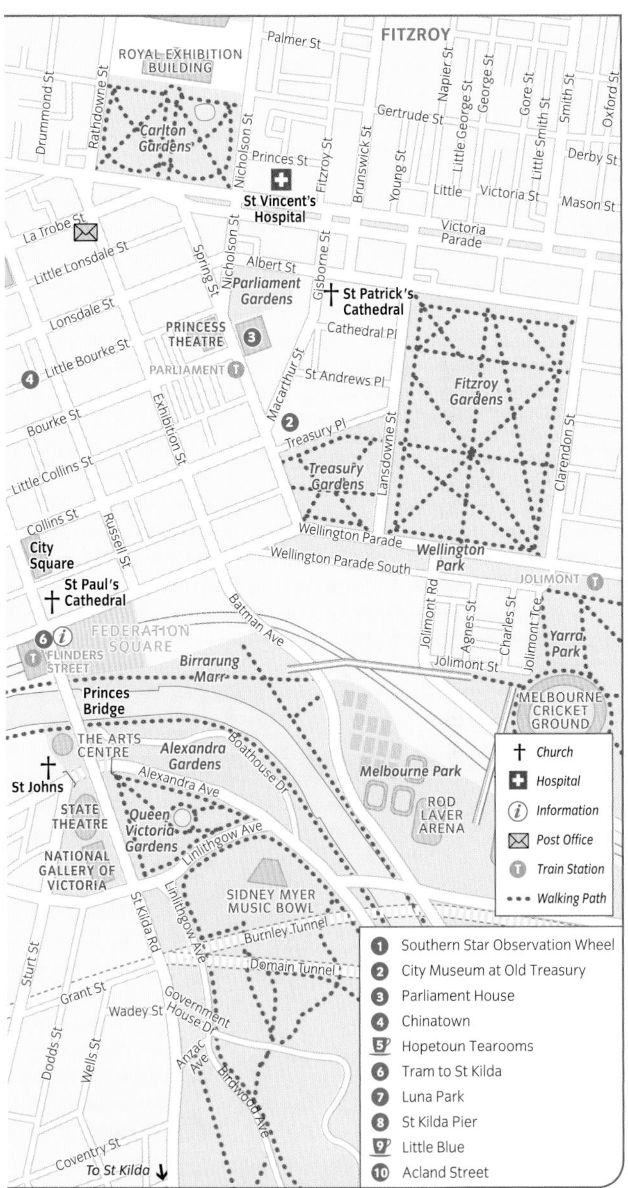
FITZROY
ROYAL EXHIBITION BUILDING
Carlton Gardens
St Vincent's Hospital
Parliament Gardens
PRINCESS THEATRE
PARLIAMENT
St Patrick's Cathedral
Fitzroy Gardens
Treasury Gardens
Wellington Park
JOLIMONT
Yarra Park
City Square
St Paul's Cathedral
FEDERATION SQUARE
FLINDERS STREET
Birrarung Marr
Princes Bridge
THE ARTS CENTRE
Alexandra Gardens
St Johns
STATE THEATRE
Queen Victoria Gardens
NATIONAL GALLERY OF VICTORIA
SIDNEY MYER MUSIC BOWL
Melbourne Park
ROD LAVER ARENA
MELBOURNE CRICKET GROUND
To St Kilda
Church
Hospital
Information
Post Office
Train Station
Walking Path
1 Southern Star Observation Wheel
2 City Museum at Old Treasury
3 Parliament House
4 Chinatown
5 Hopetoun Tearooms
6 Tram to St Kilda
7 Luna Park
8 St Kilda Pier
9 Little Blue
10 Acland Street

Start the day with a bird's-eye view of the city from one of Melbourne's newest attractions, then check out a few more sights, including vibrant Chinatown, before venturing to the seaside suburb of St Kilda for a more laid-back version of city life. Historic and hip, St Kilda has a shabby-chic appeal befitting what was once Melbourne's prime red-light district.

1 Southern Star Observation Wheel. This giant ferris wheel offers views over Port Phillip Bay and across the city, with spectacular light shows at night. Cocooned in a glass cabin at the top arc of Australia's first and only observation wheel, you're 120m (about 40 storeys) off the ground. Unlike traditional wheels, the Southern Star doesn't stop, and you step aboard while the slowly moving cabins are in motion. Hire a private cabin if you wish. Rides last 30 minutes. *30 min. Waterfront City, Docklands Dr. (03) 8688 9688. www.thesouthernstar.com.au. Tickets $29 adults, $17 children. Daily 10am–10pm. Tram: 48, 86.*

2 ★ City Museum at Old Treasury. Built in 1857 at the height of the Victorian gold rush, the imposing sandstone edifice that is the Old Treasury Building now tells the story of Melbourne. There are permanent exhibits and a variety of changing ones. 'Making Melbourne' tells the city's history, while 'Built on Gold' shows how Melbourne was built using the profits from the gold rushes. In the basement are the restored quarters of a caretaker who lived there from 1916 to 1928. *1 hr. Old Treasury Building, Spring St (at Collins St). (03) 9651 2233. Admission $8.50 adults, $5 children, $18 families. Mon–Fri 9am–5pm, weekends & public holidays 10am–4pm. Tram: City Circle. Train: Parliament.*

3 ★ Parliament House. For a glimpse inside the running of Victoria's State Parliament, sit in the public gallery or take a guided tour. Built in 1856, Parliament House

See Melbourne from above on the Southern Star Observation Wheel.

Enjoy a cup of tea in the ornate Hopetoun Tearooms.

Victoria was used as the seat of the national parliament during the time of Australian Federation (1900–27). When Parliament is in session—between March and July, and August and November, generally on Tuesday afternoon and all day Wednesday and Thursday—you can watch the action from the public gallery. At non-sitting times, both the opulent Upper House and the less ornate Lower House chambers are open to the public. Ring ahead to check sitting times, as they vary, and to book tours. 🕘 ***30 min. Spring St.*** ☎ ***(03) 9651 8568 or (03) 9651 8569. www.parliament.vic.gov.au. Mon–Fri 9am–5pm. Free guided tours Mon–Fri 10 & 11am, noon, & 2, 3, and 3.45pm when Parliament is not in session. Tram: City Circle. Train: Parliament.***

4 ★ **Chinatown.** Since the heady gold-rush days of the 19th century, Chinatown has been a meeting place for Melbourne's Chinese community. The alleys and lanes are filled with the aromas of Asian dishes, and the shops are crammed with everything from paper lanterns to herbal remedies, chinoiserie and peking duck. Unless you're after yum cha (dim sum), the best time to head here is at night, when the decorative streetlights are ablaze and the bustle is at its height. Chinatown hosts many traditional festivals throughout the year, including Chinese New Year, and there's also a Chinese Museum (see p. 37). ***Little Bourke St (between Swanston & Spring sts).***

5 **Hopetoun Tearooms.** They've been pouring tea (and latterly coffee) in this old-fashioned tearoom since 1892. The chunky cups are a bit disappointing in such genteel surroundings, but the cakes are always good. ***Block Arcade, 280–282 Collins St.*** ☎ ***(03) 9650 2777. $.***

6 Tram to St Kilda. Take tram 16 from Swanston St to St Kilda Beach. The tram ride will take you down St Kilda Road, a wide boulevard lined with trees and flanked by some of Melbourne's most expensive real estate—gleaming office towers, luxury apartments, wealthy schools—and of course the major parks and monuments you've have already visited, such as the Domain Parklands and the Shrine of Remembrance. The tram turns into St Kilda's Fitzroy Street and continues until you can see the waters of Port Phillip Bay. Get off the tram at Luna Park.

7 kids Luna Park. Pose for a photo in front of the yawning mouth and ancient wooden rollercoaster that symbolise Melbourne's oldest fun park. Kids will enjoy this tiny, ageing park (built in 1912), but for adults, this is only about nostalgia. I recommend a ride on the gorgeous restored carousel. *30 min. 18 Cavell St (Lower Esplanade). ☎ (03) 9525 5033. www.lunapark.com.au. Admission free. Unlimited ride tickets $36 adults, $26 children 4–12, $13 children 3 and under, $109 family of 4. Daily during Victorian school & public holidays, & weekends only May–Sept, 11am–6pm; Sept–Apr, Fri 7pm–11pm, Sat 11am–11pm, Sun 11am–6pm; Victorian school & public holidays Mon–Thurs & Sun 11am-6 pm, Fri–Sat 11am–11 pm. Extended hours apply over Dec–Jan. Closed Christmas Day.*

8 ★★ St Kilda Pier. Whatever the weather, a walk along this historic pier is worthwhile for the wonderful views of Port Phillip Bay, the city and—on the return—to St Kilda Beach. *30 min.*

9 ★ Little Blue. Named for the penguin colony that lives at the breakwater behind it, this smart restaurant is tucked behind the kiosk (another option for coffee or a snack) at the end of St Kilda pier. *St Kilda Pier, Pier Rd. ☎ (03) 9525 5545. $–$$.*

10 ★ Acland Street. A mixed bag of cafes, restaurants, boutiques and housewares, Acland Street is most famous for its European cake shops (see p. 50) and slightly down-at-heel reputation. It's a great spot for people-watching. *30 min.* ●

St Kilda Pier is a lovely place to stroll.

2 The Best Special-Interest Tours

Aboriginal Melbourne

Previous page: Pellegrini's Espresso Bar has been serving coffee since 1954.

The Kulin Nation, made up of five Aboriginal language groups, were the original inhabitants of the land that is now Melbourne. Among the best ways to discover more about Melbourne's Indigenous people is through the Koorie Heritage Trust. Art also offers important insights into Aboriginal culture and the 'Dreaming'.

❶ ★★ **The Koorie Heritage Trust Cultural Centre.** Much of the work that makes this such an important place goes on behind the scenes, in the form of educational programs and cultural services for the Indigenous community. For casual visitors, the main attractions are the two ground-floor gallery spaces for Koorie art and the interesting historical exhibition upstairs. The Trust is charged with preserving and promoting the living culture of south-eastern Australia's Indigenous people and fostering reconciliation, and has a vast collection of artefacts, a research library of rare books and documents, and an oral history unit. Three walking tours run daily, taking around 2 to 2½ hours, and all include time at the cultural centre. Bookings are essential. ◷ *1 hr. 295 King St.* ☎ *(03) 8622 2600. www.koorieheritagetrust.com. Free admission, guided tours $50–$60 adults, $30–$50 children 4–16. Daily 10am–4pm. Train: Flagstaff. Tram: City Circle.*

❷ **Koorie Connections—Altair.** It may look unprepossessing, but if you buy something at this small shop in the Queen Victoria Market you can be sure you're getting the real thing and your money will be supporting Indigenous artists. 'Altair' is an Aboriginal word meaning 'the beginning': owner Julie Peers was the first Aboriginal woman to trade in Melbourne. Her gallery has given many artists a start, providing recognition and respect for their talents. ◷ *15 min. Queen Victoria Specialty Shops, 155 Victoria St.* ☎ *(03) 9326 9824. Daily except Mon and Wed, 9am–4pm. Train: Flagstaff.*

❸ ★★★ **Bunjilaka.** The Melbourne Museum's Aboriginal Centre, Bunjilaka (it means 'creation place'), is thought-provoking and moving. Listen to the voices of Indigenous people telling what has been termed the 'shadow story' of official white Australian history, in the Koori Voices exhibition. As well as a large and significant collection of Aboriginal cultural heritage items, Bunjilaka has a garden of indigenous plants. Try to plan your visit to coincide with a performance of Aboriginal dance—check the website for details. *www.museumvictoria.com.au/bunjilaka.* *See p. 16, bullet* ❼.

Enjoy an Aboriginal dance performance at Bunjilaka.

❹ **Aboriginal Galleries of Australia.** The walls of this commercial gallery are lined with the dots and designs of colourful canvases based on important cultural stories, along with sculpture by contemporary artists from the central desert, including big names such as Emily Kame Kngwarray and Clifford Possum Tjapaltjarri. There's also a good collection of books on Aboriginal art and culture for sale. ⏱ *30 min. 35 Spring St (cnr Flinders Ln). ☎ (03) 9654 2516. Admission free. Mon–Sat 10am–6pm. Train: Parliament. Tram: City Circle.*

❺ **Gallery Gabrielle Pizzi.** One of Melbourne's most respected dealers in Aboriginal art, this gallery (run by the late Gabrielle's daughter, Samantha) represents the work of artists from the communities of Balgo Hills, Papunya, Utopia, Maningrida, Haasts Bluff and the Tiwi Islands, as well as showcasing urban Indigenous artists producing photography, video, paintings and installations. Prices range from $1000 to around $40 000. ⏱ *15 min. Level 3, 75–77 Flinders Ln. ☎ (03) 9654 2944. www.gabriellepizzi.com.au. Tues–Fri 10am–5.30pm, Sat 11am–5pm. Train: Flinders St.*

❻ **Flinders Lane Gallery.** Three major exhibitions of work by Aboriginal artists working at Utopia, Spinifex and Papunya are held at this commercial gallery each year. This was the first Melbourne gallery to show the colourful work of Utopia artist Minnie Pwerle, and has worked closely with Aboriginal artists and communities for nearly two decades. ⏱ *30 min. 137 Flinders Ln. ☎ (03) 9654 3332. www.flg.com.au. Tues–Fri 11am–6pm, Sat 11am–4pm. Tram: City Circle. Train: Flinders St.*

7 ★★ **Tjanabi.** Using ingredients that Indigenous Australians have been eating for thousands of years, Aboriginal elder Carolyn Briggs's restaurant, Tjanabi, offers contemporary fine-dining dishes with a bush-tucker twist. Native plants, fruits and berries are matched with Australian game like kangaroo, wild boar and barramundi, with steaks from regional Victoria also on the menu. A tasting plate provides great samples of the fare, or splash out on a six-course degustation dinner with matching wines. To complete the experience, the walls are hung with contemporary Aboriginal art and the soundtrack is likely to be Australian music. *Federation Sq. ☎ (03) 9662 2155. www.tjanabi.com.au. Daily 11am–11pm. $–$$$$$.*

Gallery Gabrielle Pizzi is one of Melbourne's most respected dealers in Aboriginal art.

Scar: A Stolen Vision *brings indigenous art outdoors.*

8 ★★★ The Ian Potter Centre: NGV Australia. The ground-floor galleries at the Ian Potter Centre feature works by such prominent Indigenous artists as Barak, Judy Watson, Emily Kame Kngwarray and Uta Uta Tjangala, in a changing display picked from the NGV's huge collection. Free guided tours with an Indigenous focus run at 1.30pm Tuesday to Friday. *30 min.* *See p. 10, bullet 7.*

9 ★★ Aboriginal Heritage Walk. Follow an Aboriginal guide through the ancestral lands of the local Boonerwrung and Woiwurrung (Wurundjeri) people, which are now part of the Royal Botanic Gardens, and make a spiritual connection with the land. You'll close your eyes and listen to the wind, put your arms around a tree and your cheek against its trunk, learn how to catch a duck (in theory), drink lemon myrtle tea, and gain an insight into Aboriginal culture and beliefs. The guide will explain how indigenous plants are used as food and medicine, let you handle traditional tools and share stories of his or her life. *90 min. Visitor Centre, Royal Botanic Gardens, Birdwood Ave. ☎ (03) 9252 2429. Most Thursdays & Fridays & some Sundays (days vary). Walk $18 adults, $9 children 6–17, $50 families of 5. Bookings essential.*

10 *Scar: A Stolen Vision.* Thirty colourful carved pier posts, decorated by Indigenous artists using ancient shield and canoe-making techniques, form this outdoor sculpture along the north bank of the Yarra River. The poles speak of the consequences of colonisation for Victoria's Aboriginal communities, and represent different aspects of their life, history and mythology. *15 min. Enterprize Park, Flinders St.*

Melbourne for Art Lovers

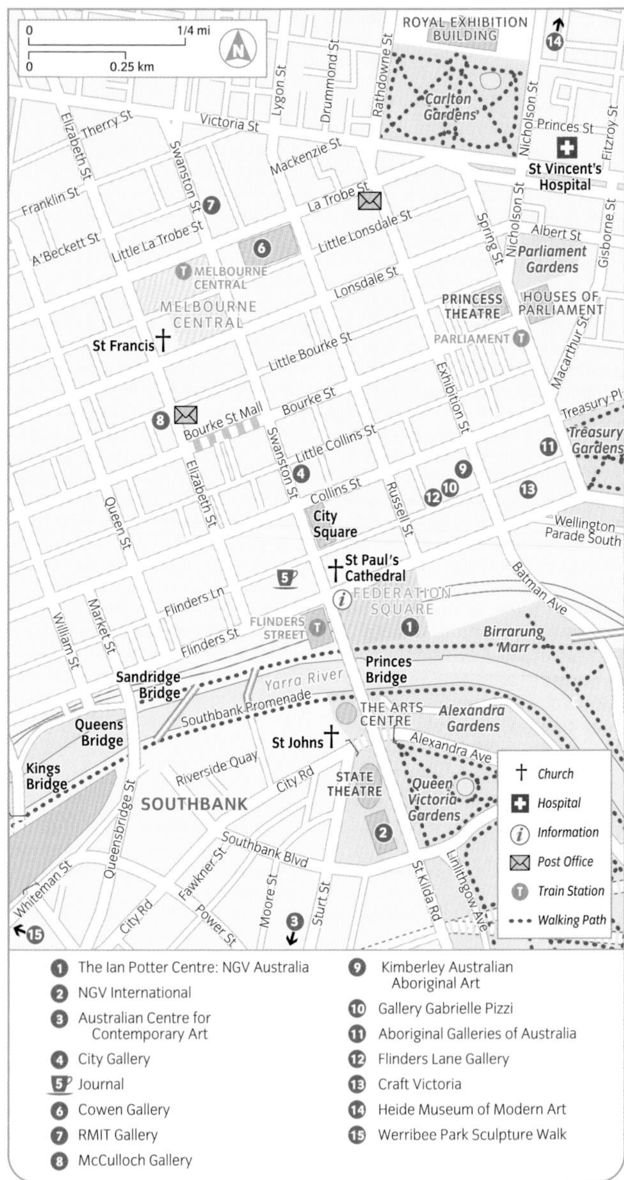

1. The Ian Potter Centre: NGV Australia
2. NGV International
3. Australian Centre for Contemporary Art
4. City Gallery
5. Journal
6. Cowen Gallery
7. RMIT Gallery
8. McCulloch Gallery
9. Kimberley Australian Aboriginal Art
10. Gallery Gabrielle Pizzi
11. Aboriginal Galleries of Australia
12. Flinders Lane Gallery
13. Craft Victoria
14. Heide Museum of Modern Art
15. Werribee Park Sculpture Walk

From large public galleries to commercial galleries to artists' cooperatives, Melbourne boasts a huge range of places to see great art. The city has more than 100 gallery spaces, including the Ian Potter Centre: NGV Australia, the world's first major public gallery dedicated to Australian art. Stroll Flinders Lane and you'll find a swathe commercial galleries, many of which specialise in Aboriginal art.

1 ★★★ **The Ian Potter Centre: NGV Australia.** Immerse yourself in Australian art and history, wandering the NGV's 20 galleries of contemporary, colonial and Indigenous works—they'll tell you much about Australia and its history. *See p. 10, bullet 7.*

2 ★★ **National Gallery of Victoria (NGV) International.** Whether your artistic tastes run to Manet or Picasso, ceramics or sculpture, there's a gallery for you here. This stunning bluestone building houses the NGV's collection of 70 000 works, including European, Asian, Oceanic and American art. *See p. 13, bullet 1.*

3 **Australian Centre for Contemporary Art.** With a building that's a sculpture in itself—the rusty steel facade is a Melbourne landmark—ACCA promises an interesting and challenging experience, and it delivers. There are four gallery spaces leading off a foyer area with the all-important coffee stand. ACCA's forecourt is also the fitting new home of one of Melbourne's most controversial artworks. *Vault*, an angular assemblage of steel panels by Sydney artist Ron Robertson-Swann, was once decried as 'the yellow peril'. *20 min. 111 Sturt St, Southbank. (03) 9697 9999. www.accaonline.org.au. Admission free. Tues–Fri 10am–5pm, Sat–Sun & public holidays 11am–6pm. Train: Flinders Street. Tram: 1 or any tram along St Kilda Rd to Grant St, then a short walk.*

4 **City Gallery.** Art and social history combine in this tiny gallery, which has a program of five annual exhibitions drawing on the City of Melbourne's art and heritage collection. The gallery shares space with the Half-Tix office. *15 min. Ground flr, Melbourne Town Hall, 90–120 Swanston St. (03) 9658 9658. www.melbourne.vic.gov.au/citygallery. Admission free. Mon 10am–2pm, Tues–Thurs 11am–6pm, Fri 11am–6.30pm, Sat 11am–2pm. Train: Flinders St.*

5 **Journal.** Bar stools running inside and out spill this smart cafe into the foyer that leads to the City Library. It offers snacks and great coffee, glasses of wine, and a vibe that's conducive to conversation. Neatly shelved books add to the atmosphere. *253 Flinders Ln. 03 9650 4399. $.*

6 ★ **Cowen Gallery.** Part of the State Library of Victoria, the Cowen Gallery has a permanent exhibition of 137 oil paintings and 13 marble busts of Victoria's early settlers and other people who made their mark in Victoria's history. There are works by some 'big names'—Frederick McCubbin, Nicholas Chevalier,

An exhibit at NGV International.

Laneway Commissions

Turn down one of the city's intriguing lanes and you could stumble on suspended sculptures, light installations, soundscapes and all sorts of artworks. Since 2001, the City of Melbourne has run a public arts program called the Laneway Commissions, for which local and international artists have created temporary works of public art. Some works become semi-permanent, but there are new discoveries to be made all the time.

Percival Ball and John Francis among them—including Charles Summers' marble bust of Sir Redmond Barry (the judge and politician who founded the library) and a large bust of Lord Melbourne, the British prime minister the city was named after. *See p. 11, bullet* ⑩.

⑦ **RMIT Gallery.** Design, fine art, craft, new media and technology can all be found in the changing exhibitions put on at this gallery from the RMIT University collection. It's mainly Australian art, including Indigenous work. ⏱ *15 min. 344 Swanston St.* ☎ *(03) 9925 1717. www.rmit.edu.au/rmitgallery. Admission free. Mon–Fri 11am–5pm, Sat 2–5pm. Tram: City Circle. Train: Melbourne Central.*

⑧ **McCulloch Gallery.** A new exhibition is launched every two weeks at this gallery, which shows a wide variety of genres and artists. It stocks works by emerging artists alongside those of leading Australian artists like John Olsen, Tim Storrier, Bill Henson, John Perceval, Kathleen Petyarre, Minnie Pwerle and George Ward Tjungurrayi. ⏱ *15 min. 8 Rankins Ln.* ☎ *(03) 9602 1101. www.mccullochgallery.com.au. Wed–Fri 12–6pm, Sat 12–5pm.*

⑨ **Kimberley Australian Aboriginal Art.** Despite its name, this commercial gallery also presents works by non-Indigenous contemporary artists, and has a good mix of styles. ⏱ *15 min. 76 Flinders Ln.* ☎ *(03) 9654 5890.*

⑩ **Gallery Gabrielle Pizzi.** Specialising in contemporary Australian Aboriginal art since 1987, this is one of Melbourne's top galleries, showing work by artists from Indigenous communities as well as non-Indigenous art. *See p. 26, bullet* ⑤.

Hosier Lane is a canvas for talented street artists.

Heide Museum of Modern Art is the home of Australian modernism.

⓫ **Aboriginal Galleries of Australia.** A good place to find the big names in Aboriginal art, this light-filled space has traditional dot paintings and contemporary sculpture from the central desert. *See p. 26, bullet* ❸.

⓬ **Flinders Lane Gallery.** New exhibitions are staged every three weeks at this longstanding commercial gallery. It represents a range of contemporary artists, both Indigenous and non-Indigenous, at affordable prices. *See p. 26, bullet* ❻.

⓭ ★ **Craft Victoria.** This small basement gallery is a treasure trove of locally made works from Melbourne's burgeoning craft scene, including textile art, jewellery, pottery, sculpture and more. A great place to pick up a unique souvenir of Melbourne. *15 min. 31 Flinders Ln. ☎ (03) 9650 7775. www.craftvic.asn.au. Admission free. Tues–Sat 10am–5pm. Tram: City Circle.*

⓮ ★ **Heide Museum of Modern Art.** If walls could talk, those of the farmhouse called Heide would have some rich tales to tell—the original house was a frequent haunt of Melbourne's bohemian set in the 1930s. It's now open to guided tours only, but a second home built in 1963 and the gallery purpose-built in 1993 form the basis of one of Australia's leading public art museums, offering changing exhibitions of the works of some of the artists who pioneered Australian modernism, such as Sidney Nolan, Albert Tucker, Arthur Boyd and Charles Blackman. The 16-acre property also has a sculpture park, a cafe, lovely gardens, and a river frontage that extends to the Heidelberg Artists' Trail. *30 min. 7 Templestowe Rd, Bulleen. ☎ (03) 9850 1500. www.heide.com.au. Tues–Fri 10am–5pm, Sat–Sun & public holidays 12–5pm. Admission $12 adults, $8 students & children (under-12s free). Tours 2pm Thurs & Sat, $10.*

⓯ ★★★ kids **Werribee Park Sculpture Walk.** This is one of my favourite places to take visitors who have an interest in sculpture—and even those who don't. With historic Werribee Mansion as its backdrop, the Sculpture Walk is made up of works acquired through the magnificently diverse and often quirky annual Helen Lempriere National Sculpture Awards. Finalists' works are on display from March to May (except in 2009) in Werribee Park's spectacular formal gardens. At other times of year, you can only see the permanent Sculpture Walk if you purchase admission to the whole property (inside and out), but it's well worth it, providing a great day out. Take a picnic or eat at the cafe. *30 min. K Rd, Werribee. ☎ (03) 8734 5100. www.werribeepark.com.au. Daily 10am–5pm, & until 4pm on weekdays May–Oct. Free admission to grounds; admission to Werribee Mansion $13 adults, $7 children 4–15, $31 families.*

Melbourne for Kids

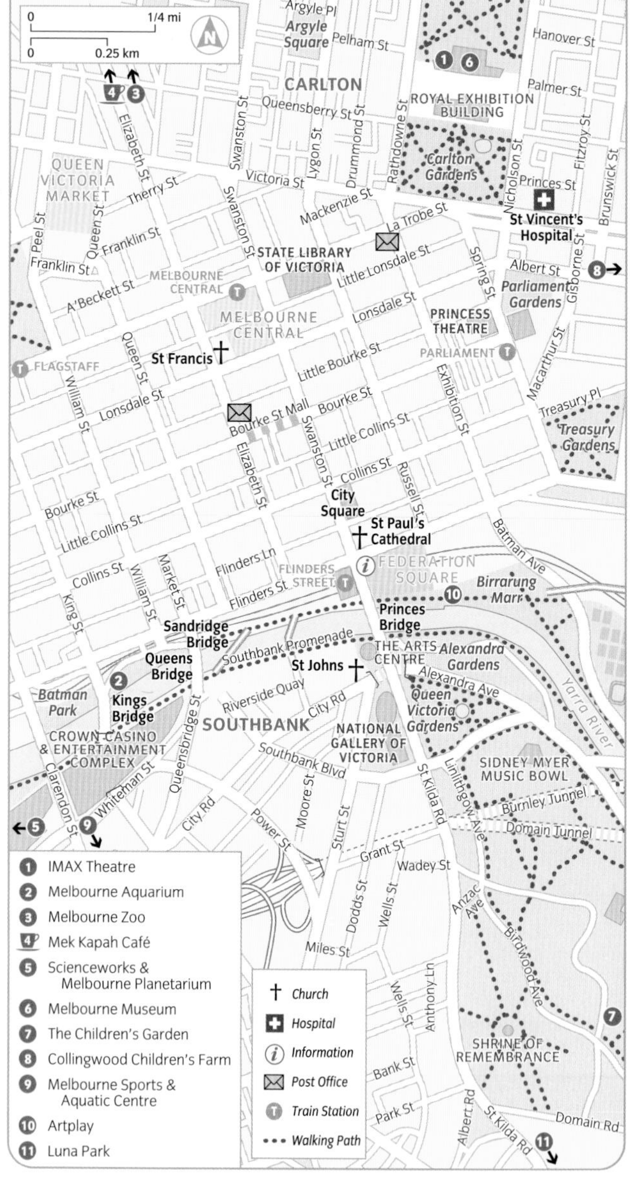

1. IMAX Theatre
2. Melbourne Aquarium
3. Melbourne Zoo
- Mek Kapah Café
5. Scienceworks & Melbourne Planetarium
6. Melbourne Museum
7. The Children's Garden
8. Collingwood Children's Farm
9. Melbourne Sports & Aquatic Centre
10. Artplay
11. Luna Park

Melbourne is a great city for kids. Not only are there wide open spaces and beaches, there is a host of indoor activities to keep them amused, along with cultural pursuits specially designed to challenge young minds on days when the city's infamous changeable weather fails to oblige with sunshine.

1 IMAX Theatre. Whether it's educational or entertaining—or both—kids will love the big screen experience. IMAX Melbourne runs a wide variety of specially made large-format films every hour on the hour—everything from mainstream movies to nature and wildlife documentaries to cartoons. Your movie ticket also gets you free admission to the Melbourne Museum. *Melbourne Museum, Rathdowne St. ☎ (03) 9663 5454. www.imaxmelbourne.com.au. Tickets $13–$18 or $50 for families of 4. Daily 10am–10pm, except Christmas Day. Tram: City Circle.*

2 Melbourne Aquarium. Fish fans will still like it, but the aquarium is looking a little tired and in need of a facelift. The highlight is a 360-degree oceanarium which houses sharks and giant stingrays, with live feeding presentations held twice daily. There's also a Great Barrier Reef exhibit, touch pools and a coral atoll with colourful fish. ⌚ *1 hr. Cnr King & Flinders sts. ☎ (03) 9620 0999. www.melbourneaquarium.com.au. Admission $27 adults, $16 children 3–15, $55–$75 families. Daily 9.30am–6pm & until 9pm Jan 1–26. Last admission 1 hr before closing. Train: Southern Cross or Flinders St. Tram: City Circle or 48.*

3 ★ Melbourne Zoo. Elephants, gorillas, orang-utans, tigers and a host of Australian animals are among the 320 species on show at Australia's oldest zoo, which opened in 1862. The zoo's newest residents, a trio of Asian elephants, are the star attractions. I also love the Butterfly House, whose colourful inhabitants, if you stand still, may alight on your hands or head. Spend another $3 for a ride on the zoo's historic carousel, which operates from 11.30am to 2pm on weekends, public holidays and school holidays. ⌚ *4 hr. Elliott Ave, Parkville. ☎ (03) 9285 9300. www.zoo.org.au. Admission $24 adults, $12 children 4–15, $54–$74 families. Daily 9am–5pm. Train: Royal Park. Tram: 55.*

Kids get among the fish at Melbourne Aquarium.

The looming face of Luna Park.

4 For an ice-cream or drink, a snack or a box of noodles, stop at Melbourne Zoo's **Mek Kapah Café** (named for one of the elephants) in the Trail of the Elephants exhibit. Note that the cafe takes cash only. **Café de Zoo**, just inside the main entrance, sells espresso coffee and drinks, bakery goods, sandwiches and wraps, and hot soup during winter. $.

5 ★★ Scienceworks and the Melbourne Planetarium. There's no other word to describe the Lightning Room than, well… sorry… electrifying. It's the highlight of this fun, educational and interactive museum. Scienceworks seems to appeal to all ages, and has several elements to it: the historic Spotswood (sewage) Pumping Station is more interesting than it sounds, and the planetarium has comfy reclining chairs from which you view simulated night skies projected onto the 16-metre dome. There's loads more! *3 hr. 2 Booker St, Spotswood. ☎ 131 102. www.museumvictoria.com.au/scienceworks. Admission $6 adults, children 3–16 enter free; an extra $5 adults & $3.50 children for Planetarium & Lightning Room shows. Daily 10am–4.30pm. Train: Spotswood.*

6 ★★ Melbourne Museum. A special Children's Gallery designed for kids aged three to eight features an exploration of how plants, animals, minerals and humans grow. 1, 2, 3, Grow tells the story of growth through the themes of size, colour and shape. Kids can size themselves up against specimens from the museum's natural history collections and compare their own growth with the world around them. It's easy to see how popular this is with families—the place is literally crawling with kids! There's a sandpit, an outdoor play area and even a corner with beanbags for those who need a nap (parents and kids!). *See p. 16, bullet 7.*

7 ★★ The Children's Garden. Water spurts from the ground, a bamboo forest rustles with mystery, mist swirls through the snow gums. Kids are scrambling over rocks, digging in the sand, building cubby houses in the Ruin Garden, using nets and microscopes to learn about insects and plants in the wetland area, and hiding in the plant tunnels. The Ian Potter Foundation Children's Garden, in the Royal Botanic Gardens, is a wonderful place for kids to explore the world of plants. There's even a kitchen garden where small hands can get dirty, and a tower to climb for a bird's-eye view!

See p. 77, bullet 2. Wed–Sun & public holidays 10am–4pm. Closed Christmas Day, Boxing Day, New Year's Day & Good Friday, & for two months after the Victorian July school holidays.

8 ★ Collingwood Children's Farm. Milk a cow, bottle-feed the lambs, collect the chooks' eggs, help with the chores or just wander around with the sheep and goats... This not-for-profit community farm offers country life in the heart of the city, and generations of Melbourne kids have loved it. Tucked into a bend of the Yarra, the farm has 7ha of paddocks, gardens, orchards, rustic buildings and shady trees. Patsy the cow is milked at 10am and 4pm. *1 hr. St Heliers St, Abbotsford. ☎ (03) 9417 5806. www.farm.org.au Admission $8 adults, $4 children, $16 families. Daily 9am–5pm. Train: Victoria Park.*

9 ★ Melbourne Sports & Aquatic Centre. A wave pool, waterslide and inflatable racers are all part of the fun at this large swimming pool complex. There are indoor and outdoor pools, a 'youngsters' pool' for toddlers and kids under 7, and special water features are run during weekends, public and school holidays. So when Melbourne's temperatures rise, head for the water! In winter, opt for one of the heated pools. *1 hr. Aughtie Dr, Albert Park. ☎ (03) 9926 1555. www.msac.com.au. Single visit $6 adults, $4.50 children 3–15. Mon–Fri 5.30am–10pm, weekends and public holidays 7am–8pm. Tram: 12 or 96.*

10 Artplay. Artplay is a specially designed centre where children under 12 can get creative. Professional artists work with kids in painting, print-making, music and drama workshops—the fun but messy stuff that parents don't like cleaning up at home. Bookings are essential and can be made online. Children under 8 must be accompanied by an adult. The centre also includes a playground overlooking the Yarra. *2 hr. Birrarung Marr, Batman Ave. ☎ (03) 9664 7900. www.artplay.com.au. Costs vary from free to about $25. Wed–Fri 10am–2pm, Sat & Sun 12–4pm; weekends and holidays only. Tram: City Circle.*

11 Luna Park. Kids seem to love the rumbling roller-coaster and the rides in this small vintage funpark. The beautifully restored heritage carousel is a delight, or try the ghost train, the upside-down Pharoah's Curse or the spinning Enterprise! Some rides have height restrictions. *See p. 22, bullet 7.*

Collingwood Children's Farm is a must for animal-loving littlies.

Melbourne's Museums

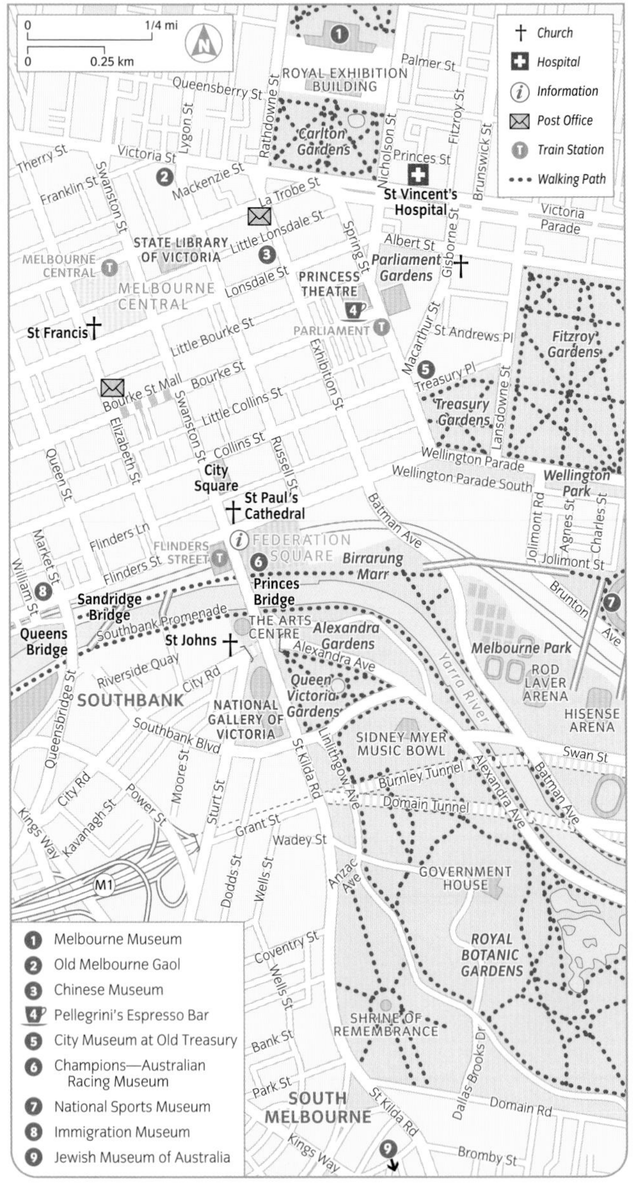

Melbourne's history—social, political, built and natural— is easily discovered and well-told in a wealth of high-quality museums scattered around the city. From gracious historic mansions to a sleek interactive sports museum, they'll help you discover what has shaped the city and what makes it tick today.

1 ★ kids **Melbourne Museum.** Phar Lap, Australia's most celebrated racehorse, is the most popular exhibit here, but the museum also provides a strong sense of Melbourne's history and of Aboriginal cultural heritage. *See p. 16, bullet 7.*

2 ★★★ **Old Melbourne Gaol.** My enthusiasm for this place knows no bounds. The Melbourne Gaol's Crime & Justice Experience has three elements to it. Start off at the historic old prison, scene of 135 hangings (including that of notorious bushranger Ned Kelly), then move to the former City Watch House next door. Your guided tour involves a bit of role-playing—and you'll be locked up! On Sundays you can also visit the former Magistrates' Court and take part in a re-enactment of a real-life court case. Night tours of the gaol run every Monday, Wednesday, Friday and Saturday. *See p. 11, bullet 9.*

3 ★ **Chinese Museum.** Start in the basement, which is the best of this museum's four levels of exhibition space. You'll find yourself immersed in the recreated story of a Chinese migrant heading for the goldfields of Victoria—complete with heaving ship's deck and other special effects. The other main attraction is the world's longest processional dragon, a 60m monster that needs 35 sets of human legs to bring it to life for Chinese celebrations. You'll also see traditional wedding costumes, tiny shoes for women with bound feet and other changing exhibitions that help tell the Chinese-Australian story. ⌚ *45 min. 22 Cohen Pl.* ☎ *(03) 9662 2888. www.chinesemuseum.com.au. Admission $7.50 adults, children $5.50. Daily 10am–5pm. Tram: City Circle. Train: Parliament.*

4 ★ **Pellegrini's Espresso Bar.** Since the first pour from one of Melbourne's first espresso machines at this cafe-bar in 1954, Pellegrini's has been buzzing with customers downing great coffee and authentic Italian food. *66 Bourke St.* ☎ *(03) 9662 1885. $–$$.*

Eerie Old Melbourne Gaol.

Historic Homes

The city's stately old homes, offering a glimpse of bygone Melbourne, are open to the public by guided tour only.

Rippon Lea Estate (192 Hotham Street, Elsternwick; ☎ (03) 9523 6095) is a grand Victorian house worth a visit to get a feel for old-money Melbourne. Sir Frederick Thomas Sargood built the Romanesque house between 1868 and 1903; a Hollywood-style pool and ballroom were added in the 1930s. The real attraction, though, is the 5ha garden, which has a conservatory, lake and lookout tower. Admission is $12 for adults, $6.50 for children 5–16, $30 for families of 6; to see the garden only is $7 adults, $3 children, $17 families. Open daily 10am–5pm. Tours of the house occur every half hour 10.30am–4pm; tours of the estate at 2pm. Closed Monday–Wednesday in May to late September, Good Friday and Christmas Day. Tram: 67. Train: Rippon Lea.

Como House (Corner Lechlade Ave and Williams Road, South Yarra; ☎ (03) 9827 2500; www.comohouse.com.au), built in 1847, is a mix of Australian Regency and classic Italianate architecture. From 1864 to 1959, the house belonged to the Armytage family, and it still seems like you're walking into their glamorous home—it's furnished as if they'd just walked out. Admission is $12 for adults, $6.50 for children under 16, $30 for families of 6; garden only $5 adults, $2 children, $10 families. Open daily 10am–5pm in summer; Wednesday, Saturday and Sunday in winter. Train: South Yarra.

5 ★ City Museum at Old Treasury. This imposing neo-classical sandstone edifice, built in 1857, once stored the booty from the Ballarat and Bendigo goldfields in its underground vaults. Today, the museum tells the story of Melbourne and how the city was 'built on gold'. *See p. 20, bullet 2.*

6 ★★ Champions—Australian Racing Museum & Hall of Fame. With famous frocks (and hats!) dating from 1872 to the present day, trophies (including myriad Melbourne Cups) and the skeleton of the racehorse Carbine, you'll find out more about the horse-racing industry and its social impact here than anywhere else—except perhaps at the track itself. Then there's Tulloch's huge heart, inkwells made from horse's hooves and much more. You'll be surprised and entertained. *1 hr. Federation Square. ☎ 1300 139 407. www.racingmuseum.com.au. Admission $8 adults, $5 children & students (under-12s free), $20 families. Daily 10am–6pm. Tram: City Circle. Train: Flinders St.*

Historic Rippon Lea Estate.

The deeply moving Immigration Museum.

7 ★★ kids **National Sports Museum.** Showcasing mementos such as Don Bradman's baggy green cap and Ian Thorpe's swimsuit, this new testament to Australia's sporting history will have sports fans in heaven. Fittingly housed at the Melbourne Cricket Ground (see p. 42), the museum tells Australia's sporting story from its beginnings to the present day and celebrates its heroes and memorable moments. Almost every imaginable sport is covered, including Australian Rules football, basketball, boxing, cricket, cycling, golf, hockey, netball, rugby union, rugby league, soccer and tennis. There's a special section on the Olympic and Paralympic games, plus an exhibition telling the story of the MCG, the Sport Australia Hall of Fame, and a large interactive area the kids will love. The extensive collection includes Australia's first-ever Olympic gold medal from 1896 and the Malvern Star bicycle that Hubert Opperman rode in his record-breaking 24-hour cycling marathon in Sydney in 1940. During major event days at the MCG (including the AFL Grand Final, Day One of the Boxing Day Test and Anzac Day football), entry to the museum is half-price, but restricted to those holding an event-day ticket. Opening hours vary on weekends when events are being held in the MCG, so check the website for details. ⏲ *1–2 hr. Gate 3, Melbourne Cricket Ground, Brunton Ave, Richmond.* ☎ *(03) 9657 8879. www.nsm.org.au. Admission $15 adults, $8 children 5–15, $45 families of 6 for museum only; $22 adults, $12 children, $50 families for museum & MCG tour. Daily 10am–5pm (last admission 4.30pm). Tram: 48, 70 or 75. Train: Jolimont.*

8 ★★ **Immigration Museum.** Visiting the Immigration Museum is often a deeply moving experience. The stories of migrants who have come to Australia over the past 200 years are varied, but taken together they explain how Melbourne has become such a multicultural city. This interactive museum, set in the beautiful Old Customs House, contains memorabilia, short films and the chance to track histories or tell your own story. It's well worth dropping into. ⏲ *1 hr. 400 Flinders St.* ☎ *(03) 9927 2700. www.museumvictoria.com.au/immigrationmuseum. Admission $6, children under 17 free. Daily 10am–5pm.*

9 ★★ **The Jewish Museum of Australia.** Located opposite the St Kilda Hebrew Congregation, one of Melbourne's most beautiful synagogues, the Jewish Museum gives a fascinating insight into Australia's Jewish history. The permanent displays—Belief and Ritual, The Jewish Year, The Australian Jewish History Gallery and The Timeline of Jewish History—are supplemented by changing exhibitions. ⏲ *30 min. 26 Alma Rd, St Kilda.* ☎ *(03) 8534 3600. www.jewishmuseum.com.au. Admission $10 adults, $5 students, $20 families. Tues–Thurs 10am–4pm, Sun 11am–5pm. Closed Jewish holy days. Tram: 3, 67.*

Sporting Melbourne

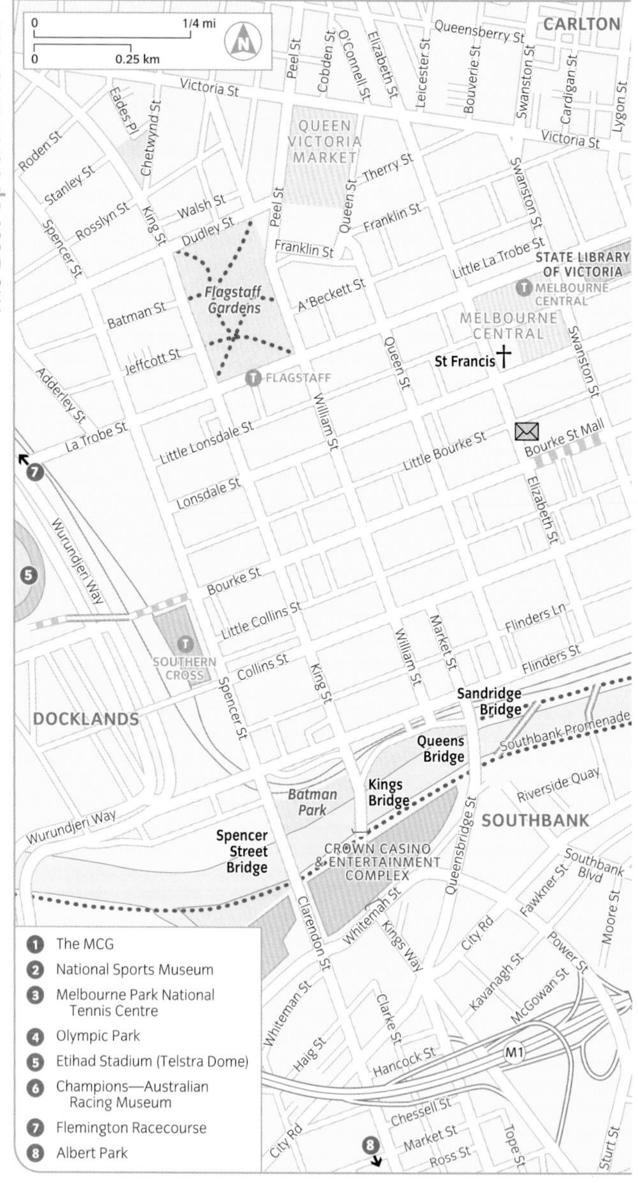

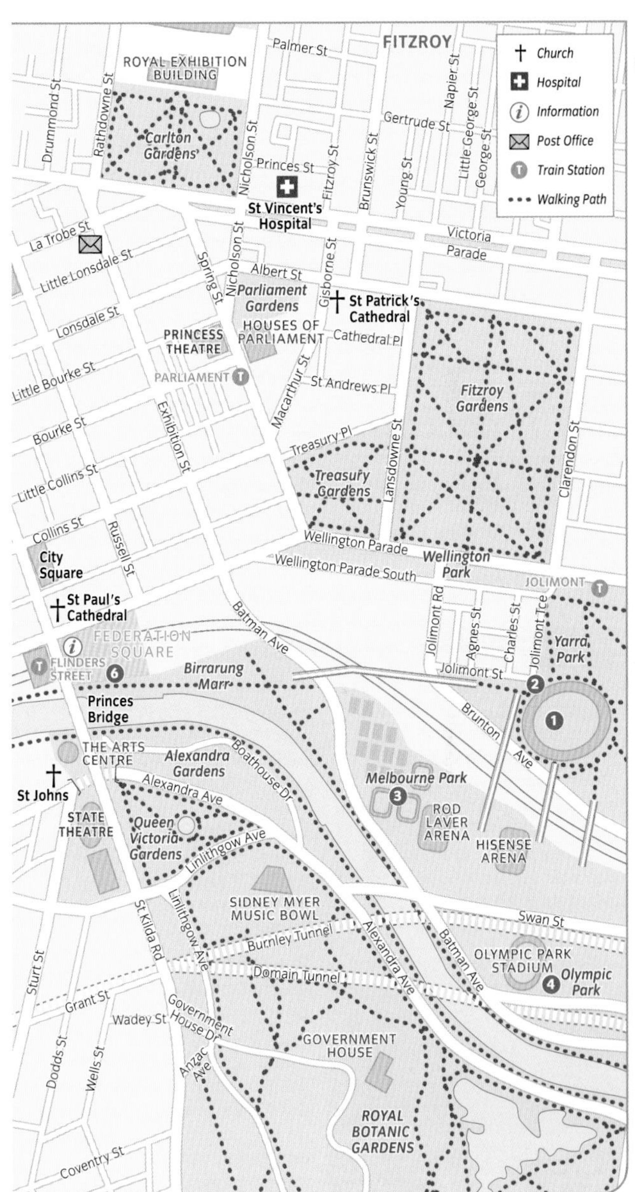
FITZROY
Church
Hospital
Information
Post Office
Train Station
Walking Path
Palmer St
ROYAL EXHIBITION BUILDING
Drummond St
Rathdowne St
Carlton Gardens
Nicholson St
Princes St
Fitzroy St
Brunswick St
Young St
Gertrude St
Napier St
Little George St
George St
St Vincent's Hospital
La Trobe St
Little Lonsdale St
Spring St
Victoria Parade
Albert St
Parliament Gardens
Gisborne St
St Patrick's Cathedral
Lonsdale St
PRINCESS THEATRE
HOUSES OF PARLIAMENT
Cathedral Pl
Little Bourke St
PARLIAMENT
Macarthur St
St Andrews Pl
Fitzroy Gardens
Exhibition St
Bourke St
Treasury Pl
Lansdowne St
Clarendon St
Little Collins St
Treasury Gardens
Collins St
Russell St
Wellington Parade
Wellington Parade South
Wellington Park
City Square
JOLIMONT
St Paul's Cathedral
Batman Ave
Jolimont Rd
Agnes St
Charles St
Jolimont Tce
Yarra Park
FEDERATION SQUARE
FLINDERS STREET
6
Birrarung Marr
Jolimont St
2
Princes Bridge
Brunton Ave
1
THE ARTS CENTRE
Alexandra Gardens
Boathouse Dr
St Johns
Alexandra Ave
Melbourne Park
3
ROD LAVER ARENA
HISENSE ARENA
STATE THEATRE
Queen Victoria Gardens
Linlithgow Ave
SIDNEY MYER MUSIC BOWL
Swan St
St Kilda Rd
Linlithgow Ave
Burnley Tunnel
Alexandra Ave
Batman Ave
OLYMPIC PARK STADIUM
4
Olympic Park
Sturt St
Domain Tunnel
Grant St
Wadey St
Government House Dr
GOVERNMENT HOUSE
Dodds St
Wells St
Anzac Ave
ROYAL BOTANIC GARDENS
Coventry St

Melbourne is sports mad. There's no way around it—and for outsiders, it's a sure-fire conversation-starter. Depending on the time of year, you can talk cricket, tennis, horse racing or football and you're almost certain to get an interested response. There's one challenge, of course: Australia has its very own football code, AFL.

❶ ★★ **The MCG.** Don't be bamboozled by the fact that the hallowed ground of the Melbourne Cricket Ground also hosts football matches. In summer, this is the home of cricket; in winter, Australian Rules ... um ... rules. The stadium (which was the venue for the 1956 Melbourne Olympic Games) can accommodate 97 500 people.When there's no game on, take an hour-long tour of the MCG. A tour ticket also gets you into the new National Sports Museum. Tours leave from Gate 3. 🕘 *1 hr. Brunton Ave, Richmond.* ☎ *(03) 9657 8864. www.mcg.org.au. Tours $22 adults, $12 children 5–15, $50 families. Tours non-event days only, every half hour 10am–3pm. Tram: 70 or 75. Train: Jolimont.*

❷ ★★ **National Sports Museum.** Sporting fans of all disciplines will be enthralled by this museum, where you can trace the history and achievements of your heroes. Few of the mainstream sports played in Australia are left out. There are trophies and blazers, cricket bats and golf clubs, a host of short films and TV clips to watch... you could spend hours here. Take an audio tour to get the best out of it. 🕘 *1 hr.* *See p. 39, bullet ❼.*

Melbourne Park National Tennis Centre.

❸ ★ **Melbourne Park National Tennis Centre.** Melbourne Park, part of the city's sports complex, is home to the Australian Open tennis each January. The central 15 000-seat Rod Laver Arena was named for one of Australia's first Wimbledon winners, and there's also Margaret Court Arena, with 6000 seats. You can even play on centre court yourself—when tournaments aren't scheduled, the six indoor and 22 outdoor courts (including the show courts) are open to the public. You can rent courts on weekdays between 7am and 11pm, and on weekends from 9am to 6pm. The fee is $26 to $40 per hour, depending on the court and time (outdoor courts are cheapest). Racquets can be hired. *Batman Ave.* ☎ *1300 836 647. www.mopt.com.au. Tram: 70. Train: Jolimont.*

❹ **Olympic Park.** With 12 000 seats, Olympic Park Stadium hosts major sporting and entertainment events through the year. In the same complex as Melbourne Park, it's also home to the Collingwood Football Club and the Victorian Institute of Sport. *Batman Ave.* ☎ *1300 836 647. www.mopt.com.au. Tram: 70. Train: Jolimont.*

❺ ★ **Etihad Stadium (formerly Telstra Dome).** Melbourne's number-one sport is Australian Rules Football—aka 'the footy'— and the home of several AFL teams is this 53 000-plus-seat stadium. Melbourne has 10 of the 16 national AFL teams (www.afl.com.au), and it seems every Melbournian worth their salt follows a team. The season runs from March, with the Grand Final on the last

A mini MCG at the National Sports Museum.

Saturday in September at the MCG. 'Behind the Scenes' tours of the stadium take you into the AFL players' change-rooms, the briefing room, coaches' box, media centre, tribunal room and much more. *1 hr. Bourke St. ☎ (03) 8625 7700. www.telstradome.com.au. Tours Mon–Fri 11am, 1pm & 3pm (except event days) from the Customer Service Centre opposite Gates 2 & 3 (Bourke St footbridge side). Tickets $14 adults, $11 students, $7 children under 15, $37 families of 4. Tram: 70, 75, 96, 109, 112. Train: Southern Cross.*

6 ★★ **Champions—Australian Racing Museum & Hall of Fame.** For a peek inside the world of horse racing, head to this interesting museum dedicated to all things equine. For those not horse-mad, the fashion gallery alone is worth the entry fee! *See p. 38, bullet 6.*

7 **The Melbourne Cup.** Break out your best hat! Australia's most over-the-top horse race, run on the first Tuesday in November at **Flemington Racecourse**, has been contested by the best of Australia's thoroughbreds (and a few from overseas) since 1861—but it's not all about the horses. Melbourne society puts on a show, dressing up for the occasion, and the entire nation stops in its tracks to go to the race, or at least to tune in on TV. *400 Epsom Rd, Flemington. ☎ 1300 727 575. www.vrc.net.au. Tram: 57 from Flinders St.*

8 **Australian Formula One Grand Prix.** The whine of engines can be heard all over inner-city Melbourne when the Australian Formula One Grand Prix is held each March at the massive **Albert Park**. If you're going, take the train or tram, as some streets around South Melbourne are closed, parking is difficult and the crowds are huge. The big program of off-track events keeps everyone entertained, if the world's fastest cars aren't enough for you. *Albert Rd, Queens Rd, Lakeside Dr & Canterbury Rd, South Melbourne. ☎ 132 849. www.grandprix.com.au. Tram: 96. Stop: Albert Park or Middle Park.*

Teeing Off in Melbourne

One of the best public golf courses in Australia is Yarra Bend in the Melbourne suburb of Fairfield (☎ (03) 9481 3729), where green fees and club rental are around $25 each. The exclusive **Royal Melbourne Golf Club** (☎ (03) 9598 6755; www.royalmelbourne.com.au) in the suburb of Black Rock, 24km from the city centre, is rated as one of the world's 10 best golf courses. If you have a letter of introduction from your golf club at home, a handicap of under 26 for men and 32 for women, and don't mind the $375 green fee for overseas visitors, you might be able to play a round. Club hire is $50. No can do? There are lots of other public and private courses close to the city that have public access. For more information contact the **Victorian Golf Association** (☎ (03) 9889 6731; www.golfvic.org.au).

Melbourne Wildlife

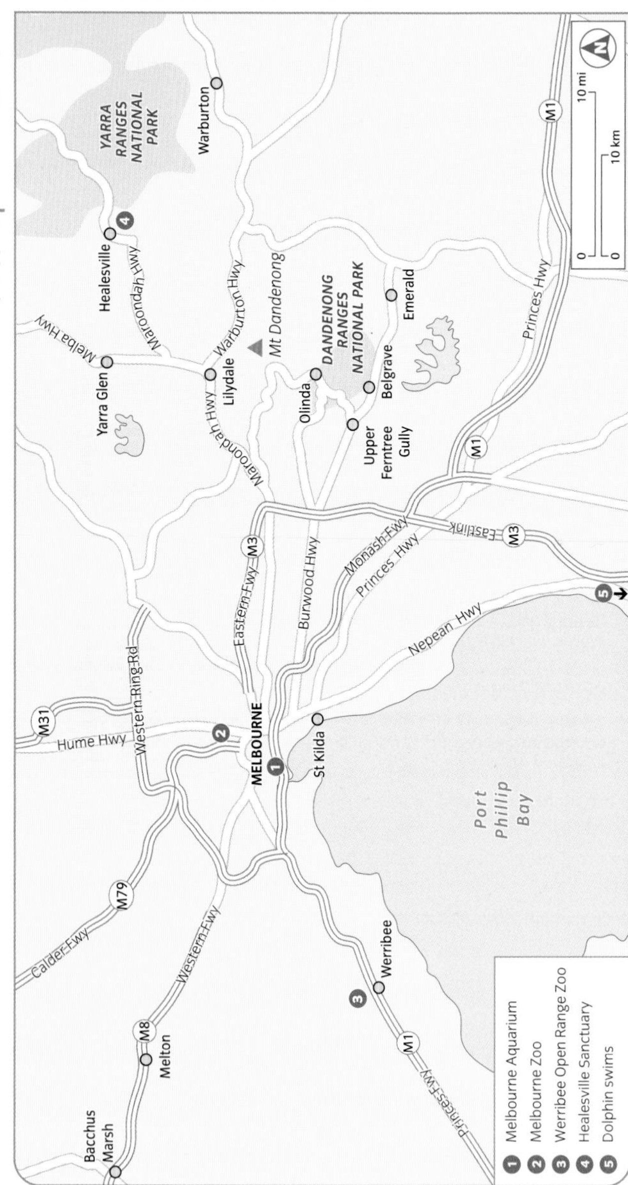

Whether you're interested in Australia's amazing and unique fauna—kangaroos, koalas, emus and echidnas—or something more exotic, Melbourne has a number of places you can see them without leaving the city. For wider open spaces you'll need to head further afield, but a day trip will easily satisfy the need to see creatures in the wild.

The Werribee Open Range Zoo: who's watching whom?

❶ kids **Melbourne Aquarium.** Giant stingrays and big sharks cruising above your head—thrilling! There's plenty here to keep the kids amused, including touch-tanks, feeding demonstrations and dazzling, darting fish—and they'll learn a lot too. *See p. 33, bullet* ❷.

❷ ★ kids **Melbourne Zoo.** This is the place to see exotic species—elephants, gorillas, orang-utans and tigers among them. Don't miss the Butterfly House and the World of Bugs (and look out for the Giant Burrowing Cockroach). *See p. 33, bullet* ❸.

❸ ★★ kids **Werribee Open Range Zoo.** Families love this African-themed zoo without (many) cages, where the only way to see the open-range animals is on a guided tour. The large safari bus is the cheapest option—it's included in the ticket price—but it's not always the best if you really want to make the most of seeing the animals. On a busy day, you could be wedged into a centre seat, making viewing and photography difficult. So consider spending a bit more to take a smaller group tour in an open-sided jeep. You'll see rhinoceros, giraffes, zebras, hippos and other animals wandering the fields. There are also walking tracks to sections featuring lions, cheetahs and monkeys, and an

Kangaroo and joey at Melbourne Zoo.

Australian section with kangaroos, wallabies and emus. The safari-bus tour takes about 50 minutes, but you could easily spend another couple of hours wandering around and picnicking. And if a day's not long enough, the zoo also offers 'slumber safari' overnight packages from September to May. ⌚ *3 hr. K Rd, Werribee. ☎ (03) 9731 9600. www.zoo.org.au. Admission $23 adults, $12 children 4–15, $52–$70 families. Open vehicle tours $75 adults, $60 children (must be over 8). Daily 9am–5pm (entrance closes at 3.30pm). Safari tours hourly 10.30am–3.40pm.*

4 ★★ kids **Healesville Sanctuary.** This is a great place to spot native animals in almost-natural surroundings. There are wedge-tailed eagles, dingoes, koalas, wombats, reptiles and lots more, all visible while you stroll through the peppermint-scented gum forest and listen to the ringing of the bellbirds. The sanctuary has been popular among Melbournians since it opened in 1921. You can also visit the Wildlife Health Centre (an animal rescue hospital) to see veterinarians caring for, and even operating on, injured or orphaned wildlife. ⌚ *2 hr. Badger Creek Rd, Healesville. ☎ (03) 5957 2800. www.zoo.org.au. Admission $23 adults, $12 children 4–15, $52–$70 families. Daily 9am–5pm. Train from Flinders St Station to Lilydale, then bus no. 685.*

5 **Dolphin swims.** Port Phillip Bay is home to a population of around 150–200 wild bottlenose dolphins, and it's possible to get up close and in the water with some of them on a tour from Sorrento on the Mornington Peninsula (see p. 130). Polperro Dolphin Swims is a family-run award winning company that runs half day tours onto the bay from October to April. You are likely to see Australian fur seals and a rich array of sea birds including cormorants and gulls, as well as dolphins. Wetsuits, masks and snorkels are supplied. Bookings are essential.. ⌚ *3–4 hr. Polperro Dolphin Swims, Sorrento Pier, Sorrento. ☎ 03/5988-8437. www.polperro.com.au. $115 swimmers, $50 observers, $30 child observers. Daily 8.30am & 1.30pm, Oct–Apr.*

Platypuses and other native creatures can be admired at Healesville Sanctuary.

3 The Best **Neighbourhood Walks**

St Kilda

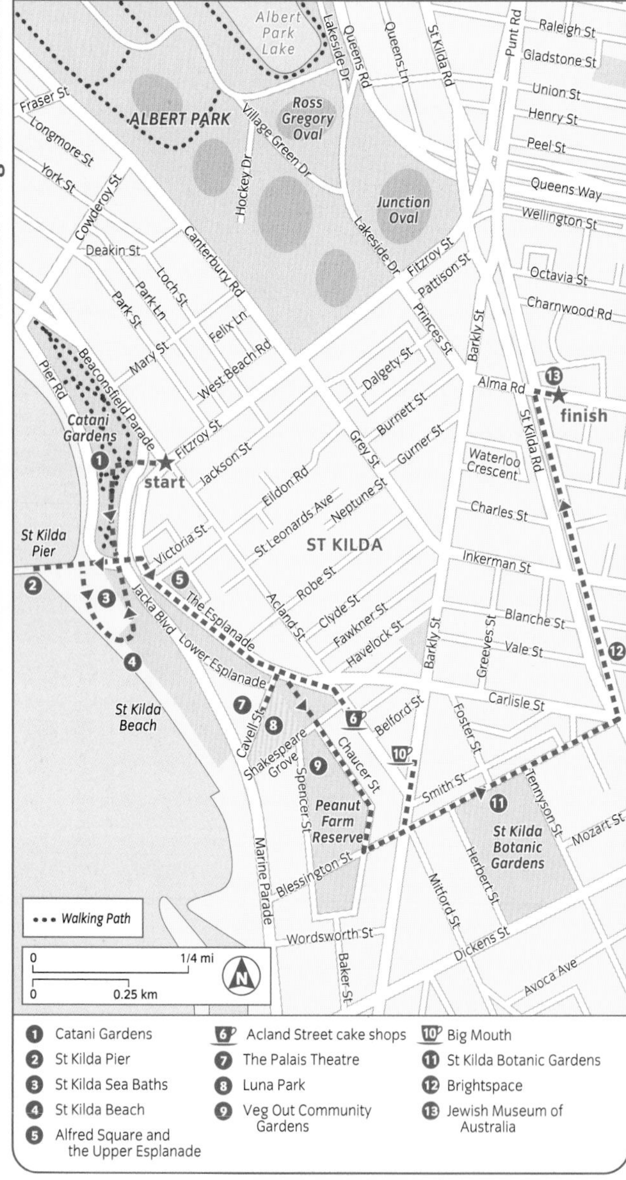

Previous page: The Royal Exhibition Building's Hochgurtel Fountain.

A bit bohemian, a bit shabby around the edges, but with corners of sleek sophistication, especially in its nightlife and restaurant scene, St Kilda has been Melbourne's seaside playground since the 1860s. It may not have the most fabulous beach in the world, but it's emphatically Melbourne's beach, and tourists rub shoulders with locals along bustling Acland Street or on the historic pier. A controversial redevelopment next to Luna Park and the Palais Theatre may soon change the face of this area, but until then, welcome to my neighbourhood. START: **Tram 16 from Federation Square to Fitzroy Street.**

❶ ★ **Catani Gardens.** Three avenues of fabulous century-old palm trees run through the heritage-listed Catani Gardens, which stretch along 6ha of the foreshore from the end of Fitzroy Street. Named for Carlo Catani, the designer of the St Kilda foreshore, the gardens are one of St Kilda's great landmarks and hugely popular with families. 🕘 *15 min.*

❷ ★★ **St Kilda Pier.** Soak up the sun or rug up against the wind and stroll along the historic pier, which stretches 700m out into Port Phillip Bay. Chat to the ever-hopeful fishermen, and have a drink or an ice-cream at the kiosk at the end of the pier. The 99-year-old building was destroyed by fire in 2003, but rebuilt a year later to the original plans. 🕘 *15 min.*

❸ **St Kilda Sea Baths.** Steam rises against the windows of the heated pool now housed inside the redeveloped 1931 sea baths. The complex has also gained a health club that looks out onto the waves, plus shops and restaurants. Its Spanish-style domes and archways are best viewed from the Upper Esplanade. Don't bother going inside unless it's to a restaurant or for a swim. Upstairs, **Soul Mama** (☎ (03) 9525 3338; www.soulmama.com.au) is a popular vegetarian cafe with great views of the bay. 🕘 *15 min.*

❹ **St Kilda Beach.** Cycle, in-line skate, walk or jog along the foreshore with everyone else—summer or winter, the esplanade is well used. St Kilda Beach sweeps from the pier to the marina, with

The kiosk at the end of St Kilda Pier was rebuilt using the original building's plans after being destroyed by fire.

Drool over delicious delicacies at Acland Street's famed cake shops.

foot and cycle paths separating the sand from grassy picnic areas. Sailors, sailboarders and kite-boarders skim the small waves, but there's no surf here; the bay protects the beach, which makes it a good spot for families. *30 min.*

5 Alfred Square and the Upper Esplanade. After your walk on the foreshore, take the pedestrian overpass from Jacka Boulevard to the Upper Esplanade. The Catani memorial clock tower, erected in 1932, stands opposite Alfred Square; St Kilda's Memorial to the Boer War is in the square itself. If you can, come on a Sunday, when the Upper Esplanade becomes a colourful craft market selling art-works, pottery, clothing and other handmade souvenirs. *15 min.*

6 ★★ Acland Street cake shops. Monarch Quality Cakes may well be the oldest business in St Kilda: it opened at 103 Acland Street in 1934. More than 70 years later it and its cluster of near neighbours are still offering the best Eastern European cakes in Melbourne. They taste as sweet and rich as they look: you won't be disappointed once you get past the crowds outside the window. Take your pick from Monarch, the Europa Cake Shop, Le Bon Continental Cake Shop and Acland Cakes. And try not to drool on the windows.

7 ★ The Palais Theatre. This imposing Art Deco theatre is on the Victorian Heritage Register, so it is remaining untouched by the controversial St Kilda Triangle redevelopment. Since its opening in 1927, the Palais's stage has been graced by some of the biggest international names in showbusiness. *Lower Esplanade. ☎ (03) 9525 3240. www.palaistheatre.net.au.*

8 kids Luna Park. Take a moment to pause for photos at the iconic entrance of Melbourne's oldest fun park, but unless you have kids don't plan to spend much time in it. Just take a quick turn on the beautiful carousel. *See p. 22, bullet 7.*

9 ★ Veg Out Community Gardens. For a fun look at how those without gardens keep their thumbs green, step through the gate at Veg Out and wander in this creative and quirky community garden. You'll come across odd sculptures, chooks (chickens), garden gnomes and other unexpected creations among the 140 lovingly tended organic vegetable patches. A namesake farmers' market runs on the first Saturday of every month from 8.30am to 1pm in the Peanut Farm Reserve next door. *15 min. Cnr Shakespeare Gr & Chaucer St. www.vegout.asn.au. Admission free.*

10 ★ Big Mouth. Take a seat in the window of one of my favourite cafes and watch Acland Street go by. The coffee's good and so are the cakes, snacks and meals. *Cnr Acland & Barkly sts. ☎ (03) 9534 4611. $–$$.*

St Kilda Festival

All roads lead to the beach during the St Kilda Festival each January, when the suburb hosts a huge array of live music, entertainment and activities. On Festival Day, there are usually around 50 bands performing at various venues. The streets are closed, the crowds are huge. After Festival Day there's a week-long program of music, dining and drinking. See www.stkildafestival.com.au.

⓫ ★★ **St Kilda Botanic Gardens.** Established in 1859, the St Kilda Botanic Gardens are an oasis that hosts early-morning tai chi and meditation classes, dog-walkers, chess games on the giant chess board and, on fine weekends, the occasional wedding. There's a lovely rose garden with a gazebo, a rainforest conservatory, a kid's playground and the EcoCentre, which has displays on sustainable living. My favourite thing in the gardens is the Rain Man, a fountain in the lake that runs on solar power and uses recycled water. 🕘 *15 min. Between Dickens, Tennyson & Blessington sts. Open daily dawn to dusk; conservatory open weekdays 10.30am–3.30pm, weekends & public holidays 1pm–4.30pm.*

⓬ **Brightspace.** A two-room gallery, the aptly named Brightspace shows contemporary work by emerging and established artists, including a number of Aboriginal artists. 🕘 *15 min. 8 Martin St. ☎ (03) 9593 9366. Open Wed–Sat 12–6pm, Sun 1–5pm.*

⓭ ★★ **The Jewish Museum of Australia.** For an insight into Melbourne's Jewish community and its history, take a tour of the museum or one of the nearby synagogues. The Jewish Museum offers tours of the adjacent and architecturally unique St Kilda Synagogue, and of Melbourne's principal progressive synagogue, Temple Beth Israel. Tours of the St Kilda Synagogue run Tuesday to Thursday at 12.30pm and Sundays at 12.30pm and 3pm. Tours to Temple Beth Israel, just along the street, are by arrangement. Each tour takes about 40 minutes. *See p. 39, bullet ❾.*

A sign shows the way at quirky Veg Out Community Gardens.

Williamstown

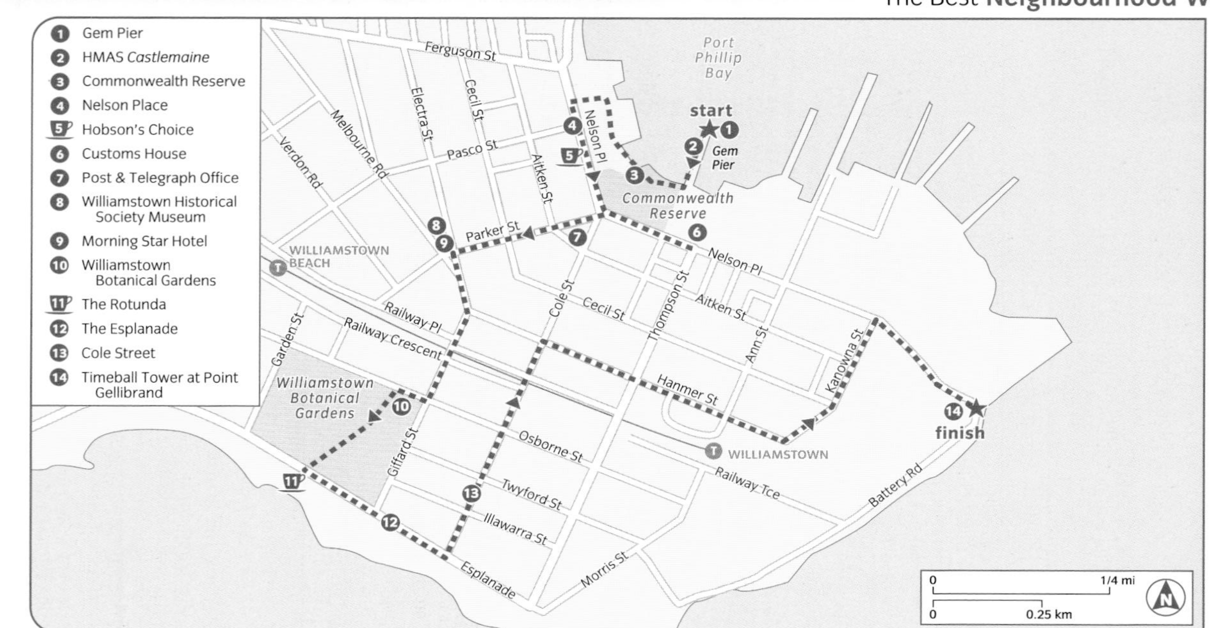

A stroll by the bay is one of the highlights of Williamstown, on Melbourne's south-west corner. The suburb has been home to naval shipbuilding since 1860 and retains much of its maritime village charm. The historic buildings of Nelson Place now house cafes and restaurants, with views of the city skyline through the masts of boats bobbing on Port Phillip Bay. START: **Take the 50-minute ferry trip from Southbank to Gem Pier.**

❶ **Gem Pier.** As soon as you alight from the ferry, you're surrounded by Williamstown's nautical history. The first jetty on this site was completed in 1839; the present pier is named after the ferry *Gem*, which plied the waters between Port Melbourne and Williamstown in the mid-1800s. Numerous boat tours—and even a seaplane tour—offer visitors the chance to get out on the bay. *15 min.*

❷ ★ kids **HMAS *Castlemaine*.** Step aboard this World War II naval minesweeper and get a feel for how life was for the seamen of yesteryear. The ship, a product of the Williamstown dockyards, is now a maritime museum, and you can clamber up and down ladders, take a seat at the four-inch gun, and wonder how so many men managed to live in such a confined space. The interesting nautical exhibits and memorabilia are viewed with the soundtrack of a chattering ship's radio, and volunteer guides are on hand to explain anything you want to know. *30 min. Gem Pier. ☎ (03) 9397 2363. www.hmascastlemaine.com. Admission $5 adults, $2.50 children, $13 families of 4. Sat–Sun 12–5pm.*

❸ kids **Commonwealth Reserve.** A green space at the waterfront, Commonwealth Reserve's points of interest include the band rotunda, the anchor from HMAS Nelson, the stone Tide Gauge House, the Message Tree (once used for posting messages to those disembarking from sailing ships), and the drinking fountain donated by Reverend John Wilkinson to discourage alcohol consumption. Every third Sunday of the month, the reserve hosts a bustling craft market with live entertainment. *15 min.*

❹ **Nelson Place.** Running almost the length of the waterfront, Nelson Place is lined with interesting

Historic Gem Pier.

historic buildings, but is perhaps best appreciated from the other side of the road, along the foreshore, where you can get a great view of the upper facades. There are former hotels, newspaper offices, banks and a barber shop from the 19th century, as well as the 'Modern Buildings', built in 1909. Along the stretch of waterfront between Cole and Ann streets, most buildings date back to 1870. At number 139 is the Gothic Revival–style bank erected in 1873; further along is the former Royal Hotel, a white-pointed red-brick building in the Queen Anne style, built in 1893. Many buildings now house restaurants and cafes. *15 min.*

5 **Hobson's Choice.** The brick walls of this spacious cafe are lined with historic photographs. In winter there's an open fire, in summer take a table on the footpath. The substantial sandwiches and focaccias with interesting fillings can be supplemented by cakes and pastries made on the premises, and there are full meals for those who want more. *213–215 Nelson Pl. ☎ (03) 9397 1891. $.*

6 **Customs House.** The Customs House was constructed in 1874 to the design of notable architect William Wardell. The Port Phillip Pilot Service, formed in 1852, had its offices here. *5 min. Cnr Syme St & Nelson Pl.*

7 **Post & Telegraph Office.** Built in 1859, this attractive building sits on a triangle at the junction of Parker Street and Cole Street, just back from Nelson Place. It housed the telephone exchange from 1893 and was substantially remodelled in 1895. Today, it—like many of the other edifices here—houses a restaurant. *5 min.*

8 **Williamstown Historical Society Museum.** Everything you'll ever need to know about Williamstown can be found here in one of Hobsons Bay's oldest structures—the Mechanic's Institute, a National Trust building dating from 1860. There are two 'period rooms' (a bedroom and dining room), two maritime rooms and another large room for everything else—furniture, costumes and photographs, as well as books and research services. *30 min. 5 Electra St. ☎ (03) 9397 5423. Admission $3. Open Sun 2–5pm.*

9 **Morning Star Hotel.** There's been a hotel on this site since 1869, and the present pub has been here since 1889. The outside hasn't changed, but inside, the dining room is graced with white

Nelson Place is lined with beautiful historic buildings

The delightfully green Williamstown Botanical Gardens.

linen tablecloths and offers modern gastro-pub cuisine—with fish and chips still on the menu, of course. *3 Electra St. ☎ (03) 9397 6082. Open 12–2pm & 6–9pm.*

⑩ ★★ **Williamstown Botanical Gardens.** Ornate iron gates open into these gardens, where the four lawns—Golden Elm, Liquidambar, Sunset and Four Corners—are well used, especially when the sun's shining. Established in 1860, remodelled in 1905 and recently restored, these gardens originally belonged to a small group of 'scientific and pleasure' gardens that tested how well European species would grow in the new colony of Australia. A stroll through the palm-lined pathways will bring you out to the seafront. *15 min. Cnr Osborne & Giffard sts.*

11 ★ **The Rotunda.** A seat by the window in this octagonal cafe ensures you great views of Williamstown beach and the sea to accompany your coffee and cake. The Rotunda offers simple fare all day, including breakfast and light meals, but the best time to stop in is for a sunset drink. *The Esplanade. ☎ (03) 9397 7834. $.*

⑫ **The Esplanade.** Several colonial houses run along the stretch of the Esplanade that overlooks Hatts Reserve and the sea. At number 16 is the Convent of St Joseph, built for Captain James Ogilvie in 1888 and bought by the Sisters of St Joseph in 1927. 'Ellerslie', on the corner of Cole Street, was built for shipbuilder James Gray in 1899. There's another interesting house at number 12–13, built in 1858 for Captain Matthews, master of the ship *Great Britain*. *15 min.*

⑬ **Cole Street.** More colonial cottages to look at as you head back towards the village centre. The pair of two-storey houses at numbers 73 and 75, built from rough-cut basalt in 1859, were first owned by a sailor and then by sea pilot William Murrell. The row of lovely cottages (numbers 66–52) were built in 1872 for railway workers and sailors. *15 min.*

⑭ **Timeball Tower at Point Gellibrand.** Set on the point at the eastern end of Nelson Place, this bluestone tower was built in the late 1840s using convict labour. Originally a lighthouse, it operated as a timeball for passing ships until 1926. *5 min.*

Carlton

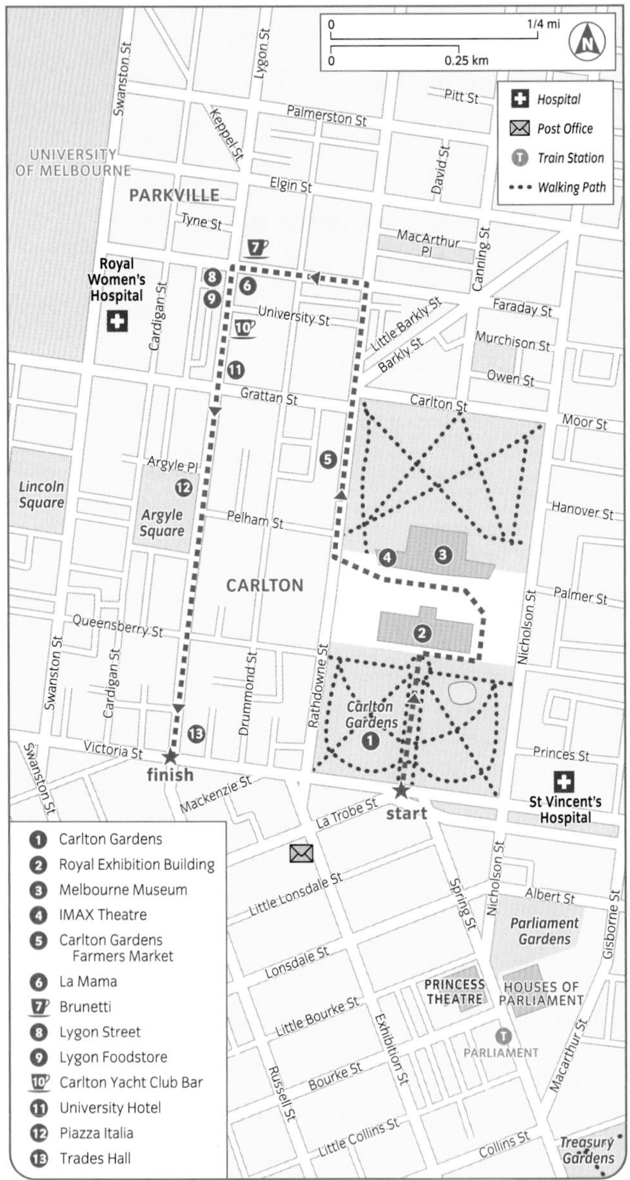
0
1/4 mi
0
0.25 km
Hospital
Post Office
Train Station
Walking Path
UNIVERSITY OF MELBOURNE
PARKVILLE
Royal Women's Hospital
CARLTON
Lincoln Square
Argyle Square
Carlton Gardens
St Vincent's Hospital
Parliament Gardens
PRINCESS THEATRE
HOUSES OF PARLIAMENT
PARLIAMENT
Treasury Gardens
start
finish
Swanston St
Lygon St
Keppel St
Palmerston St
Pitt St
Elgin St
David St
Tyne St
MacArthur Pl
Canning St
Cardigan St
University St
Little Barkly St
Barkly St
Faraday St
Murchison St
Owen St
Grattan St
Carlton St
Moor St
Argyle Pl
Pelham St
Hanover St
Palmer St
Nicholson St
Queensberry St
Drummond St
Rathdowne St
Victoria St
Princes St
Mackenzie St
La Trobe St
Little Lonsdale St
Spring St
Albert St
Gisborne St
Lonsdale St
Little Bourke St
Exhibition St
Macarthur St
Russell St
Bourke St
Little Collins St
Collins St
1 Carlton Gardens
2 Royal Exhibition Building
3 Melbourne Museum
4 IMAX Theatre
5 Carlton Gardens Farmers Market
6 La Mama
7 Brunetti
8 Lygon Street
9 Lygon Foodstore
10 Carlton Yacht Club Bar
11 University Hotel
12 Piazza Italia
13 Trades Hall

Carlton is Melbourne's Little Italy. Italian migrants made their homes in this inner-city suburb between the 1920s and the 1950s, and it still retains the traditions—and the flavours—they brought with them. The heart of Carlton is Lygon Street; walking down it you may wonder which country you're in. START: **City Circle tram, tram 86 or tram 96 from Bourke Street to Victoria Street.**

❶ ★★ kids **Carlton Gardens.** For the greatest impact, enter the gardens from Victoria Street through the avenue of plane trees. The path leads to the Hochgurtel Fountain—spurting water even in the drought—in front of the Royal Exhibition Building. Established in 1857, the classical and quite formal Victorian-era gardens are popular for picnics; behind the museum there's a playground that will keep kids happy. The gardens and the Royal Exhibition Building are also the venue for the Melbourne International Flower & Garden Show (www.melbflowershow.com.au) each April, which is rated among the top five flower and garden shows in the world. ⌚ *15 min. Between Victoria, Carlton & Nicholson sts.*

❷ ★★ **Royal Exhibition Building.** One of the world's oldest remaining exhibition pavilions, built for the Great Exhibition of 1880, this wonderful structure is as stunning inside as it is viewed from the gardens that surround it. *See p. 17, bullet* ❽.

❸ ★★ kids **Melbourne Museum.** Find out what sets Melbourne apart from other cities by exploring Australia's largest museum. The Melbourne Gallery focuses on the city's history, and kids will find a lot of fun interactive spaces. Don't miss an insight into Aboriginal culture at the Bunjilaka centre. *See p. 16, bullet* ❼.

❹ kids **IMAX Theatre.** Films run every hour on the really big screen of this special theatre next to the Melbourne Museum. *See p. 33, bullet* ❶.

❺ **Carlton Gardens Farmers Market.** Inner-city dwellers flock to this market to buy fresh organic fruit and vegetables straight from the growers. It also does a good trade in dairy and deli goodies, alongside home-baked cakes, bread, jams and more. The school parents run a fundraiser sausage sizzle, too! ⌚ *1 hr. Carlton Gardens Primary School, 215 Rathdowne St. 9am–1pm 3rd Saturday of the month.*

The Royal Exhibition Building is surrounded by lovely gardens that come alive in spring.

6 La Mama. A much-loved part of the Melbourne theatre scene, since the 1960s La Mama has been the launch pad for many of Australia's best playwrights, actors and directors. Set back from the street in an old factory, the theatre recently won the battle to survive closure—raising enough funds from its passionate supporter base to buy the building from the long-time landlords. *205 Faraday St. ☎ (03) 9347 6948. www.lamama.com.au.*

7 ★★ Brunetti. For some of my out-of-town guests, a trip to Melbourne isn't complete without a visit to Brunetti—and they'll happily travel across the city for it. More than a cake shop, more than a great Italian restaurant, Brunetti is an institution that offers a dazzling array of sweet treats in its *pasticceria*—and they're as good as they look! In summer, don't go past the gelati. *194–204 Faraday St. ☎ (03) 9347 2801. www.brunetti.com.au.*

8 Lygon Street. The crowds of tourists have taken some of the charm from Lygon Street in recent years, but it remains the heart of Carlton, where Melbourne cafe culture was born. Imitate the university students, elderly Italians and dog-walkers you'll be rubbing shoulders with—ignore the touts trying to get you into their restaurants, and wander in and out of the street's bookshops, boutiques and small galleries instead. The leafy stretch from Queensberry Street to Elgin Street is where most of the action is, its Victorian terrace houses now crammed with restaurants, cafes and shops. 🕐 *1 hr.*

9 ★ Lygon Foodstore. Stock up on cheese cut from a great wheel, savour the deli aromas, or perch on a stool at the bar down the back for a short black and a bruschetta or panini with your choice of fillings. There are tables out the front for those who love people-watching. 🕐 *30 min. 263 Lygon St. ☎ (03) 9347 6279.*

Lygon Foodstore is a foodie's delight.

Argyle Square's Piazza Italia is home to a giant sundial.

10 **Carlton Yacht Club Bar.** It's easily missed in this busy street, but the oddly named CYC Bar is worth a look for novelty value. It gets its moniker from a 1920s entrepreneur, Sam Nelson, who unsuccessfully petitioned the city fathers to build a canal from Port Phillip Bay to Lygon Street, so he could indulge his passion for yachting. The appropriately nautical-themed CYC stands on the site of Nelson's former offices. Stop in for a drink or a pizza. ***298 Lygon St.*** ☎ ***(03) 9347 7080. www.carltonyachtclubbar.com.au.***

11 **University Hotel.** Established in 1873, this longstanding Lygon Street pub has a colourful past. It's claimed that lengthy discussions over a few beers led to the founding of the famous Carlton Football Club—and that makes it, for Melbournians, almost a heritage site. ***15 min. 272 Lygon St.*** ☎ ***(03) 9347 7299. www.unihotel.com.au.***

12 **Piazza Italia.** Only a few years old, Piazza Italia is a redevelopment of Argyle Square, a pocket-handkerchief of green in the city. The piazza has traditional Italian porphyry stone paving, a giant sundial and plenty of places to sit and rest after the rigours of shopping. ***15 min. Between Lygon St & Argyle Pl Nth.***

13 **Trades Hall.** At the city end of Lygon Street, this 1874 monument to the labour movement may look forbidding, but it has a lighter side. As well as being the headquarters for trade unions, the hall is a venue for performing arts events, including the Melbourne Comedy Festival. Inside, you'll find the New International Bookshop, which specialises in books on politics, opinion and world issues. Across the street is the Eight Hour Day monument, which honours the Victorian workers who won the first eight-hour working day in the world in 1856. ***15 min. 54 Lygon St.*** ☎ ***(03) 9659 3549. www.tradeshallarts.com.au***

Lygon Street Festa

A waiters' race and pizza-throwing and spaghetti-eating competitions, along with more sedate pursuits like bocce and ballroom dancing, make the Lygon Street Festa one of Melbourne's most popular street festivals. Held each October, the weekend festival celebrates all things Italian and attracts around 600 000 people.

East Melbourne

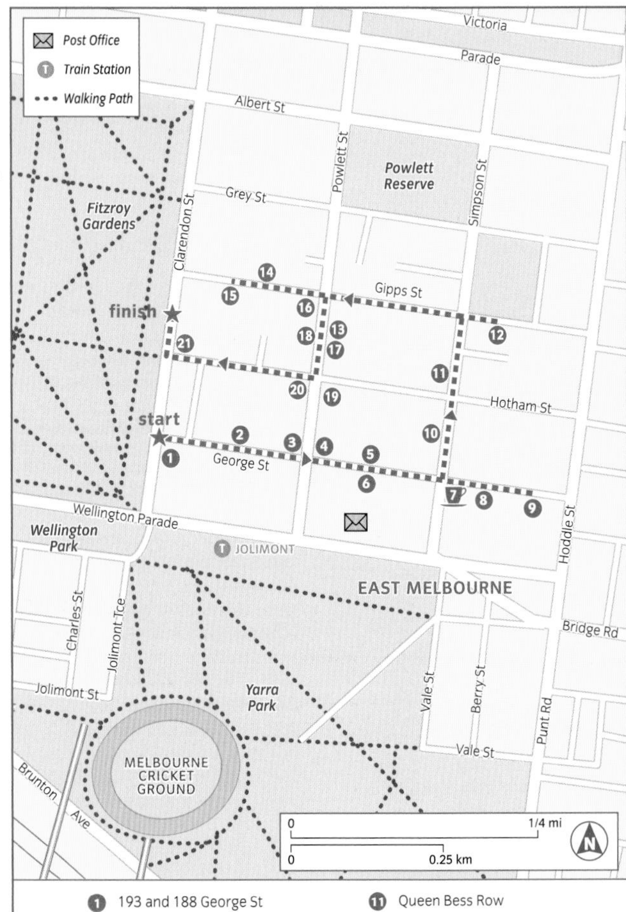

1. 193 and 188 George St
2. 182 George St
3. Canally
4. Foynes & Eastcourt
5. East Melbourne Library & Community Centre
6. 125b George St
7. George Street Café
8. 49 George St
9. Georgian Court
10. Elizabeth Terrace & Victoria Terrace
11. Queen Bess Row
12. Ola Cohn Centre for the Arts
13. Powlett Street
14. Nepean Terrace
15. Chrysalis Gallery and Studio
16. 107 Powlett St
17. Canterbury Terrace
18. 85 Powlett St
19. Cairns Memorial Church
20. The Gothic House
21. Bishopscourt

One of the city's most elegant and historic residential areas, East Melbourne will delight anyone with an interest in architecture. You'll find a mix of styles from Art Deco to contemporary, but most buildings date from the Victorian era. The mansions and terraces here were built between the 1850s (the gold-rush era) and the 1880s, and are often elaborate and always charming. START: **City Circle tram from Federation Square to Spring Street. Walk through the Treasury and Fitzroy Gardens to Clarendon Street and cross into George Street.**

❶ ★ **193 and 188 George Street.** Standing opposite each other, these two restored mansions are among East Melbourne's finest. Number 188 was built in 1886. You can see the lovely leadlight windows from the side. *5 min.*

❷ ★ **182 George Street.** This 1856 black-and-white terrace is one of East Melbourne's oldest homes. A three-storey row house, it has original timber balustrades and two verandahs. *5 min.*

The grand old building Canally.

❸ **Canally.** Sometimes known as 'Koorine', this grand house was once home to Sir Benjamin Benjamin, the first Jewish Lord Mayor of Melbourne (1887 and 1889), who lived here with his family of 13 children. The house was built in the 1860s and extended in the 1930s, and is now four apartments. *5 min. Cnr George & Powlett sts.*

❹ **Foynes and Eastcourt.** On the corner of George Street, these two white terraces, with their intricate iron lacework, resemble wedding cakes! Both were built in the 1880s. *5 min. 52 & 54 Powlett St.*

❺ **East Melbourne Library and Community Centre.** This fabulous modern building may stop you in your tracks. Opened in 2006, it was built to feature ecologically sustainable design and house an Environment Resource Centre, and is the focus of local environmental practices. Its striking glass front certainly contrasts with the Victorian homes around it! *5 min. 122 George St.* ☎ *(03) 9658 9500. www.citylibrary.org.au.*

❻ **125b George Street.** Peep down the laneway to see this purple house, believed to be one of East Melbourne's oldest homes and to have once been part of a farm. The Italian cypress tree in the driveway is more than 120 years old. *5 min.*

7 George Street Café. A corner store opened on this site in 1867 and went through several incarnations before this popular haunt opened. At breakfast time you may have to queue! At afternoon tea, the scones are served with homemade raspberry jam. Take a seat outside to gaze across at the beautiful and historic Clivedon Hill Private Hospital. *65 George St. ☎ (03) 9419 5805. $.*

8 49 George Street. At number 49 is the 1865 home of Melbourne's first surveyor, Robert Russell, who also designed St James' Old Cathedral in King Street. *5 min.*

9 Georgian Court. This 1860s apartment block sits in a leafy stretch of road bordered by English elms, opposite a converted 1920s post office. It's now run as a B&B. *5 min. 21–24 George St.* *See p. 122.*

10 ★★ Elizabeth Terrace & Victoria Terrace. These white single-storey terraces are notable for their decorative chimneys and other flourishes—Victoria Terrace has the faces of lions and cherubs moulded into its roofline. Victoria Terrace was built in 1873 and Elizabeth Terrace was constructed in 1886. *5 min. 51–57 & 59–65 Simpson St.*

11 Queen Bess Row. A landmark in East Melbourne, this wonderful four-storey red-brick building, with its arched entrances, was built in 1886 as three apartments—the first apartments purpose-built in Australia—connected with interior archways. Not surprisingly, it's classified by the National Trust. For many years it served as a boarding house, but it's now three private homes again. *5 min. Cnr Simpson & Hotham sts.*

12 ★★ Ola Cohn Centre for the Arts. Ola Cohn OBE, the Melbourne sculptor who carved the Fairies' Tree in the Fitzroy Gardens in the 1930s (see p. 85), had her home and studio here, opposite Darling Square. Her ashes—and those of several of her pets—are

Sample the delicious fare on offer at George Street Café.

buried in the lovely cobbled courtyard at the front of the house, which began life as Taylor's Livery Stables and Coach Service. Ola bought it in 1937 and turned the hayloft into her home and the stables and coach house into her studio. When she died in 1964, she left the property to the Council of Adult Education to be used as an arts centre. Now heritage-listed, the property has a permanent gallery of her work. In the courtyard there's a stone carving representing Mother Earth carrying humanity on her shoulders. *15 min. 41–43 Gipps St.*

13 ★ Powlett Street. The section of Powlett Street between Grey Street and George Street is listed on the Register of the National Estate for its outstanding historical and architectural value. Of particular note are the houses at number 130 and 138 (the latter with a large opera-box balcony), and 'Crathre', an 1873 mansion which has been a hospital and a boarding house and is now a private home. *10 min.*

14 Nepean Terrace. Built in 1864, this terrace is one of many local buildings saved from demolition by residents' action groups in the 1970s. Number 128 was the home of actor Frederick Baker, who died on stage at the Princess Theatre in 1888 and whose ghost is said to haunt it (see p. 115). *5 min. 128–132 Gipps St.*

15 Chrysalis Gallery and Studio. Number 179 was the home of Constance Stone, who became Australia's first female doctor in 1890. After being refused entry to the University of Melbourne's Medical School because she was a woman, Constance Stone went to America to train, and later worked in Canada and London. When she returned to Melbourne, she became

188 George Street (p. 61) was built in 1886.

the first woman to register with the Medical Board of Victoria—a milestone for women's rights. The house is now home to the Chrysalis Gallery and Studio, which sells fine art prints of works by Australian artists. *15 min. 179 Gipps St.* ☎ *(03) 9415 1966. www.chrysalis.com.au.*

16 107 Powlett Street. This is the former home of Australian author Joan Lindsay, famed for her novel *Picnic at Hanging Rock* (see p. 173). Her husband, Sir Daryl Lindsay, was head of the National Gallery of Victoria. *5 min.*

17 ★★ Canterbury Terrace. With 16 homes taking up the whole block, this stunning terrace is Melbourne's longest. Completed in 1878, it has 12 arches in the centre and six at either end. *5 min. 82–112 Powlett St.*

18 85 Powlett Street. Number 85 was once the home of Peter Lalor, who led the goldminers' revolt at the Eureka Stockade at Ballarat in 1854. Lalor didn't escape the uprising unscathed—he lost an arm—but went on to become a Victorian Member of Parliament, and was Speaker of the Legislative Assembly from 1880 to 1887. *5 min.*

⑲ ★★★ **Cairns Memorial Presbyterian Church.** Say a prayer outside the magnificent sandstone edifice that used to be the Cairns Memorial Presbyterian Church, because you can't get in now. Built in 1883, the church was reduced to its shell in a fire in 1988, and later converted to luxury apartments. The new additions have been cleverly done and don't detract from the original building at all. *5 min. Cnr Hotham & Powlett sts.*

⑳ ★ **The Gothic House.** This 1861 bluestone house was designed by architect Joseph Reed, who also designed the Melbourne Town Hall, State Library and Royal Exhibition Building. It was built for deputy surveyor-general Clement Hodgkinson, who designed the Fitzroy and Treasury Gardens (see p. 84). *5 min. 157 Hotham St.*

㉑ ★★ **Bishopscourt.** The oldest remaining house in the city that still has its original garden, Bishopscourt has been home to Melbourne's Anglican bishops and archbishops since it was built in 1853. It also served as Victoria's Government House from 1874 to 1876. The Italianate-style bluestone mansion is partly hidden behind a high black fence, but you can get a reasonable view through the front gates. The red-brick wing was added in 1903. *5 min. 120 Clarendon St.* ●

The Johnston Collection is an antique-filled house museum.

Behind Closed Doors

One of Melbourne's most exclusive house museums, The **Johnston Collection** (☎ (03) 9416 2515. www.johnstoncollection.org), is in this neighbourhood. I can't tell you where, because planning permits aimed at controlling parking and preserving the peace and privacy of residents make it illegal to publish the address—but don't worry, there's a way you can see it. The Johnston Collection is made up of English and French antiques that belonged to antique dealer William R Johnston, who died in 1986. It features Georgian, Regency and Louis XV furniture and decorative arts, with pieces dating from the 17th to the 19th century. Entry is by guided tour only. When you call to book, arrangements will be made to pick you up at the Hilton on the Park near the Fitzroy Gardens. You'll be delivered to the house for your tour, then dropped back to the hotel. The cloak-and-dagger approach might seem over the top, but it certainly adds to the experience! Ninety-minute tours run three times a day on weekdays and occasionally on Saturday mornings and evenings, and cost $29 Saturdays and evenings, and $22 all other times. There's a maximum of eight people in each group.

4 The Best **Shopping**

Shopping **Best Bets**

Best **Aboriginal Art**
★★★ Aboriginal Galleries of Australia, *35 Spring St (p. 68)*; and ★ Koorie Connections—Altair, *155 Victoria St (p. 68)*

Best **Arcade**
★★★ Block Arcade, *between Collins, Little Collins & Elizabeth sts (p. 74)*

Best **Art & Craft Market**
★★★ St Kilda Esplanade Art & Craft Market, *Upper Esplanade, St Kilda (p. 73)*

Best **Aussie Surf Wear**
Ozmosis, *Melbourne Central, Lonsdale St (p. 69)*

Best **Australiana**
★★ Australian Geographic, *Shop 253 Melbourne Central, La Trobe & Elizabeth sts (p. 69)*

Best **Bargain Books**
★★ Books @ Fed Square, *Flinders St (p. 73)*

Best **Designer Duds**
Alice Euphemia, *Cathedral Arcade, 37 Swanston St. (p. 71)*

Best **Made in Melbourne**
★ Counter, *31 Flinders Lane (p. 69)*

Best **Music Cavern**
The Basement Discs, *24 Block Place. (p. 70)*

Best **Suburban Shopping Street**
★★★ Chapel Street, *South Yarra (p. 71)*

Best **Vintage Clothes**
Retrostar, *37 Swanston St (p. 74)*

Previous page: Alice Euphemia is filled with designer delights.

Design a Space (p. 72) is a platform for up-and-coming designers to sell their wares.

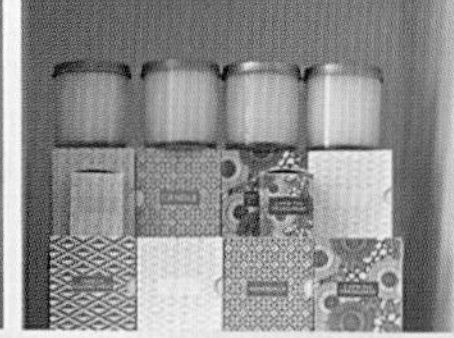

City Centre Shopping

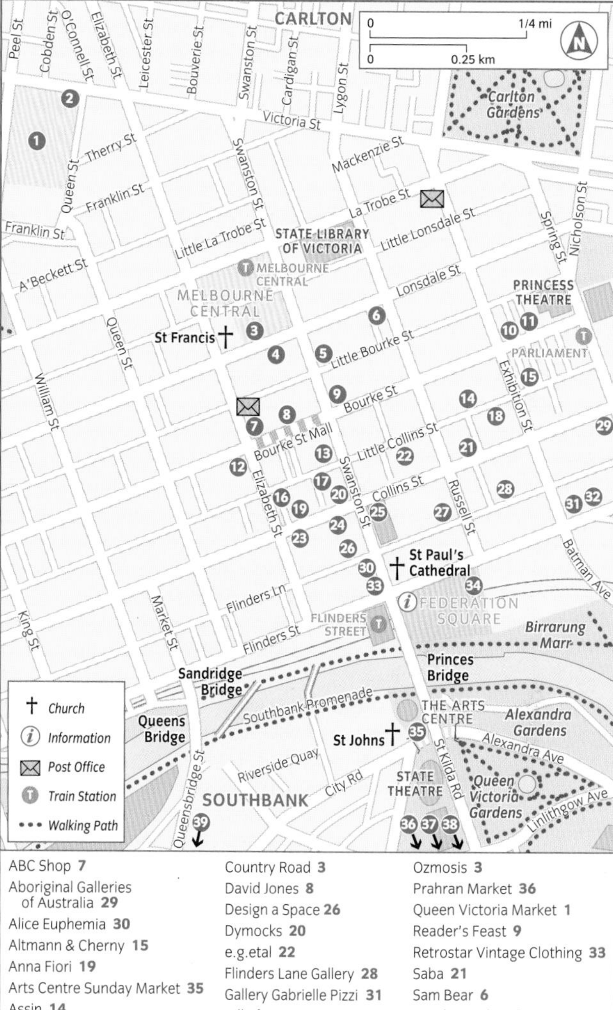

ABC Shop **7**
Aboriginal Galleries of Australia **29**
Alice Euphemia **30**
Altmann & Cherny **15**
Anna Fiori **19**
Arts Centre Sunday Market **35**
Assin **14**
Australian Geographic Shop **3, 12**
The Basement Discs **23**
Bettina Liano **13**
Books @ Fed Square **34**
Christine **27**
Counter **32**
Country Road **3**
David Jones **8**
Design a Space **26**
Dymocks **20**
e.g.etal **22**
Flinders Lane Gallery **28**
Gallery Gabrielle Pizzi **31**
Hill of Content **11**
Koorie Connections **2**
mag nation **16**
Metropolis **5**
Miss Louise **25**
Myer **4**
Original & Authentic Aboriginal Art **10**
Ozmosis **3**
Prahran Market **36**
Queen Victoria Market **1**
Reader's Feast **9**
Retrostar Vintage Clothing **33**
Saba **21**
Sam Bear **6**
Scanlan & Theodore **17**
Shag **24**
South Melbourne Market **39**
St Kilda Esplanade Art & Craft Market **38**
Veg Out St Kilda Farmers' Market **37**
Verve Boutique **18**

Melbourne Shopping A to Z

Aboriginal Art

★ **Aboriginal Galleries of Australia** CITY CENTRE Private gallery with an extensive range of paintings by some of Australia's most famous Indigenous artists, including Emily Kame Kngwarray. *35 Spring St. ☎ (03) 9654 2516. www.agamelbourne.com. MC, V. Tram: City Circle. Train: Parliament. Map p. 67.*

Flinders Lane Gallery CITY CENTRE The place to find work by central and western desert Aboriginal artists including those from the Utopia, Spinifex and Papunya communities. *137 Flinders Ln. ☎ (03) 9654 3332. www.flg.com.au. MC, V. Tues–Fri 11am–6pm, Sat 11am–4pm. Tram: 109 or 112. Train: Flinders St or Parliament. Map p. 67.*

Gallery Gabrielle Pizzi CITY CENTRE Respected dealer in Aboriginal art, representing artists from traditional communities including the Tiwi Islands, as well as urban Indigenous artists. *Lvl 3, 75–77 Flinders Ln. ☎ (03) 9654 2944. www.gabriellepizzi.com.au. MC, V. Tues–Fri 10am–5.30pm, Sat 11am–5pm. Train: Flinders St. Tram: City Circle. Map p. 67.*

Koorie Connections—Altair CITY CENTRE Crammed with painted boomerangs, T-shirts, large paintings, decorated emu eggs, pottery and didgeridoos, this small shop at the Queen Victoria Market may look like any other souvenir shop, but it's much more.

Flip-flops from Ozmosis are an Aussie summer essential.

Is It Authentic?

How do you know if the Aboriginal artwork you're buying is authentic? Fakes have been an issue since the popularity—and prices—of Indigenous art soared a decade or so ago, so it's important to ask the right questions before parting with your hard-earned cash. The City of Melbourne has introduced a Code of Practice for galleries and retailers, with guidelines on the ethical sale of Indigenous art. Check if the shop you're dealing with has adopted it. Also ask for the details of the artists: where they come from, whether they're part of a co-operative, whether they've they signed the work. For crafts and souvenirs such as boomerangs and didgeridoos, ask what kind of wood it is made of (fakes are often bamboo or teak). For more information and a list of dealers who subscribe to the Code of Practice, visit www.melbourne.vic.gov.au/indigenousarts or call ☎ (03) 9658 9658.

Owner Julie Peers and her husband Les pride themselves on selling only authentic work—and will give advice on how to spot a fake when you see it. Works on display come from all around Australia. *Queen Victoria Specialty Shops, 155 Victoria St. ☎ (03) 9326 9824. MC, V. Daily except Mon & Wed 9am–4pm. Train: Flagstaff. Map p. 67.*

Original & Authentic Aboriginal Art CITY CENTRE Stop here for artworks and traditional bark paintings from the Central Western Desert region, the Kimberley and Arnhemland, as well as boomerangs, didgeridoos, clap sticks and Aboriginal glass art. *90 Bourke St. ☎ (03) 9663 5133. www.authaboriginalart.com.au. AE, MC, V. Tram: 86, 96. Train: Parliament. Map p. 67.*

Aussie Apparel

Country Road CITY CENTRE One of Australia's best-known names for men's and women's fashion, Country Road has cool, classic looks that don't come cheap, but are good quality. *Shop 125 Melbourne Central, Lonsdale St. ☎ 1800 801 911. www.countryroad.com.au. MC, V. Train: Melbourne Central. Map p. 67.*

Ozmosis CITY CENTRE Hip beachwear at reasonable prices, as well as surfboards, boogie boards and sunglasses. All the big names in Australian surfwear are here, including Rip Curl, Quiksilver and Billabong. *Shop 2 Melbourne Central, Lonsdale St. ☎ (03) 9662 3815. www.ozmosis.com.au. MC, V. Train: Melbourne Central. Map p. 67.*

Saba CITY CENTRE Australian designer Joseph Saba has several very expensive, in-vogue boutiques for men and women in Melbourne, including this one on Collins Street and one in the Melbourne Central complex. *234 Collins St. ☎ (03) 9654 3524. www.saba.com.au. MC, V. Tram: 11, 12, 31, 42, 109. Train: Flinders St. Map p. 67.*

Sam Bear CITY CENTRE Sam Bear is a good bet for Outback-style fashions: things like Driza-Bone coats, Akubra bush hats, R.M. Williams boots and clothing and Blundstone boots. It also sells camping equipment. *225 Russell St. ☎ (03) 9663 2191. www.sambear.com.au. AE, MC, V. Tram: 86, 96. Train: Parliament. Map p. 67.*

Australiana

★ **Australian Geographic Shop** CITY CENTRE You'll find high-quality and often quirky Australiana in this chain store, including crafts, books, educational and science-based toys and gadgets. *Shop 253 Melbourne Central, La Trobe & Elizabeth sts. ☎ (03) 8616 6725. Train: Melbourne Central. Shop B02B Galleria Shopping Plaza, cnr Elizabeth & Little Collins sts. ☎ (03) 9670 5813. Train: Flinders St. www.australiangeographicshop.com.au. MC, V. Map p. 67.*

★ **Counter** CITY CENTRE Lovely scarves, hand-made shoes, jewellery, glass art and ceramics are among the pieces, made by emerging and established Australian craftsworkers, in this basement shop and gallery run by Craft Victoria. *31 Flinders Ln. ☎ (03) 9650 7775. www.craftvic.asn.au. MC, V. Tues–Sat. Tram: City Circle. Train: Parliament or Flinders St. Map p. 67.*

Sam Bear is the place to come for R.M. Williams boots.

Books & Music

★ **ABC Shop** CITY CENTRE ABC Shops are linked to the national broadcaster, and the books in them often reflect that. Great for Australian books, music, DVDs of your favourite shows, and they have a good range of kids' books and audio. *Shop M01 Mezzanine level, Melbourne GPO, cnr Elizabeth & Bourke sts.* ☎ *1300 360 111. www.abcshops.com.au. MC, V. Train: Flinders St. Map p. 67.*

★★ **The Basement Discs** CITY CENTRE Hidden down a flight of stairs, this cavernous space is a treasure trove for music lovers, especially those who favour artists outside the mainstream. If you can't find what you're after, helpful staff will hunt it out for you. *24 Block Pl.* ☎ *(03) 9654 1110. www.basementdiscs.com.au. MC, V. Train: Flinders St. Map p. 67.*

★ **Dymocks** CITY CENTRE This large basement store is part of a well-regarded national chain of bookstores that also sells music and DVDs. This one also has a small ABC Shop within it. *234 Collins St.* ☎ *(03) 9663 0900. www.dymocks.com.au. AE, DC, MC, V. Train: Flinders St. Map p. 67.*

★★ **Hill of Content** CITY CENTRE Established in 1922, this is one of Melbourne's treasures, with a fine collection of books, including a whole floor devoted to the arts, classics and poetry. *86 Bourke St.* ☎ *(03) 9662 9472. www.hillofcontentbookshop.com.au. AE, DC, MC, V. Tram: 86, 96. Train: Parliament. Map p. 67.*

Hill of Content bookstore.

★★ **mag nation** CITY CENTRE Two levels of escapism where you'll find almost any magazine on any subject your heart and mind desire. Buy or browse…they don't seem to mind. There are more than 4000 titles to dip into. *88 Elizabeth St.* ☎ *(03) 9663 6559. www.magnation.com.au. MC, V. Train: Flinders St. Map p. 67.*

Metropolis CITY CENTRE This specialist bookstore has a huge range of books about architecture, design, pop culture, film, music, photography, fashion and the performing arts, complemented by CDs and vinyl representing a similarly interesting range of music. *Lvl 3 Curtin House, 252 Swanston St.* ☎ *(03) 9663 2015. www.metropolisbookshop.com.au. MC, V. Train: Flinders St. Map p. 67.*

★★ **Reader's Feast** CITY CENTRE Head down the escalator to this enormous Aladdin's Cave of books, music and more. If you can't find something, it's likely the knowledgeable staff will be able to help. *Midtown Plaza, cnr Bourke & Swanston sts.* ☎ *(03) 9662 4699. www.readersfeast.com.au. AE, DC, MC, V. Tram: 86, 96. Train: Flinders St. Map p. 67.*

Department Stores

David Jones CITY CENTRE DJs—as this massive store is affectionately known—spans two blocks, separated into men's and women's stores. You'll find designer names such as Collette Dinnigan, Veronika Maine, Saba, Lisa Ho and Easton Pearson here. And be sure not to miss the wonderful food hall! *310 Bourke St Mall.* ☎ *(03) 9643 2222. www.davidjones.com.au. AE, DC, MC, V. Tram: 86, 96. Train: Flinders St or Melbourne Central. Map p. 67.*

mag nation is heaven for magazine aficionados.

Myer CITY CENTRE The grande dame of Melbourne's department stores, Myer also straddles Bourke and Lonsdale streets. The store is undergoing a massive redevelopment, and all but two floors of the Bourke Street store will be closed until the end of 2009. However, most of the stock, apart from the furniture section, will remain in the Lonsdale Street store. Myer stocks a wide range of designer labels, including Ben Sherman, Vivienne Westwood, Paule Ka, Armani Jeans and Seafolly. Featured Australian designers include Toni Maticevski, Jayson Brunsdon, Nicola Finetti, Josh Goot and camilla and marc. Each December, the Myer Christmas windows are a huge attraction. ***295 Lonsdale St. ☎ (03) 9661 1111. www.myer.com.au. AE, DC, MC, V. Tram: 86, 96. Train: Flinders St or Melbourne Central. Map p. 67.***

Designer Duds

★★ Alice Euphemia CITY CENTRE A champion of upcoming Australian and New Zealand designers, this boutique stocks labels by around 80 different fashion geniuses. Look for labels such as Antipodium and Mjolk, and quirky jewellery. ***Cathedral Arcade, 37 Swanston St. ☎ (03) 9650 4300. www.aliceeuphemia.com. MC, V. Train: Flinders St. Map p. 67.***

Assin CITY CENTRE Top-line labels and current European season stock fight for attention in this basement boutique. It stocks both men's and women's ranges for most designers, and there are shoes and accessories, too. ***138 Little Collins St. ☎ (03) 9654 0158. www.assin.com.au. MC, V. Train: Flinders St. Map p. 67.***

Bettina Liano CITY CENTRE This Melbourne label is for the young and skinny and those with supermodel proportions! Famed for her jeans, Liano's gear is said

Shopping Streets

Some of Melbourne's most famous shopping streets are outside the city centre, but are well worth the tram or train fare. Bargain-hunters flock to **Bridge Road, Richmond**, renowned for its factory outlets and clearance stores. For the latest fashions and labels—think Alannah Hill, Saba and Wayne Cooper—**Chapel Street** in South Yarra and Prahran can take all day to do properly. **Greville Street** is great for retro clothing, streetwear and young designers. On Sunday afternoons, catch the Greville Street Market for new and secondhand fashion, art, craft, books and bric-a-brac.

to have made it into the closets of Paris Hilton, Dannii Minogue, Courtney Love and other celebs… and nothing much over a size 8 hangs on the racks here. But it's not just jeans, there are also gorgeous dresses, skirts and suits in silk, jersey, cotton and knits. *269 Little Collins St. ☎ (03) 9654 1912. www.bettinaliano.com. MC, V. Train: Flinders St. Map p. 67.*

★ **Christine** CITY CENTRE Bags, scarves, hats, belts, brooches… whatever the accessory you need (or think you need), you're likely to find it in this store, where women, it's said, have been known to faint with joy at the fabulous range. *181 Flinders Ln. ☎ (03) 9654 2011. MC, V. Train: Flinders St. Map p. 67.*

Design a Space CITY CENTRE A vehicle for new talent to show their stuff (and sell it), this 'retail gallery' has new designers rotating monthly, with pieces from about 70 independent Australian designers in store at any time. *20 Manchester Ln. ☎ (03) 9663 8991. www.designaspace.com.au. MC, V. Train: Flinders St. Map p. 67.*

Scanlan & Theodore CITY CENTRE This Australian designer brand offes elegant and timeless creations for women. Whatever you choose may cost you a lot, but you'll very likely keep it forever. *285 Little Collins St. ☎ (03) 9650 6195. www.scanlantheodore.com.au. MC, V. Train: Flinders St. Map p. 67.*

Miss Louise (p. 74): bright and often bizarre footwear.

★★ **Verve Boutique** CITY CENTRE Only in Melbourne! Where else would you find a trendy boutique combined with a tempting coffee shop? The clothes hang along one wall and up the stairs to a small mezzanine; the rest is pure cafe! Sip while you think your purchases over. *177 Little Collins St. ☎ (03) 9639 5886. AE, DC, MC, V. Train: Flinders St. Map p. 67.*

Jewellery

Altmann & Cherny CITY CENTRE Even if you're not going to buy anything, it's worth popping in here to get a look at 'Olympic Australis', the largest opal in the world. The store offers tax-free shopping for international visitors. *120 Exhibition St. ☎ (03) 9650 9685. www.altmanncherny.com.au. AE, DC, MC, V. Train: Parliament. Map p. 67.*

★★ **e.g.etal** CITY CENTRE These two stores have fresh, innovative, exquisite jewellery by 80 or so of Australia and New Zealand's leading and emerging designers. Rings to die for … and much more. *185 Little Collins St. ☎ (03) 9663 4334. 167 Flinders Ln. ☎ (03) 9639 5111. www.egetal.com.au. MC, V. Train: Flinders St. Map p. 67.*

Markets

★ **Arts Centre Sunday Market** CITY CENTRE Spilling along the pavement and into the underpass below, the 150 or so stalls at this market offer an endless array of gift and souvenir ideas. *100 St Kilda Rd. ☎ (03) 9281 8000. www.theartscentre.net.au/sundaymarket. Sun 10am–5pm. Train: Flinders St. Map p. 67.*

★★ **Books @ Fed Square** CITY CENTRE Bargain-hunting bookworms should mark the calendar for this monthly book market—the only one in Melbourne. It offers more than 5000 books, and the chatty booksellers provide recommendations and reviews.

Fresh produce at Queen Vic market.

Cnr Swanston & Flinders sts. ☎ (03) 9655 1900. Every Sat & 3rd Sun 11am–5pm. Tram: City Circle. Train: Flinders St. Map p. 67.

Prahran Market PRAHRAN This where everyone, from students to famous faces, buys their weekly produce. Prahran Market is Australia's longest running market—since 1864—and offers top-quality fresh produce in a lively buzz. Pop along on Sundays for live jazz in the market square, where you can sit at one of the cafes and soak up the atmosphere. There are also kids' activities and cooking classes on offer. *163–185 Commercial Rd. ☎ (03) 8290 8220. www.prahranmarket.com.au. Tues & Thurs–Fri 6.30am–6pm, Sat 6.30am–5pm, Sun 10am–3pm. Tram: 72. Train: Prahran. Map p. 67.*

Queen Victoria Market CITY CENTRE It has a lot of junk, but people still flock here. The best bits of the market are the deli section and the cheap eats. A two-hour Foodies Dream Tour runs on Tuesday, Thursday, Friday and Saturday at 10am and costs $30 per person, including tastings. Night markets run in summer on Wednesdays from 5.30pm to 10pm. *513 Elizabeth St (between Peel, Victoria & Therry sts). ☎ (03) 9320 5822. www.qvm.com.au. Tues & Thurs 6am–2pm, Fri 6am–6pm, Sat 6am–3pm; Sun 9am–4pm. Closed Mon, Wed & public holidays. Food stalls closed Sun. Tram: 19, 55, 57, 59, 68. Map p. 67.*

South Melbourne Market SOUTH MELBOURNE Established 127 years ago, the South Melbourne Market has super-fresh fruit and vegetables, deli fare and household goods, and also offers the usual cheap clothing and knick-knacks. *Cecil St. ☎ (03) 9209 6295. www.southmelbournemarket.com.au. Sat, Sun & Wed 8am–4pm, Fri 8am–6pm. Tram: 12, 96.*

★ **St Kilda Esplanade Art & Craft Market** ST KILDA Under the palms along the Upper Esplanade overlooking the bay, more than 200 artists—painters, potters, photographers, jewellers, woodworkers and others—sell their wares. Colourful and sometimes quirky. *Upper Esplanade. ☎ (03) 9209 6777. Sun 10am–5pm. Tram: 3, 16, 96, 112.*

★★ **Veg Out St Kilda Farmers' Market** ST KILDA Bring your own bag to this authentic farmers' market, because you're likely to shop up big and it's a plastic-bag-free zone. Organic vegetables, free-range eggs, herbs, meat and fish vie for attention with breads, berries, cheeses, chutneys, pâtés and so much more. Come early! *Peanut Farm Reserve, Chaucer St. www.vegout.asn.au. 1st Sat of the month 8.30am–1pm. Tram: 3, 16, 96, 112.*

Shoes

Anna Fiori CITY CENTRE Melbourne-made Anna Fiori shoes have been gracing the feet of local women since the 1960s, offering

Come to Shag for pre-loved glamour gear.

European style, designer touches and practical comfort. *Shop 22, Block Arcade.* ☎ *(03) 9650 5333. MC, V. Train: Flinders St. Map p. 67.*

Miss Louise CITY CENTRE Bright and sometimes bizarre footwear, from boots to strappy stilettos. All the big names are here: Dolce & Gabbana, Chloé, Jimmy Choo, Valentino, Balenciaga, Sergio Rossi and Bottega Veneta. There are also bags, sunglasses and more. *205 Collins St.* ☎ *(03) 9654 7730. www.misslouise.com.au. MC, V. Train: Flinders St. Map p. 67.*

Vintage Clothing

★★ Retrostar Vintage Clothing CITY CENTRE Get lost inside this massive time warp. Whether your penchant is for 1960s bellbottoms or fabulous hats, denim or sheepskin, kaftans or even a bridal gown ... you'll have fun turning back the fashion clock to anywhere between the '40s and the '80s. *Upstairs, Cathedral Arcade, 37 Swanston St.* ☎ *(03) 9663 1223. www.retrostar.com.au. AE, DC, MC, V. Train: Flinders St. Map p. 67.*

★★ Shag CITY CENTRE This wonderful emporium mixes retro and vintage wear with a limited range of brand-new 'vintage-style' clothing. Mix and match! It's especially good for pre-loved glamour gear. *Shop 20, Centreway Arcade, 259–268 Collins St.* ☎ *(03) 9663 8166. MC, V. Train: Flinders St. Map p. 67.* ●

Addicted to Arcades

Some of the best discoveries you'll make in Melbourne will be hidden away in the laneways and arcades that proliferate in the city centre. Sometimes I think the arcades themselves are more beautiful than the stores. Soaring ceilings, intricate archways, fine frescos, stained glass and quirky little surprises abound, as if the architects had fun with them. Explore the stunning 19th-century Block and Royal arcades and Art Deco Cathedral Arcade—if you resist spending any money, you'll go home richer in two senses. My favourite is the gorgeous **Block Arcade**, built in the early 1890s, which has a glass roof and a lovely mosaic floor. Tours of the arcade are run on Tuesdays (☎ (03) 9650 2777) and Thursdays (☎ (03) 9654 5244) at 1pm. In **Royal Arcade**, look up to see the effigies of mythical figures Gog and Magog either side of a clock which chimes each hour. In the **Centreway Arcade**, look closely at the wall of brass Helvetica type at one end, which spells out the message: 'We live in a society that sets an inordinate value on consumer goods and services'.

5 The **Great Outdoors**

Royal Botanic Gardens

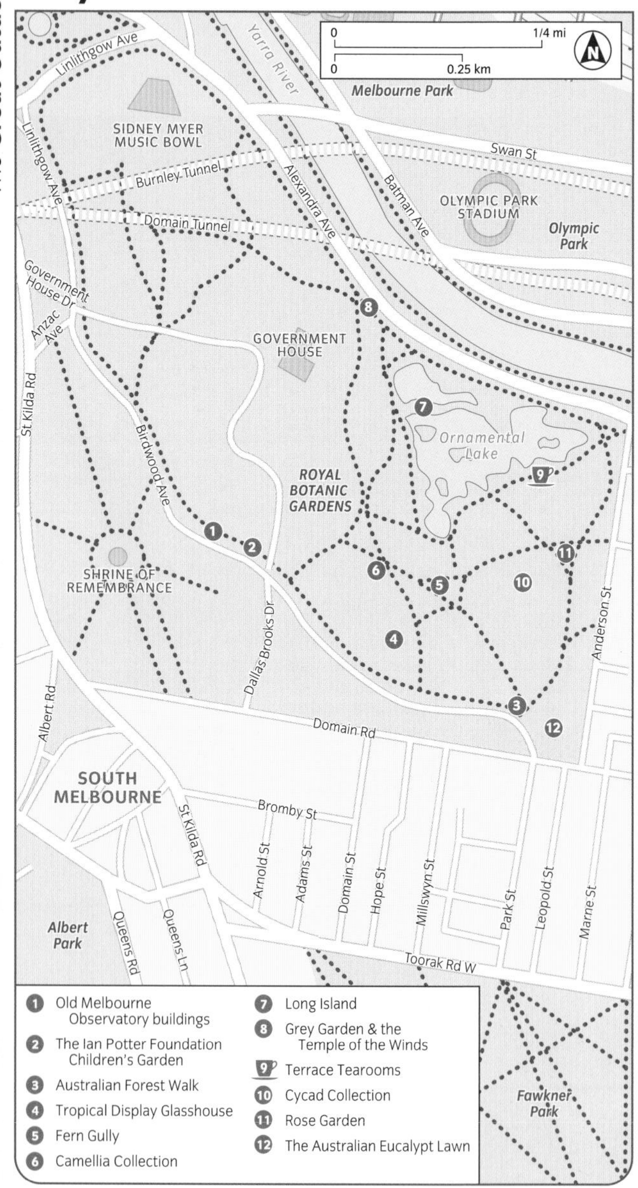

Previous page: The iconic Brighton Beach bathing boxes.

Laid out with an artist's eye, the Royal Botanic Gardens were established in 1846 and are a sanctuary for native birds and Melbournians looking for a green and tranquil spot. On the southern banks of the Yarra, the RBG covers nearly 40ha, but is still within walking distance of the city centre. The oldest part of the gardens is the Tennyson Lawn, with its 120-year-old English elms. START: **Tram 8 from Swanston Street and walk from the Shrine of Remembrance on St Kilda Rd to Birdwood Ave.**

The Old Melbourne Observatory is a great place to stargaze.

1 **Old Melbourne Observatory buildings.** Built in 1862, the Old Melbourne Observatory was once home to a 48-inch telescope—then the world's largest—known as the 'Great Melbourne Telescope'. Special evenings run by astronomy experts are held at the Observatory throughout the year to watch the night skies, the moon and the planets. Bookings are essential; times and costs vary. ☎ *(03) 9252 2429.*

2 ★★ kids **The Ian Potter Foundation Children's Garden.** A dedicated garden for kids so they can explore the world of plants. It's fun, but also a learning experience, and has been cleverly created so that kids just love it. *See p. 34, bullet 7.*

The Australia Garden

For the kind of red earth and dry-country plants you might only normally see in the outback, head to the **Royal Botanical Gardens Cranbourne** (cnr Ballarto Rd & Botanic Drive, Cranbourne; ☎ (03) 5990 2200), about an hour's drive southeast of Melbourne. It makes a great day trip. Covering more than 300ha, the gardens' key features are a large area of natural bushland and the fabulous Australia Garden (for which you pay an entry fee). Start at the Red Sand Garden, inspired by the arid lands of Australia and planted with grey-blue saltbush. There's also the Eucalypt Walk, Arid Garden and Dry River Bed and the amazing 90m-high Escarpment Wall sculpture flanking a flowing 'river' of water. In spring, wildflowers bloom. Guided tours run daily at 1pm, with specialised tours at other times. Admission is $9.50 for adults, $7.10 for students, free for children under 16; tours cost $5 for adults, $4 for children. Open daily 9am–5pm; see www.australiangarden.com.au for more details.

Visiting the Gardens

The Royal Botanic Gardens can be accessed from four gates on Birdwood Avenue, three gates on Anderson Street, South Yarra, and three on Alexandra Avenue, beside the river. The gates are open daily 7.30am–8.30pm between November and March, 7.30am–6pm in April, September and October, and 7.30am–5.30pm between May and August. The visitors centre, for guided tour bookings and information, is on Birdwood Avenue opposite the Shrine of Remembrance, and is open daily 9am–5.30pm. Call ☎ (03) 9252 2300 or visit www.rbg.vic.gov.au for more information.

3 ★ **Australian Forest Walk.** Stroll through a lush rainforest with plants from all over the country, from the Queensland tropics to Tasmania, and learn about their habitats.

4 **Tropical Display glasshouse.** This 'hot house' is full of wonderfully exotic plants like pineapple, ginger, vanilla orchids and rubber trees. *Daily 10am–4pm.*

5 **Fern Gully.** Follow a sadly too-dry stream through this cool gully, shaded by towering Moreton Bay fig trees with their amazing root systems. Look up to see the palms and ferns growing high in their branches. In the gully you'll also see the rare cabbage-tree palm, *Livisona australis*, Victoria's only native palm. It's easy to imagine for a moment that you're far from the city, deep in a subtropical rainforest.

6 **Camellia Collection.** More than 300 varieties of camellia are planted in the gardens, creating a spectacular display when they flower in the winter.

7 **Long Island.** This island at the north-western end of the Ornamental Lake has been restored to near what the Lower Yarra region and the Melbourne CBD would have been like before European settlement. Indigenous plants restored here include 29 wetland species and 57 land species known to have been native to the area.

8 ★ **Grey Garden and the Temple of the Winds.** Created in the 1980s, this interesting garden has only grey and white plants, chosen both for their visual impact and because they survive well in dry conditions. The Grey Garden surrounds the Temple of the Winds,

The lovely greenery of the Tropical Display glasshouse.

A rotunda in the Botanic Gardens.

built in honour of Charles La Trobe. It has wonderful views across the Yarra.

9 **Terrace Tearooms.** This is a large, open and usually crowded place, where you'll find the usual snack foods and ice-creams. At weekends, it can be difficult to get a seat. It's near the lake at the northern end of the gardens. A better bet, for my money, is the Observatory Café (p. 15, bullet 4). *Gate A, Alexandra Ave.* ☎ *(03) 9820 9590. Daily 9am–5pm Oct–May; 9.45am–4pm April–Sept. $.*

10 ★ **Cycad Collection.** Dinosaur plants—or, to give them their proper name, 'endangered living fossils cycads'—are one of the highlights of the RBG. These ancient cone-bearing plants existed 140 to 200 million years ago and are now under threat, but they still flourish in the gardens. Several cycads are in danger of extinction; today only about 80 species naturally occur in Australia.

11 ★ **Rose Garden.** What self-respecting botanical gardens would be without a collection of the world's most popular flower? The RBG has two—for 'species' and 'hybrid tea' roses—which allow visitors to revel in the wonderful colours and fragrances of many varieties.

12 **The Australian Eucalypt Lawn.** Stroll beneath Australia's most famous native tree—the eucalyptus or gum—on this lawn. In spring, native wildflowers from across Australia also burst into life on this lawn.

Please Don't Feed the Birds

It's an offence under the Royal Botanic Gardens Regulations to feed the birds—or any other animals—in the gardens. So although it may be tempting to slip them a tasty morsel, please don't. Foreign foods such as bread are not good for their health, and there are plenty of natural food sources for them in the gardens. To learn more about the birds you'll see in the gardens, take a guided Bird Walk (☎ (03) 9252 2429).

Melbourne's **Beaches**

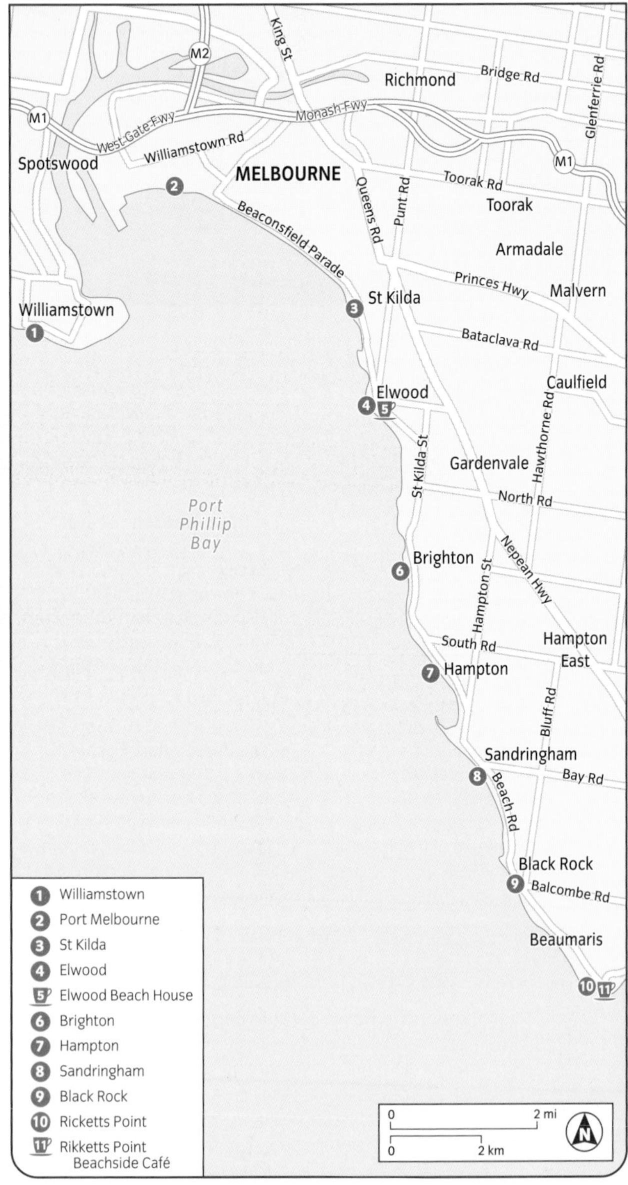

Port Phillip Bay—or just 'the bay'—is lined with beaches to which the locals flock in summer to swim and sunbathe and in winter to walk, run or cycle. Hardy Victorians brave the often chilly waters, sometimes year-round. The bay is sheltered, so there's no surf here, but more sedate pleasures remain. Here are just a few of the beaches where you can throw your towel.

1 **Williamstown.** Tucked between the greens of Hatt Reserve and Gloucester Reserve on the western side of the bay, Williamstown Beach has always been popular with families because of its shallow waters and nearby parks. There are cycling paths and a kiosk, and the old bathing pavilion is now a smart beachfront restaurant. *Train: Williamstown.*

2 ★ **Port Melbourne.** The closest beach to Melbourne's CBD, Port Melbourne is flanked by Sandridge Beach and the South Melbourne/Middle Park beach, which stretches all the way to St Kilda. Sandridge is a small beach between Webb Dock and Station Pier, with close up views of the cruise ships and Tasmanian ferry. Port Melbourne is one of Melbourne's most popular bathing beaches, with grass lawns, palms and low dunes. The path that runs along the coastline is popular with cyclists, in-line skaters, joggers and walkers. At South Melbourne/Middle Park, take a walk out on Kerferd Road Pier. *Tram: 109.*

3 ★★ **St Kilda.** When summer comes and the temperatures soar, St Kilda Beach can get awfully crowded. It may not be the most beautiful of beaches, but it has wide lawns, the famous pier, beachfront cafes and a kiosk, and is the venue for many big outdoor events. *See p. 49.*

4 **Elwood.** Popular with families, Elwood Beach's backdrop of native coastal vegetation and a wide stretch of parkland protect it from the road. There are quite a few clubs here—lifesaving, sailing, angling, sea scouts—plus a kiosk, cafe and an absolute-beachfront restaurant. Point Ormond provides a high vantage point for a great view of the bay, or you can just sit on the rock walls and dangle your feet. It's a popular area for kite-flying, so make sure to look up! *Tram: 96 to St Kilda and walk along the beachfront.*

5 **Elwood Beach House.** Set a bit back from the beach behind the surf club, this cafe/restaurant has simple kitchen-style tables and chairs and an area with lounges to relax in. There's an enclosed playground so you can watch the kids while you're sipping a latte or a cold beer. *63a Ormond Esplanade.* ☎ *(03) 9531 7788. $–$$$.*

St Kilda beach puts on a show at sunset.

Relax on the wide strech of grass at Elwood Beach (p. 81).

6 ★★★ **Brighton.** Famous for its colourful historic bathing boxes, Brighton is one of Melbourne's sandiest and safest swimming beaches. The 82 brightly painted timber boxes on the beach, where Dendy Street meets the Esplanade, have been admired and coveted (they're hot property and now fetch large sums when—rarely—they're sold) for more than a century. While there are similar bathing boxes on other parts of the Victorian coast, these are the closest to the city. Other attractions at Brighton include Middle Brighton Pier, the historic Middle Brighton Sea Baths and a host of seaside restaurants and cafes. There is a shared bicycle and walking path between Bay Street and Middle Brighton Baths. ***Train: Brighton Beach or Middle Brighton***.

7 **Hampton.** Secluded and sheltered, Hampton Beach is a bit of a secret. There's less of a crowd here, and you can stroll

The Bayside Coastal Art Trail

The Coastal Art Trail follows the paint trail left by the many notable Australian artists who have painted Port Phillip Bay's eastern coastline. Nearly 40 signboards along 17km between Middle Brighton Pier and Mentone identify the landscapes that inspired painters, including Heidelberg School founders Tom Roberts, Arthur Streeton and Frederick McCubbin. They painted here during summer camps between 1886 and 1907. Detailed signs have been erected as close as possible to where the artists set up their easels, so you can see how things have changed (or not) over the past century. For information, call ☎ (03) 9599 4444 or visit www.bayside.vic.gov.au/artstrail.

along the bike path and admire the public artworks or watch the windsurfers. The foreshore is studded with indigenous plants. *Train: Hampton.*

8 **Sandringham.** Walk or ride along the bike path or simply stroll along the wide sandy beach. Sandringham Beach has adjacent parkland, barbecues and a playground so families love it. It's also a great place to watch the yachts sail past. *Train: Sandringham.*

9 **Black Rock.** Activity on Black Rock Beach centres on Half Moon Bay and Red Bluff. The beach beyond the yacht club is wide and clean, and there's a lookout with cliff views and a couple of benches. The wreck of the HMVS *Cerberus*, which sits in Half Moon Bay, is now on the National Heritage List. Another small beach around the corner from the surf-lifesaving club is a find, but still gets a bit crowded in summer. *Train: Black Rock.*

10 **Ricketts Point.** Ricketts Point Nature Reserve is part of the Beaumaris foreshore reserve, and is a great place for families. It is shallow and sheltered and kids love paddling in the rock pools. It's also a great place to start the Coastal Art Trail. *Train: Mentone.*

11 **Ricketts Point Beachside Café.** This large open cafe, with its wide verandahs on the beachfront, is a good place for an ice-cream, a coffee or a meal. It's unpretentious, busy and the service is quick. *Beach Rd, Beaumaris. ☎ (03) 9589 3040. $.*

A lifesaver patrols Hampton Beach.

Swim Between the Flags

Lifesavers patrol many of Melbourne's beaches during summer and peak holiday times—and if you're at a patrolled beach you should swim only in the area between the red-and-yellow flags on the beach. The flags mean that lifesavers are on duty. Lifesaving patrols in Victoria usually start at the end of November and run until Easter Monday. Patrols are usually provided on weekends and most public holidays on city beaches. Daily patrols are provided during the peak summer period at the most popular holiday spots on the coast, such as those along the Great Ocean Road like Lorne, Torquay, Apollo Bay, Warrnambool and Port Fairy, and Portsea and Sorrento on the Mornington Peninsula (see Chapter 10).

Treasury & Fitzroy Gardens

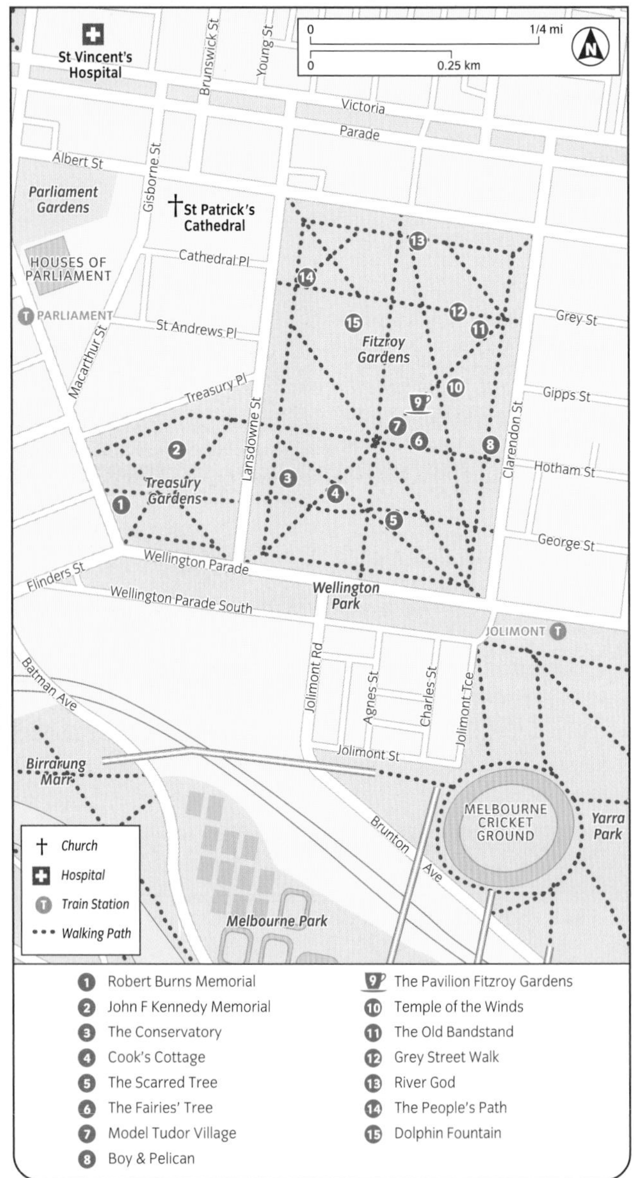

1. Robert Burns Memorial
2. John F Kennedy Memorial
3. The Conservatory
4. Cook's Cottage
5. The Scarred Tree
6. The Fairies' Tree
7. Model Tudor Village
8. Boy & Pelican
9. The Pavilion Fitzroy Gardens
10. Temple of the Winds
11. The Old Bandstand
12. Grey Street Walk
13. River God
14. The People's Path
15. Dolphin Fountain

Two of Melbourne's most popular and loved inner-city parks, these gardens are separated only by a street. Begin your escape from the city in the smaller Treasury Gardens, developed in the 1860s to set off the government buildings beside them, then cross Lansdowne Street into Fitzroy Gardens. START: **City Circle tram to Spring Street or train to Parliament.**

1 Robert Burns Memorial. First erected in St Kilda in 1904, this bronze statue of Scottish poet Robert Burns was moved to the Treasury Gardens in 1970. It's a replica of one in Burns's birthplace, the Scottish town of Ayr.

2 John F Kennedy Memorial. A small bust of the assassinated US president is attached to a rock beside the lake in the centre of the gardens. The lake is part of the original garden plan from 1867; the Kennedy memorial was erected in 1965, two years after his death.

3 ★ The Conservatory. Built in 1929, this Art Deco conservatory is a popular backdrop for wedding parties, and is as lovely inside as it is out. Statues, water features, masses of colourful flowers and even a tiny bridge make for a fine oasis. The bronze statue standing in the lily pond at the front of the conservatory is called 'Diana and the Hounds'.

4 ★★ kids Cook's Cottage. The childhood home of explorer Captain James Cook was transported from England brick by brick and reassembled in the Fitzroy Gardens in 1934 to celebrate Victoria's centenary. The tiny house was built in Yorkshire in 1755 and its interior reflects homes of that era. The kitchen garden at the back is delightful, but the large statue of Cook is slightly overbearing and the cardboard cut-outs for photos are tragic. The small shop will only take you a minute. ☎ *(03) 9419 4677. www.cookscottage.com.au. Daily 9am–5pm. Admission $4.50 adults, $2.20 children, $12 families.*

5 The Scarred Tree. Look at the trunk of this river red gum, now just a stump. It's easy to see where the land's Aboriginal inhabitants removed bark to make a shield or canoe.

6 kids The Fairies' Tree. Kids are fascinated by this carved tree, and can spend ages looking for their

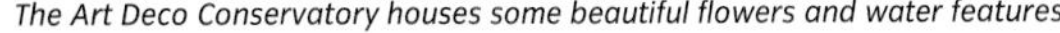

The Art Deco Conservatory houses some beautiful flowers and water features.

favourites among the elves, goblins, fairies and Australian animals etched into the bark by sculptor Ola Cohn in the 1930s (see p. 70, bullet 12). Each of the carved figures is an individual. Too many years of wear from kids' fingers and feet mean the tree is now fenced off, but the magic remains.

7 kids **Model Tudor Village.** The good folk of Lambeth gave this model village to the people of Melbourne as a thank you for food parcels sent to London during World War II. It's been in the gardens since 1948 and is still a source of delight for children of all ages.

8 **Boy and Pelican.** William Bowles' two sculptures—a boy and pelican, and a mermaid and a fish—are at the Hotham Street gate. The sculptures, carved from Pyrmont stone and sandstone, won the 1935 Fitzroy Gardens Sculpture Competition.

9 **The Pavilion Fitzroy Gardens.** The coffee, cakes and simple lunch fare are all very good here, but the service can be slow and erratic, especially when there's a big crowd or a bus tour. Still, indoor or out, it's a pleasant setting. *Wellington Pde. ☎ (03) 9417 2544. www.thepavilionfitzroygardens.com.au. $.*

10 **Temple of the Winds.** This rotunda was built in 1873 and sits on a platform of bluestone rock quarried from the gardens.

11 **The Old Bandstand.** The days of regular brass band recitals may be over, but this lovely bandstand, built in 1864, is still popular for garden weddings.

12 kids **Grey Street Walk.** The Grey Street Fountain, erected in the 1860s, stands at the Clarendon St end of the Grey Street Walk. Turning back down the walk towards Parliament, you'll find two empty pedestals—the remains of sculptures which once graced the gardens. There's also a children's playground on this stretch.

13 **River God.** The gardens' first fountain, erected in 1862, River God was built to commemorate Melbourne's first piped water supply, before which such fountains weren't possible.

14 kids **The People's Path.** Thousands of tiles, decorated and inscribed by the people of Melbourne as part of a crafts festival in 1978, are embedded in this circular path. It's colourful and fun, but the inscriptions vary from the deep and meaningful to the mundane.

15 **Dolphin Fountain.** One of the newer additions to the gardens, this 1982 fountain is now sadly often dry due to Melbourne's ongoing water shortage. Bronze dolphins, turtles and other sea creatures flounder until it rains. ●

The intricately carved Fairies' Tree is a must for children

6 The Best Dining

Dining Best Bets

Best **Beachfront Dining**
★★ Donovans $$$$ *40 Jacka Blvd, St Kilda (p. 92)*

Best **Bush Tucker**
★★ Tjanabi @ Fed Square $$$ *Flinders St (p. 96)*

Best **Cafe**
★★ Café Segovia $$ *33 Block Pl (p. 91)*

Best **Cheap Eats**
★ Lentil as Anything $ *41 Blessington St, St Kilda (p. 92)*

Best **Chinese**
★★★ Flower Drum $$$$ *17 Market Ln (p. 93)*

Best **Dumplings**
Camy Shanghai Dumpling Restaurant $ *23–25 Tattersalls Ln (p. 91)*

Best **Eat Street**
★ Acland St, St Kilda *(p. 90)*

Best **Fine Dining**
★★★ Vue de Monde $$$$$ *430 Little Collins St (p. 96)*

Best **Meals on Wheels**
★ Colonial Tramcar Restaurant *(p. 94)*

Best **Secret Rendezvous**
★ The Pantry $$ *Sofitel Melbourne, 25 Collins St (p. 96)*

Best **Spanish**
★★★ MoVida $$$ *1 Hosier Ln (p. 94)*

Best **Vegetarian**
★ Shakahari $$ *201–203 Faraday St, Carlton (p. 95)*

Previous page: Vue de Monde combines creative dishes with out-there presentation.

The cozy interior of Donovans (p. 92).

City Centre Dining

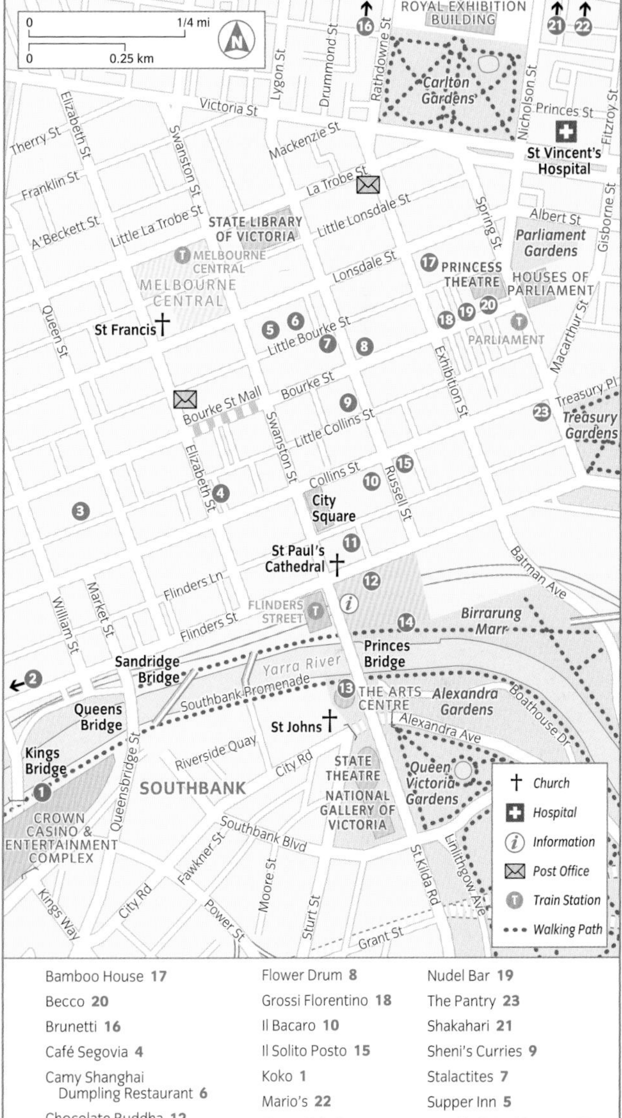

Bamboo House **17**
Becco **20**
Brunetti **16**
Café Segovia **4**
Camy Shanghai Dumpling Restaurant **6**
Chocolate Buddha **12**
EQ Café Bar **13**
Flower Drum **8**
Grossi Florentino **18**
Il Bacaro **10**
Il Solito Posto **15**
Koko **1**
Mario's **22**
Mecca Bah **2**
MoVida **11**
Nudel Bar **19**
The Pantry **23**
Shakahari **21**
Sheni's Curries **9**
Stalactites **7**
Supper Inn **5**
Tjanabi @ Fed Square **14**
Vue de Monde **3**

St Kilda Dining

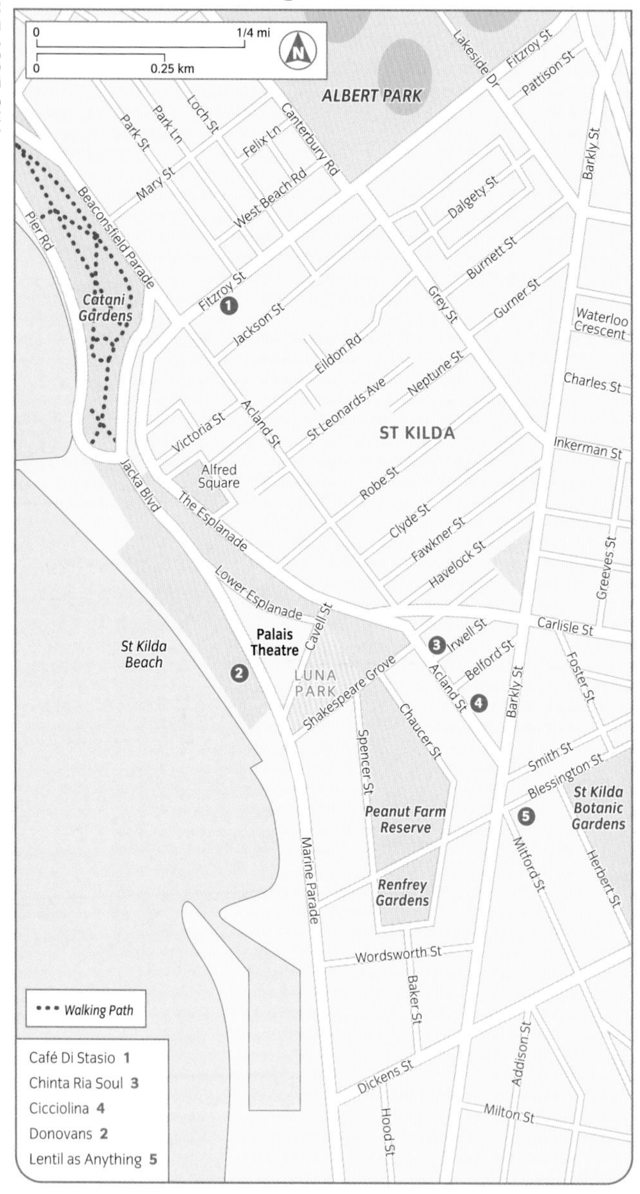

Melbourne Dining A to Z

★ **Bamboo House** CITY CENTRE *CHINESE* Attentive waiters will help you choose from the long menu of Cantonese and northern Chinese dishes; the service here is a pleasure. Order ahead for the signature Szechuan crispy fragrant duck. *47 Little Bourke St. ☎ (03) 9662 1565. www.bamboohouse.com.au. Mains $15–$33. AE, DC, MC, V. Lunch Mon–Fri; dinner daily. Tram: City Circle. Train: Flinders St. Map p. 89.*

★★ **Becco** CITY CENTRE *ITALIAN* Stylish service and stylish customers, all without pretension, make this a hit whether you're settling in for the full experience or sampling the bar menu. Finish off with the best tiramisu in town. *11–25 Crossley St. ☎ (03) 9663 3000. www.becco.com.au. Mains $26–$43. AE, DC, MC, V. Lunch Mon–Sat; dinner daily. Tram: 86, 96. Train: Parliament. Map p. 89.*

Brunetti CARLTON *ITALIAN* For a real Italian experience, walk past the mouth-watering range of excellent cakes and head to the quiet little à la carte restaurant section at the side. The lunch and dinner menu offers authentic Italian cuisine, done very well. *198–204 Faraday St. ☎ (03) 9347 2801. Mains $19–$30. AE, DC, MC, V. Breakfast, lunch & dinner Mon–Sat; brunch Sun. Tram: 1, 15, 21, 22 from Swanston St. Map p. 89.*

★★ **Café Di Stasio** ST KILDA *ITALIAN* Even after years as one of Melbourne's top restaurants, Di Stasio manages still to evoke a love-hate relationship with its clientele. While service can depend on the mood of the staff sometimes, the food is consistently excellent. At night it's intimate and low lit, but lunch offers one of the best bargains around: a $30 set menu (if you can stick to it!). *31a Fitzroy St. ☎ (03) 9525 3999. Mains $35–$40. AE, MC, V. Lunch & dinner daily. Tram: 16, 96, 112. Map p. 90.*

★ **Café Segovia** CITY CENTRE *CAFE* One of my favourites, Café Segovia is always friendly, always busy, and sits in an atmospheric laneway. It has an intimate interior and there's also seating outside in the arcade, but you'll have to come early at lunchtime to nab a table. Meals are light but servings generous. *33 Block Pl. ☎ (03) 9650 2373. Mains $16–$27. AE, DC, MC, V. Breakfast, lunch & dinner daily; closed Sun night. Tram: City Circle. Train: Flinders St. Map p. 89.*

★★ **Camy Shanghai Dumpling Restaurant** CITY CENTRE *CHINESE* Some believe this noisy, crowded place cooks the best Shanghai food outside Shanghai. Test it out! Have the spring onion pancake, but otherwise concentrate on the generous serves of dumplings, large and small, savoury and sweet. Yum! *23–25 Tattersalls Ln. ☎ (03) 9663 8555. Mains $5–12. No cards. Lunch & dinner daily. Train: Melbourne Central. Map p. 89.*

Mouth-watering sugary delights at Brunetti.

★ **Chinta Ria Soul** ST KILDA *MALAYSIAN* Head to this very popular eatery if you're looking for simple, satisfying Malaysian food with a touch of spice. The big sellers are the laksa, mee goreng, chicken curry and sambal spinach. It's nearly always crowded and buzzy here, so don't expect privacy! ***94 Acland St. ☎ (03) 9525 4664. Mains $13–$25. AE, MC, V. Lunch & dinner daily. Tram: 16 or 96. Map p. 90.***

★ **Chocolate Buddha** CITY CENTRE *NOODLES* This is the place to head if you like mostly organic produce (including some organic wines) served up in homestyle Japanese dishes. The noodles and donburi are fresh and hearty, and the space is big, casual and creative. ***Federation Square, Flinders St. ☎ (03) 9654 5688. www.chocolatebuddha.com.au. Mains $19–$25. AE, MC, V. Lunch & dinner daily. Tram: City Circle. Train: Flinders St. Map p. 89.***

★★★ **Cicciolina** ST KILDA *CONTEMPORARY* I'm not fond of places with 'no booking' policies but this is worth an exception! Cicciolina is intimate, crowded and well-run, and has superb but simple food. There's a cosy back bar to wait in, and it's definitely worth it. ***130 Acland St. ☎ (03) 9525 3333. Mains $23–$37. AE, DC, MC, V. Lunch & dinner daily. Tram: 16 or 96. Map p. 90.***

★★ **Donovans** ST KILDA *CONTEMPORARY* Beach-house style with sunset views over the sand—who can beat that? This 1920s bathing pavilion serves up a mind-boggling array of wonderful dishes. Many are big enough for

Lentil as Anything provides food for the soul.

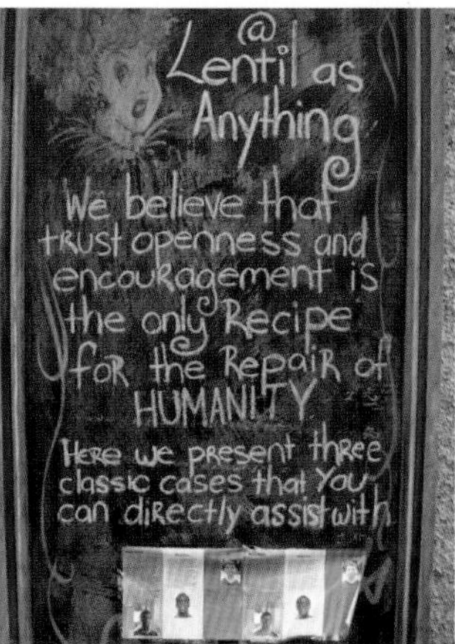

Lentil as Anything

Was it worth the money? If that's a question you sometimes ask after dining out, then you'll love **Lentil as Anything**. In a novel approach that's not surprisingly become a hit, these not-for-profit vegetarian restaurants ask customers to pay whatever they feel the meal and service were worth after they've eaten. That means you get a menu without prices...and before you leave, you put your money in a box anonymously. The food is fresh and organic, with lots of noodles and vegetables and tofu, curries and stir-fries, and the concept has been so popular that there are now three restaurants in Melbourne—at Abbotsford (☎ (03) 9419 6444), St Kilda (☎ (03) 9534 5833) and East Brunswick (☎ (03) 9388 0222). There's also a café at Artplay in Birrarung Marr. Opening hours vary, so check the website, www.lentilasanything.com. No cards.

two, including Donovans' trademark steamed mussels, linguine with seafood, and stuffed squid. *40 Jacka Blvd.* ☎ *(03) 9534 8221. www.donovanshouse.com.au. Mains $30–$45. AE, DC, MC, V. Lunch & dinner daily. Tram: 16 or 96. Map p. 90.*

★ **EQ Café Bar** SOUTHBANK *CONTEMPORARY* For dinner before or after a show at the Arts Centre, don't go past EQ. The service is prompt but not rushed; they know what they're doing. The menu offers simple fare like lamb shanks and sausage and mash, but it's all done with flair. Open till midnight. *Riverside Tce.* ☎ *(03) 9645 0644. www.eqcafebar.com.au. Mains $17–$35. MC, V. Breakfast, lunch & dinner daily. Train: Flinders St. Map p. 89.*

★★★ **Flower Drum** CITY CENTRE *CHINESE* It's formal and somewhat clubby, but the Flower Drum has long held the reputation of having the best Cantonese food in town. Whether you order the signature Peking duck or let your waiter guide you through the chef's specials, expect something exceptional. But be prepared to pay for the privilege. *17 Market Ln.* ☎ *(03) 9662 3655. Mains $30–$45. AE, DC, MC, V. Lunch Mon–Sat; dinner daily. Tram: City Circle. Train: Flinders St. Map p. 89.*

★★★ **Grossi Florentino** CITY CENTRE *ITALIAN* This family-run restaurant serves up the best Italian food in Melbourne. Choose whether you'd like to eat in The Grill downstairs (a bistro), the Cellar Bar, or the fine-dining restaurant with its chandeliers and murals. The signature dish is wet-roasted suckling lamb or pork. *80 Bourke St.* ☎ *(03) 9662 1811. www.grossiflorentino.com. Mains $38–$48. AE, DC, MC, V. Lunch Mon–Fri; dinner Mon–Sat. Tram: 86, 96. Train: Parliament. Map p. 89.*

★ **Il Bacaro** CITY CENTRE *ITALIAN* A little slice of Venice, Il Bacaro is packed with small tables and waiters

Spice is the order of the day at Chinta Ria Soul.

delivering dishes like organic baby chicken wrapped in prosciutto. Dominated by a horseshoe-shaped bar, it's a favourite with suits sampling the excellent wine list. *168–170 Little Collins St.* ☎ *(03) 9654 6778. Mains $26–$42. AE, DC, MC, V. Lunch & dinner Mon–Sat. Train: Flinders St. Map p. 89.*

Il Solito Posto CITY CENTRE *ITALIAN* Choose between the casual bistro, its blackboard menu offering good pastas, soups and salads, and the more upmarket trattoria, which provides à la carte dining. Both are good. *113 Collins St (enter through George Pde).* ☎ *(03) 9654 4466. www.ilsolitoposto.com.au. Mains $15–$20 in bistro; $36–$40 in trattoria. AE, DC, MC, V. Breakfast, lunch & dinner Mon–Sat. Tram: 11, 12, 31, 42, 109. Train: Flinders St. Map p. 89.*

Koko SOUTHBANK *JAPANESE* Let the goldfish pond soothe you while you select your food, or just opt for the easy way out: a set menu. There are separate teppanyaki grills and screened tatami rooms where you sit on the matted floor. Be brave and try the grilled freshwater eel, and order some sake to aid digestion. *Lvl 3, Crown Towers, Yarra Promenade.* ☎ *(03) 9292 6886. www.kokoatcrown.com.au. Mains $30–$49. AE, DC, MC, V. Lunch & dinner daily. Tram: 55, 112. Map p. 89.*

Colonial Tramcar Restaurant

I was reluctant to take my mother to dinner on the tramcar restaurant when she visited Melbourne, because I thought it might be a tourist trap serving inferior food and cheap wines. But she was insistent—and it turns out mothers are often right. From the efficient greeting and checking off as we board the tram, to the well-cooked food (the kangaroo loin starter is very good) and excellent staff, it was a fun experience. The two old-style burgundy trams rattle along the tracks between South Melbourne and St Kilda, taking a circuitous route through the city. I've done the trip twice now, and the dinner journey beats the lunchtime trip by a whisker, because of the city lights. Your booth is softly lit and there's a flower for every woman as you leave. Lunch ($75) is three courses, dinner (early dinner—5.45–7.15pm—$70, dinner Sunday–Thursday $115, Friday–Saturday $130) is a choice of four or five depending on the time, with two choices of entree, main course and dessert. Book as far ahead as you can; we had to wait weeks to get on. Call ☎ (03) 9696 4000 or visit www.tramrestaurant.com.au for more information. All cards accepted.

★★★ **Mario's** FITZROY *ITALIAN* The quintessential Melbourne cafe, this place has ambience, groovy '60s decor, great coffee and impeccable service. Menu offerings include pastas, cakes and an all-day breakfast. Ponder the passing parade over an espresso, and don't forget to check out the works by local artists on the walls. ***303 Brunswick St. ☎ (03) 9417 3343. Mains $11–$21. AE, DC, MC, V. Breakfast, lunch & dinner daily. Tram: 11.*** ***Map p. 89.***

★★ **Mecca Bah** DOCKLANDS *MIDDLE EASTERN* The best way to eat at Mecca Bah is to order several of the meze plates—little dishes of delicacies. Expect things like pastries filled with Middle Eastern cheeses, silverbeet rolls filled with chickpeas, rice and herbs, or spicy lamb and pine-nut boureks (meat-filled pastries). Whatever you choose, you'll love it. ***55 Newquay Promenade. ☎ (03) 9642 1300. www.meccabah.com. Mains $16–$20. AE, DC, MC, V. Lunch & dinner daily. Tram: 30, 48 or City Circle.*** ***Map p. 89.***

★★★ **MoVida** CITY CENTRE *SPANISH* Melbournians flock here, and it's truly one of the places I was tempted to keep a secret—if that's possible when everyone talks about how great it is. Order a feast

The Colonial Tramcar Restaurant: surprisingly classy.

MoVida mussels are a delight for the senses.

of tapas (small individual dishes) or choose a racíon (a plate to share among two or more people, or a larger dish for one). This is seriously good food in a relaxed atmosphere. *1 Hosier Ln.* ☎ *(03) 9663 3038. www.movida.com.au. Tapas $3–$8; Raciones $10–$32. AE, DC, MC, V. Lunch & dinner daily. Tram: City Circle. Train: Flinders St. Map p. 89.*

Nudel Bar CITY CENTRE *NOODLES* A favourite with city slickers, the Nudel Bar serves a variety of noodle dishes—but they're not just Asian. You can get everything from macaroni cheese to cold, spicy green-tea soba. Try the sticky rice pudding for dessert. *76 Bourke St.* ☎ *(03) 9662 9100. Mains $13–$24. AE, DC, MC, V. Lunch & dinner Mon–Sat. Tram: 86, 96. Train: Parliament. Map p. 89.*

★ **Shakahari** CARLTON *VEGETARIAN* Creative and tasty dishes that will appeal to everyone. The 'Satay Legend'—skewered, lightly fried vegetables and tofu pieces with a mild but spicy peanut sauce—is a winner, as is the tagine of spiced turmeric couscous with a Moroccan herbal eggplant, zucchini and tomato ratatouille. Vegans will find the menu a pleasant surprise. *201–203 Faraday St.* ☎ *(03) 9347 3848. www.shakahari.com.au. Mains $15–$17. AE, DC, MC, V. Lunch Mon–Sat; dinner daily. Tram: 1, 15, 21, 22. Map p. 89.*

Sheni's Curries CITY CENTRE *SRI LANKAN* This tiny and very busy place offers a range of excellent-value, authentic Sri Lankan curries. Choose from three vegetable dishes and a selection of meat and seafood options. *Shp 16, 161 Collins St.* ☎ *(03) 9654 3535. Mains $5.50–$12. No cards. Lunch Mon–Fri. Tram: 11, 12, 31, 42, 109. Train: Flinders St. Map p. 89.*

Stalactites CITY CENTRE *GREEK* You can get takeaway here, but it's worth the (hopefully short) wait for a table in the superbly kitsch 'cave', complete with fake stalactites. Melbournians have been coming here since the 1970s for good-value family-style giros and souvlaki. And if you're planning to be out late, make a note of the address—it's open 24/7. *177 Lonsdale St.* ☎ *(03) 9663 3316. www.stalactites.com.au. Mains $18–22. AE, DC, MC, V. Breakfast, lunch & dinner daily. Train: Melbourne Central. Map p. 89.*

Supper Inn CITY CENTRE *CANTONESE* Another spot to head if you get the munchies late at night (it's open till 2.30am). This is a friendly, well-worn place that draws a mixed crowd tucking in to steaming bowls of congee, barbecued suckling pig, mud crab or stuffed scallops. In the wee small hours, it's a favourite stop for chefs coming off shift. *15 Celestial Ave.* ☎ *(03) 9663 4759. Mains $13–$55. AE, DC, MC, V. Dinner daily. Train: Melbourne Central. Map p. 89.*

Stalactites is great for souvlaki 24/7.

★★ **Tjanabi @ Fed Square** CITY CENTRE *INDIGENOUS AUSTRALIAN* Bush tucker meets fine dining. For a taste of what Indigenous Australians have been eating for thousands of years, book a table at Tjanabi to try native produce matched with kangaroo, wild boar or steaks from regional Victoria. For the best value and biggest range of dishes, order a selection of small plates or a tasting plate. *Federation Square, Flinders St. ☎ (03) 9662 2155. www.tjanabi.com.au. Tasting plates $20–$35; mains $24–$34. AE, DC, MC, V. Lunch & dinner daily. Tram: City Circle. Train: Flinders St. Map p. 89.*

★★★ **Vue de Monde** CITY CENTRE *FRENCH* This is a dining experience like no other, with wonderfully creative dishes rivalled by the out-there presentation—one of mine came in a test-tube! The theatrics don't detract from the menu, though, and the hefty price tag is worth it for a special occasion. The à la carte menu in the bistro is easier on the hip pocket if your budget won't stretch to the restaurant. *430 Little Collins St. ☎ (03) 9691 3888. www.vuedemonde.com.au. Menu du jour (lunch only) $55 for 2 courses, $70 for 3; Menu gourmand (degustation) $100 for lunch, $150 for dinner. Bistro Vue mains $29–$55. AE, DC, MC, V. Lunch Tues–Fri; dinner Tues–Sat. Train: Southern Cross or Flinders St. Map p. 89.* ●

Tjanabi is the place to come for Indigenous tucker.

The Pantry

The Pantry is one of the city's best kept dining secrets: you'll literally need a guide to find it, and bookings are essential. Hidden in the basement of the Sofitel Melbourne, the food and service at this training restaurant are provided by final-year apprentice chefs and hospitality students—with flair and aplomb. It's imaginative and experimental and very good, a sort of behind-the-scenes preview of up-and-coming chefs. The surroundings are pleasant too—white linen, artworks and a good ambience. You'll be met in the lobby and escorted through the back-of-house maze to your table. Open only for lunch and dinner Wednesday and Thursday at selected times during the year (usually April to September), the Pantry's worth seeking out. The Sofitel Melbourne is at 25 Collins St; call ☎ (03) 9653 0000 for more information. The $30 set menu is three courses; all cards are accepted. Tram: City Circle. Train: Parliament. Map p. 89.

7 The Best Nightlife

Nightlife Best Bets

Best Beer Selection

★ Belgian Beer Café Bluestone, *557 St Kilda Rd (p. 100)*

Best Cocktail Bar

★★★ 1806, *169 Exhibition St (p. 100)*

Best Heritage Pub

★★ Young & Jackson, *cnr Flinders & Swanston sts (p. 104)*

Best Hideaway

★★ Cicciolina Back Bar, *130 Acland St, St Kilda (p. 101)*

Best Jazz Club

★★ Bennetts Lane Jazz Club, *25 Bennetts Ln (p. 100)*

Best Powder Room

★ Tony Starr's Kitten Club, *267 Little Collins St (p. 103)*

Best Pub Music

★ The Prince of Wales Hotel, *29 Fitzroy St, St Kilda (p. 103)*; and ★ The Esplanade Hotel, *11 Upper Esplanade, St Kilda (p. 102)*

Best Value City Drinks

★★ Troika, *106 Little Lonsdale St (p. 104)*

St Kilda Nightlife

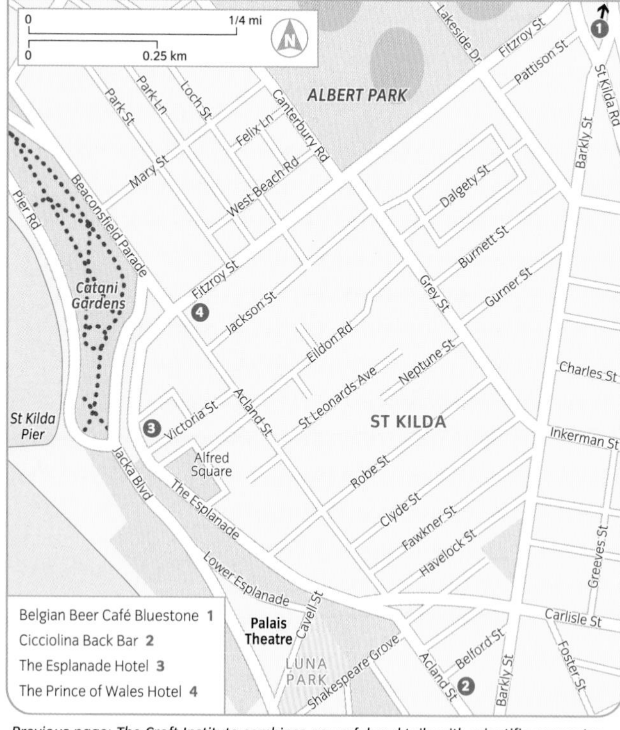

Previous page: The Croft Institute combines powerful cocktails with scientific apparatus for a truly wacky experience.

City Centre Nightlife

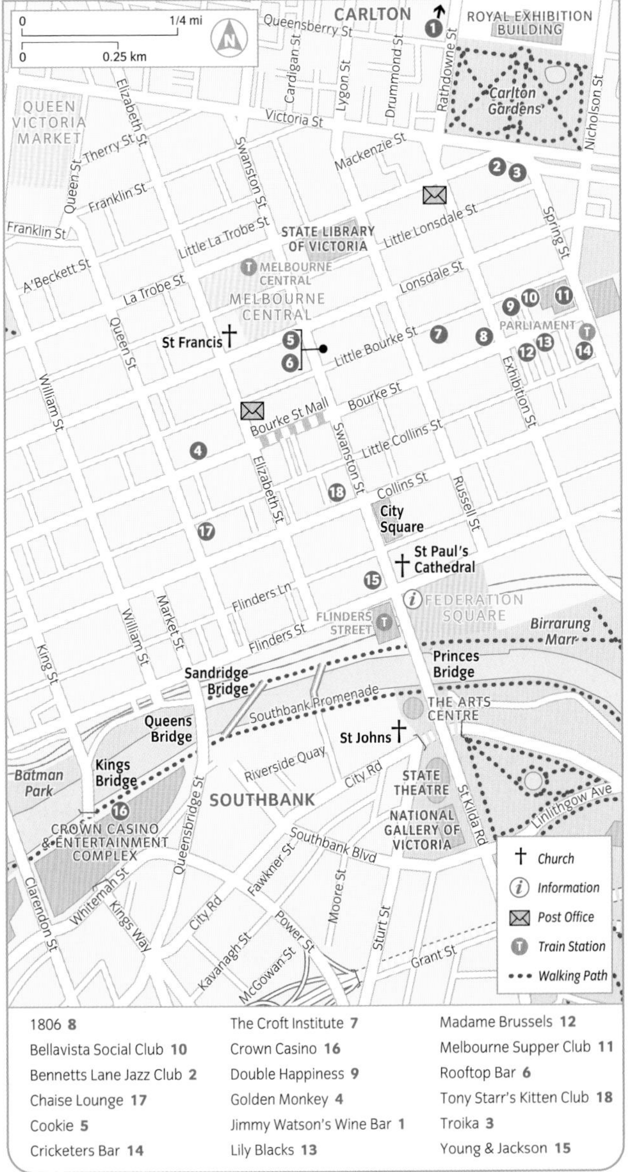

1806 **8**	The Croft Institute **7**	Madame Brussels **12**
Bellavista Social Club **10**	Crown Casino **16**	Melbourne Supper Club **11**
Bennetts Lane Jazz Club **2**	Double Happiness **9**	Rooftop Bar **6**
Chaise Lounge **17**	Golden Monkey **4**	Tony Starr's Kitten Club **18**
Cookie **5**	Jimmy Watson's Wine Bar **1**	Troika **3**
Cricketers Bar **14**	Lily Blacks **13**	Young & Jackson **15**

Melbourne Nightlife A to Z

★★★ **1806** CITY CENTRE Behind a discreet red door that you could easily miss lie rich red velvet drapes, antique leather wing-chairs and dazzling chandeliers. Seductive and smooth, with a mixed crowd, fabulous staff and award-winning cocktails, this is indisputably one of Melbourne's gems. *169 Exhibition St. ☎ (03) 9663 7722. www.1806.com.au. Train: Parliament. Map p. 99.*

★ **Belgian Beer Café Bluestone** PRAHRAN Full-bodied Belgian brews dominate the drinks list in this atmospheric joint. Down your pint in either the enormous beer garden or the historic bluestone bar. There's live music on Sunday afternoons, too. *557 St Kilda Rd. ☎ (03) 9529 2899. www.belgianbeercafemelbourne.com. Tram: 3, 5, 6, 16, 64, 67. Map p. 98.*

★ **Bellavista Social Club** CITY CENTRE This ultramodern place jumps with a late-night crowd of arty young types and suits, all watching the action in the laneway below via a big-screen hook-up. *11–25 Crossley St. ☎ (03) 9663 3000. Tram: 86, 96. Train: Parliament. Map p. 99.*

★★ **Bennetts Lane Jazz Club** CITY CENTRE Often exceptional and always varied, this venue is one of the best in Australia for jazz, and the audience is eclectic. The back-lane location is a little hard to find, but it's worth the trouble. Music starts around 8.30pm and it pays to come early to get a table, otherwise it's standing room only or a perch on the stairs. *25 Bennetts Ln. ☎ (03) 9663 2856. www.bennettslane.com. Cover from around $15. Train: Melbourne Central. Map p. 99.*

Whether you want tasty Thai food, beer or a fabulous cocktail, Cookie is the place to be.

Atmospheric Double Happiness.

Chaise Lounge CITY CENTRE Throw away any preconceived ideas of what a bar should be like. This chic boudoir-style basement features lipstick-coloured walls, a bust of a Roman god, diamanté-strung curtains, ornate sofas and glitter balls. *105 Queen St.* ☎ *(03) 9670 6120. www.chaiselounge.com.au. Tram: 11, 12, 31, 42, 109. Train: Flinders St. Map p. 99.*

★★ Cicciolina Back Bar ST KILDA This softly lit, alluring hideaway offers plush leather booths and a fine range of cocktails. Add attentive staff and you've got one of the best little bars in St Kilda, tucked away down an arcade. *130 Acland St.* ☎ *(03) 9525 3333. Tram: 16, 96. Map p. 98.*

★ Cookie CITY CENTRE The hottest place to hang out in town is an unlikely combination of good-value Thai eatery, beer hall and smart cocktail bar, complete with plastic doilies and murals. *Lvl 1, 252 Swanston St.* ☎ *(03) 9663 7660. Train: Melbourne Central. Map p. 99.*

★★ Cricketers Bar CITY CENTRE In this popular English-style pub you're surrounded by reminders of Australia's summer passion—glass cases full of cricket memorabilia. It's very masculine, with plush green carpets, woodwork and big-screen TVs. *Windsor Hotel, 103 Spring St.* ☎ *(03) 9633 6000. Tram: City Circle. Train: Parliament. Map p. 99.*

★ The Croft Institute CITY CENTRE This laneway bar is a small, lurid, bottle-green establishment, famous for its powerful cocktails and the city's largest private collection of laboratory apparatus. For the young. *21–25 Croft Alley.* ☎ *(03) 9671 4399. www.thecroftinstitute.com.au. Tram: 86, 96. Map p. 99.*

★★★ Crown Casino SOUTHBANK Round-the-clock gambling may not be your style, but Australia's largest casino is a plush place with other drawcards. A major venue for international acts, it also has 11 bars, and there are more in the extended Southgate complex. *Clarendon St, Southbank.* ☎ *(03) 9292 6868. www.crowncasino.com.au. Tram: 55, 96. Map p. 99.*

★ Double Happiness CITY CENTRE This tiny but hugely atmospheric bar has a retro-Asian theme that would make Mao proud. Mix with the hip business crowd to try the 'Gang of Four' cocktail (mango, vodka, Cointreau and lemon). *21 Liverpool St. ☎ (03) 9650 4488. www.double-happiness.org. Tram: 86, 96. Train: Parliament. Map p. 99.*

★ The Esplanade Hotel
ST KILDA A true Aussie pub overlooking the bay, with pool tables, three live-music rooms that host local and international bands, and no dress code. What more could young travellers, students and almost anyone else ask for? The Espy, a shabby-chic grand old dame of a building, is considered by many to be almost a national treasure. *11 Upper Esplanade. ☎ (03) 9534 0211. www.espy.com.au. Tram: 16, 96. Map p. 98.*

★ Golden Monkey CITY CENTRE Opium-den chic rules here, with dim lighting, Chinese lanterns, fancy cocktails and cosy corners. There's Asian tapas if you get peckish, and table service from staff in glamorous cheongsams and suits. *389 Lonsdale St (enter off Hardware La). ☎ (03) 9602 2055. www.goldenmonkey.com.au. Tram: City Circle. Map p. 99.*

Jimmy Watson's Wine Bar
CARLTON Jimmy's is something of an institution. One of Melbourne's oldest wine bars, established in 1932, it's a cosy affair drawing all types of people – from university students to serious wine buffs — in to chat and sample the vast range of wines. Inside, it has white-washed walls and is slightly old-fashioned, and there's a great courtyard for sunny days. *333 Lygon St. ☎ (03) 9347 3985. Tram: 1, 8. Map p. 99.*

★ Lily Blacks CITY CENTRE Sleek and sophisticated, Lily Blacks has cool jazz playing till the wee hours, interesting cocktails and palm trees at the door to give an exotic touch on a cold Melbourne night. Prop yourself at the large bar or seek out one of the private booths at the back. *Lvl 3, 12–18 Meyers Pl. ☎ (03) 9654 6499. www.lilyblacks.com.au. Tram: 86, 96. Train: Parliament. Map p. 99.*

For cupcakes with your cocktails, come to Madame Brussels.

The slick bar at Tony Starr's Kitten Club.

★★ **Madame Brussels** CITY CENTRE Naughty but nice, if nice is not too bland a word for a place that's named for a brothel-keeper and has a hostess called Miss Pearls. Add bright green fake grass and ... no, not bland at all. See it to believe it. *Lvl 3, 59–63 Bourke St.* ☎ *(03) 9662 2775. www.madamebrussels.com.au. Tram: 86, 96. Train: Parliament. Map p. 99.*

★★ **Melbourne Supper Club** CITY CENTRE The perfect post-theatre venue to linger in, with deep leather lounges and a giant circular window that looks onto the illuminated Parliament House buildings. Or head to the rooftop to the new Siglo Bar (where smoking's permitted). *161 Spring St.* ☎ *(03) 9654 6300. Tram: City Circle. Train: Parliament. Map p. 99.*

★ **The Prince of Wales Hotel** ST KILDA This pub is a legend among both locals and backpackers. It's huge, with several different bars, pool tables and live music every night. A huge blackboard at the front announces which bands will be playing (some of which will be big names). You can buy tickets for the gigs at the bar. *29 Fitzroy St.* ☎ *(03) 9536 1111. www.princebars.com.au. Tram: 16, 96, 112. Map p. 98.*

★ **Rooftop Bar** CITY CENTRE Work up a thirst by climbing the six flights of stairs to this eyrie (the lift is sometimes unreliable), and admire some of Melbourne's architecture from above while you sip on sangria or have a snack. Best on summer nights, but a favourite with smokers year-round, and there are heaters in winter. *Lvl 6, Curtin House, 252 Swanston St.* ☎ *(03) 9639 8770. Train: Melbourne Central. Map p. 99.*

★ **Tony Starr's Kitten Club** CITY CENTRE Don't be put off by the name—this is a fun place. The action is in the upstairs Galaxy Space, where the entertainment ranges from the peculiar to the animated to just plain bizarre. Don't miss the Love Lounge, with its floor-to-ceiling red fabric, heart-shaped lounges and secluded booths. Girls will spend probably a little longer than usual in the Powder Room, lured by its huge mirrors, comfy lounges and sometimes resident make-up artist. *267 Little Collins St.* ☎ *(03) 9650 2448. Cover Fri–Sat $5. www.kittenclub.com.au. Train: Flinders St. Map p. 99.*

★★ **Troika** CITY CENTRE Pull back the heavy metal sliding door and step into a cool interior of concrete floors and spots of colour. Stylish and just-funky-enough, with a clever covered courtyard at the back for smokers. Popular for its great-value drinks, it's considered a good first-date bar. The regular crowd includes design students, and mostly under-30s. *106 Little Lonsdale St.* ☎ *(03) 9663 0221. Train: Parliament or Melbourne Central. Map p. 99.*

★★ **Windsor Castle** WINDSOR Look for the pink elephants flying across the roofline and you'll find this tucked-away pub. Windsor Castle is a perfect spot for meeting friends for a good pub meal. On weekends there are DJs and a barbecue. *89 Albert St.* ☎ *(03) 9525 0239. Train: Windsor. Map p. 98.*

Chloe *has a special place in the hearts of Melbournians.*

Having a Beer With Chloe

A visit to Melbourne's oldest and most famous pub, Young & Jackson (corner Flinders and Swanston Streets; ☎ (03) 9650 3884; www.youngandjacksons.com.au) is always a pleasure, whether it's for a drink or a meal in the stylish upstairs restaurant or bistro areas. It's a must to head upstairs to see the nude *Chloe*, a famous painting brought to Melbourne for the Great Exhibition in 1880, too. The pub was built in 1853 and started selling beer in 1861, so it has a few years on *Chloe*, who was painted in Paris in 1875 and has a special place in the hearts of Melbournians. Free tastings and tales of the hotel's history can be had in Chloe's Bar every Saturday at 3pm. Tram: 30, 48 or City Circle. Train: Flinders St. Map p. 99.

8 The Best Arts & Entertainment

Arts & Entertainment **Best Bets**

Best **Arthouse Movies**
★★ Cinema Nova, *380 Lygon St (p. 109)*

Best **Australian Drama**
★★★ Malthouse Theatre, *113 Sturt St (p. 111)*

Best **Cabaret**
The Famous Speigeltent, *The Arts Centre forecourt, 100 St Kilda Rd (p. 113)*

Best **Family Night Out**
Circus Oz, *Big Top, Birrarung Marr (p. 110)*

Best **Festival**
Melbourne International Arts Festival, *various venues (p. 111)*

Best **Freebie**
★★★ Summertime concerts, *Sidney Myer Music Bowl (p. 116)*

Best **Haunted Theatre**
Princess Theatre, *163 Spring St (p. 115)*

Best for **Laughing Your Socks Off**
Melbourne Comedy Festival, *various venues (p. 111)*

Most **Opulent Surrounds**
★★★ State Theatre, *The Arts Centre, 100 St Kilda Rd (p. 116)*

Best **Outdoor Venue**
★★★ Sidney Myer Music Bowl, *Kings Domain Gardens (p. 116)*

Best **Peek Behind the Scenes**
★★★ Backstage tour at The Arts Centre, *100 St Kilda Rd (p. 112)*

Best for **Talent Spotting**
National Theatre, *20 Carlisle St, St Kilda (p. 114)*

Best **Theatre Restoration**
★★★ Regent Theatre, *191 Collins St (p. 116)*

Previous page: The iconic Arts Centre spire.

A performance by the Australian Ballet (p. 109).

City Centre Arts & Entertainment

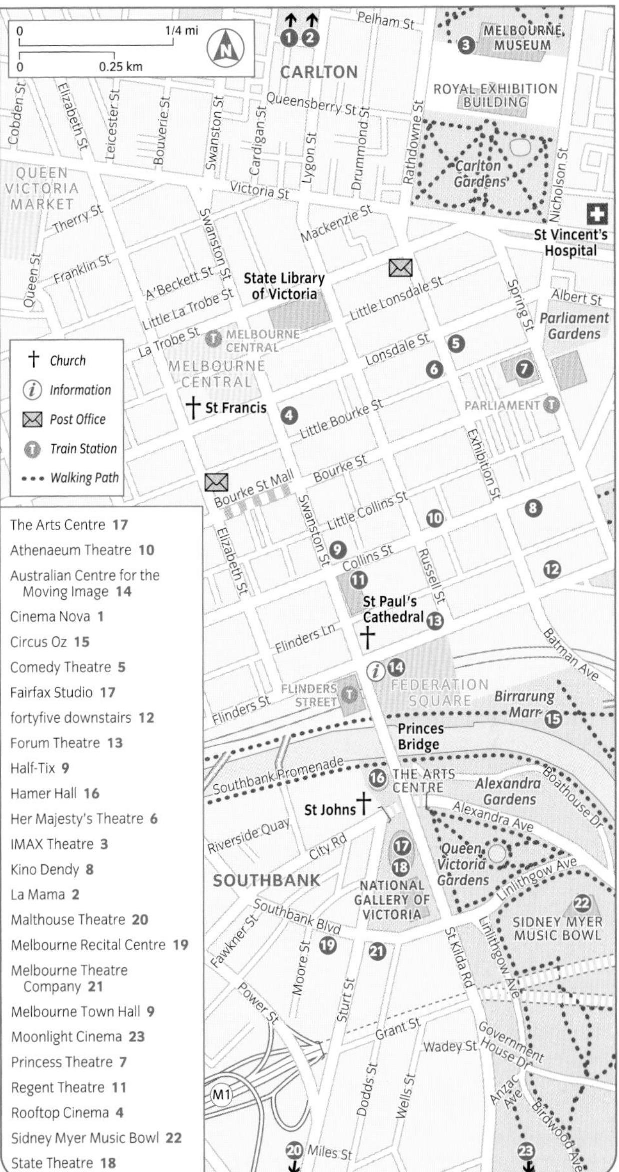

St Kilda Arts & Entertainment

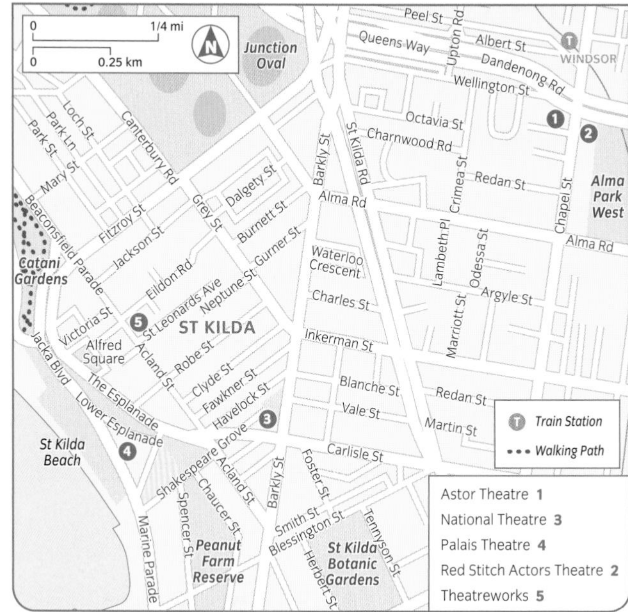

Arts & Entertainment A to Z

Classical Music

★★ Melbourne Symphony Orchestra SOUTHBANK The acclaimed MSO has been entertaining Melbourne for more than a century. It gives around 90 concerts a year under the baton of Oleg Caetani, at various venues around the city, but predominantly at The Arts Centre's **Hamer Hall**. Performances usually take place on Monday and Thursday to Saturday evenings, with matinees on Saturday and morning chamber recitals on Sunday. *Hamer Hall, The Arts Centre, 100 St Kilda Rd. ☎ (03) 9626 1111. www.mso.com.au. Train: Flinders St. Map p. 107.*

Orchestra Victoria CITY CENTRE Orchestra Victoria is the Melbourne performance partner of the Australian Ballet, Opera Australia, Victorian Opera and The Production Company. It also schedules free concerts in and around Melbourne, at venues including the NGV International's Great Hall and the Melbourne Town Hall. Check the website for details. *☎ (03) 9694 3600. www.orchestravictoria.com.au.*

Comedy

Last Laugh Comedy Club CITY CENTRE The Last Laugh is a Melbourne institution. Come here to see local and international comedy acts, musicals and special shows. It offers a dinner and show package on Fridays and Saturdays. Ask what's on offer, as discount ticket

Enjoy the sounds of the acclaimed Melbourne Symphony Orchestra.

deals can bring the show-only prices down to as low as $8 sometimes. *Athenaeum Theatre, 188 Collins St. ☎ (03) 9650 6668. www.thecomedy-club.com.au. Tickets $15–$35. Train: Flinders St. Map p. 107.*

Dance

★★ The Australian Ballet SOUTHBANK Australia's national company, the Australian Ballet is Melbourne-based and presents four to five seasons each year at the Arts Centre. *100 St Kilda Rd. ☎ (03) 9669 2700. www.australianballet.com.au. Ticket prices vary. Train: Flinders St. Map p. 107.*

Chunky Move SOUTHBANK Unconventional, energetic and sometimes hard-edged are just some of the terms that have been used to describe this contemporary Australian dance company. When it's not touring overseas, you'll find its productions usually running at the Malthouse Theatre. *111 Sturt St. ☎ (03) 9645 5188. www.chunkymove.com. Ticket prices vary. Train: Flinders St. Map p. 107.*

Film

ACMI Cinemas CITY CENTRE What better place to explore your love of film than at The Australian Centre for the Moving Image? ACMI has two state-of-the-art cinemas and large areas where visitors can view movies, videos and digital media. *Federation Square, Flinders St. ☎ (03) 8663 2200. www.acmi.net.au. Tickets $10–$18. Train: Flinders St. Map p. 107.*

The Astor Theatre ST KILDA Going to the Astor is an event in itself. One of Melbourne's few remaining independent cinemas, this lovely 1930s Art Deco theatre still has curtains that sweep across the screen, plus stalls and a dress circle. The single screen shows a mix of new releases, older films and classics such as Hitchcock's *Rear Window*. You can also take a backstage tour. *1 Chapel St. ☎ (03) 9510 1414. www.astor-theatre.com. Tickets $11 single feature, $13 double feature; $8 on selected Wednesdays. Backstage tours $30 including movie & refreshments. Train: Windsor. Map p. 108.*

★★ Cinema Nova CARLTON The best place to go for quality Australian, arthouse and foreign-language films. Monday is discount day, when tickets are $6 until 4pm and $8 after 4pm, except on public holidays. *380 Lygon St. ☎ (03) 9347 5331 or (03) 9349 5201 for Saturday-night bookings. www.cinemanova.com.au. Tickets $6–$15.50. Tram: 1, 8. Map p. 107.*

IMAX Theatre CARLTON With 478 seats and the Southern Hemisphere's biggest 3D screen, IMAX Melbourne runs a wide variety of large-format films every hour on the hour. Some are specially made, some are mainstream feature films digitally remastered into the IMAX format (which may or may not be

Circus Oz is all about acrobatics.

also converted to 3D). IMAX is part of the Melbourne Museum precinct, so your movie ticket also gets you free admission to the museum. *Melbourne Museum, Rathdowne St. ☎ (03) 9663 5454. www.imaxmelbourne.com.au. Tickets $13–$18 or $50 families of 4. Daily 10am–10pm except Christmas Day. Tram: City Circle. Map p. 107.*

Kino Dendy CITY CENTRE Plush surroundings and a great selection of local and international feature films, arthouse films and documentaries make this one of Melbourne's best cinema experiences. The Kino also runs special film festival programs, retrospectives and events such as premieres, forums and Q&As with actors and directors. *Collins Place, 45 Collins St. ☎ (03) 9281 3300. www.kinodendy.com.au. Tickets $7 Mon, $15.50 all other days. Train: Flinders St. Map p. 107.*

Opera

Opera Australia SOUTHBANK Presenting new works as well as much-loved classics such as *Carmen* and *Madama Butterfly*, Opera Australia brings its soaring arias to Melbourne for two seasons each year (April/May and November/December), usually at The Arts Centre. *☎ (03) 9685 3700. www.opera-australia.org.au. Tickets $52–$209. Train: Flinders Street. Map p. 107.*

Victorian Opera SOUTHBANK This young company, only formed in 2006, bases its program on innovation. It both performs new works and stages standard repertoire in unusual venues. *Horti Hall, 31 Victoria St. ☎ (03) 9001 6400. www.victorianopera.com.au. Tickets $37–$134.*

Circus Oz

Born in Melbourne 30 years ago, Circus Oz grew up and ran away to tour the world. You won't find performing elephants or animals of any kind in this amazing circus—it's all about the skill and agility of the human performers. Trapeze, acrobatics, juggling and other incredible stunts, all with colourful costumes, live music and a liberal dose of Aussie humour, will keep all ages entertained. It's playful, energetic and often topical—this is a circus with a social conscience. The 1400-seat Big Top goes up alongside the Yarra in Birrarung Marr when Circus Oz comes home. Tickets are usually $44–$64. Call ☎ (03) 9646 8899 or visit www.circusoz.com for more information.

A Feast of Festivals

Melbourne loves a good arts festival, and has plenty to choose from! The city is home to some of Australia's most prestigious fiestas, kicking off with the annual **Melbourne International Comedy Festival** (www.comedyfestival.com.au) in April. **The Melbourne International Film Festival** (www.melbournefilmfestival.com.au) between late July and mid-August, features new releases, shorts and avant-garde movies at venues around the city. The **Melbourne International Arts Festival** (www.melbournefestival.com.au) is arguably Australia's premier celebration of international performing and visual arts, and Melbourne's flagship cultural event. Every year since 1986 the festival has been held over 17 days each October, and debuts some of the finest national and international artists and companies in dance, theatre, music, visual arts and multimedia events. There are a wide variety of venues and ticket prices, plus many free events, and around 500 000 people are drawn to the nearly 600 performances. On at the same time, the **Melbourne Fringe Festival** (running during the first three weeks of October; www.melbournefringe.com.au) sees an eclectic array of performers—from jugglers to fire-eaters—fill the streets, pubs, theatres and restaurants. Keep in mind that hotels fill up fast during festival times, so book early.

Theatre

La Mama CARLTON Established 40 years ago as one of the first modern Australian theatre companies, La Mama has launched the careers of many leading actors, directors and playwrights, including Oscar-winner Cate Blanchett. The company focuses on new, bold and local works, often with a strong social message. *205 Faraday St. ☎ (03) 9347 6948 or bookings (03) 9347 6142. www.lamama.com.au. Tickets $25. Tram: 1, 8. Map p. 107.*

★★ Malthouse Theatre SOUTHBANK Dedicated to Australian contemporary theatre, the Malthouse regularly commissions new work as well as undertaking major reinterpretations of classics. It aims to amaze and sometimes shock, so come prepared for the unexpected. *113 Sturt St. ☎ (03) 9685 5111. www.malthousetheatre.com.au. Tickets $26–$40. Train: Flinders St. Map p. 107.*

★★★ Melbourne Theatre Company SOUTHBANK Australia's oldest professional theatre company, the MTC regularly premieres Australian and international plays and stages

October's Melbourne Fringe Festival sees an eclectic array of performers.

new productions of Broadway hits. The company has long attracted many of Australia's best actors and directors. Performances take place at The Arts Centre or the CUB Malthouse Theatre until the new MTC Theatre (under construction at the corner of Southbank Boulevard and Dodds Street) opens in June 2009. *129 Ferrars St. ☎ (03) 9684 4500. www.mtc.com.au. Tickets $36–$75. Train: Flinders St. Map p. 107.*

Red Stitch Actors Theatre ST KILDA This new theatre company, run 'by actors, for actors', is made up of a core ensemble of 15 young members dedicated to championing contemporary work. *2 Chapel St. ☎ (03) 9533 8083. www.redstitch.net. Tickets $18–$30. Train: Windsor. Tram: 5, 64. Map p. 108.*

Theatreworks ST KILDA Established around 25 years ago, Theatreworks is well known for its work with emerging artists and its close community ties. It's based in a lovely old brick church hall in the heart of St Kilda, with 160 seats. *14 Acland St. ☎ (03) 9534 4879 or bookings (03) 9534 3388. www.theatreworks.org.au. Tickets $10–$30. Tram: 16, 69, 79, 96, 112. Map p. 108.*

The exterior of the Comedy Theatre is a replica of a Florentine palace.

Venues

★★ The Arts Centre SOUTHBANK The Theatres Building is the venue that shelters under the Arts Centre's landmark spire. (The Arts Centre also runs neighbouring Hamer Hall and the Sidney Myer Music Bowl in the nearby Kings Domain Gardens.) The Arts Centre is Melbourne's premier venue, and where you'll find many of the major events and the top performing arts companies. Guided tours of the building are run at 11am daily (except Sunday) from the information desk in the Theatres Building, and cost $11 for adults or $28 for families of two adults and two or more children. Backstage tours run on Sundays at 12.15pm, taking about 90 minutes and costing $13.50 (no children under 12 are permitted). A $128-million, three-year redevelopment of the Arts Centre is expected to begin in 2010. *100 St Kilda Rd. ☎ (03) 9281 8000. www.theartscentre.com.au. Ticket prices vary. Train: Flinders St. Map p. 107.*

Comedy Theatre CITY CENTRE With an ornate Spanish rococo interior, this theatre feels intimate even though it seats more than 1000 people. Plays and musicals usually fill the bill here, but dance companies and—yes—comedians also appear. Built in 1928, the theatre's exterior is a replica of a Florentine palace. *240 Exhibition St. ☎ (03) 9299 4950. www.comedytheatre.com.au. Ticket prices vary. Train: Parliament. Map p. 107.*

CUB Malthouse SOUTHBANK Originally built in 1892 as a brewery and malting works, the Malthouse

Travelling cabaret and music salon Spiegeltent comes to Melbourne in October.

was converted into a stylish three-theatre complex in 1990, and is home to the Malthouse Theatre company. It is also used by the Melbourne Symphony Orchestra, the Melbourne Writers Festival, the Melbourne International Festival of the Arts and contemporary dance and theatre companies. *113 Sturt St. ☎ (03) 9685 5111. www.malthousetheatre.com.au. Ticket prices vary. Train: Flinders St. Map p. 107.*

Fairfax Studio SOUTHBANK This 376-seat drama space is often used by the Melbourne Theatre Company, as well as featuring the work of Victoria's artists and companies in smaller contemporary productions. It also hosts an annual season of experimental short plays called 'Short & Sweet' in December each year. *Lvl 5, Theatres Building, The Arts Centre, 100 St Kilda Rd. ☎ (03) 9281 8000. www.theartscentre.com.au. Ticket prices vary. Train: Flinders St. Map p. 107.*

fortyfive downstairs CITY CENTRE An intimate little theatre that leans towards the avant-garde, with good local talent and plenty of first-time productions. *45 Flinders Ln. ☎ (03) 9662 9733. www.fortyfivedownstairs.com. Tickets $25–$30. Train: Flinders St. Map p. 107.*

Forum Theatre CITY CENTRE Walking into the Forum's foyer is like entering a walled Roman garden,

The Famous Spiegeltent

Each year from mid-October to mid-December, this lush and exotic travelling cabaret and music salon—a 1920s European mirror tent once graced by Marlene Dietrich—comes to Melbourne. Step inside and be swept away, not just by the music, but by the red-velvet canopies, circular teak dance floor and wonderful Art Nouveau chandelier. Slip into a booth for a dazzling night you won't forget. You'll find the tent on the forecourt outside the Arts Centre on St Kilda Road. Visit www.spiegeltent.net for more information.

The Palais Theatre is a St Kilda icon.

complete with statues, blue sky and twinkling stars. There are two parts to the theatre—upstairs is a 520-seat theatre for film screenings and live performances, downstairs is a space seating 800 people and hosting acts such as comedians, magicians, dancers and live bands. Built in 1929, the Forum has had its fair share of famous artists working their magic in it over the years (including Midnight Oil, Powderfinger, Bob Geldof and Tim Finn). *154 Flinders St. ☎ (03) 9299 9700. www.marrinertheatres.com.au/forum. Ticket prices vary. Train: Flinders St. Map p. 107.*

★ Hamer Hall CITY CENTRE Home of the Melbourne Symphony Orchestra and often host to visiting orchestras. Many international stars have graced Hamer Hall's stage, which is known for its excellent acoustics. *100 St Kilda Rd. ☎ (03) 9281 0000. www.theartscentre.com.au. Ticket prices vary. Train: Flinders St. Map p. 107.*

Her Majesty's Theatre CITY CENTRE A fire destroyed the original theatre here, but the current structure retains the original 1886 facade and the Art Deco interior added during a 1936 renovation. The stage house and backstage areas were revamped between 2000 and 2002, and musicals such as *Chicago*, *Miss Saigon* and *Spamalot* frequent the boards. *219 Exhibition St. Bookings through Ticketek ☎ 1300 792 012. www.hmt.com.au. Ticket prices vary. Train: Parliament. Map p. 107.*

★★ Melbourne Recital Centre SOUTHBANK This brand new 1000-seat recital hall was designed specifically for the performance and recording of chamber music, jazz, new music, chamber opera, world music and popular song. Named in honour of Victoria's greatest philanthropist, the Elisabeth Murdoch Hall opened in February 2009 with a design expected to combine great acoustics, state-of-the-art technology and an intimate atmosphere. *Cnr Southbank Blvd & Sturt St. ☎ (03) 9954 5105. www.melbournerecital.org.au. Ticket prices vary. Train: Flinders St. Map p. 107.*

National Theatre ST KILDA Melbourne's dance schools—notably the National Theatre Ballet School—use this 1920s theatre

Half-Tix Means Cheap Tix

Melbourne's two major ticketing outlets are Ticketek (☎ 132 849; www.ticketek.com.au) and Ticketmaster (☎ 136 100; www.ticketmaster.com.au). Bargain tickets for entertainment including opera, dance and drama can be obtained on the day of the performance from the **Half-Tix Desk** in the Melbourne Town Hall on Swanston Street. The booth is open on Monday from 10am to 2pm, between Tuesday and Thursday from 11am to 6pm, on Friday from 11am to 6.30pm, and on Saturday from 10am to 4pm (when it also sells tickets for Sunday shows). Tickets must be purchased in person and paid for with cash. Available shows are displayed on the booth door and on the website, www.halftixmelbourne.com. Train: Flinders St. Map p. 107.

for their performances, so you're likely to find the stars of the future on the stage here in student shows, alongside the mainstream productions and opera. *20 Carlisle St. ☎ (03) 9534 0221. www.nationaltheatre.org.au. Ticket prices vary. Tram 16, 96. Map p. 108.*

Palais Theatre ST KILDA A wonderful venue for big-name acts, after major renovations in 2008 the Palais is once again able to stage major productions and musicals. *Lower Esplanade. ☎ (03) 9525 3240; tickets 136 100. www.palaistheatre.net.au. Ticket prices vary. Tram 16, 96. Map p. 108.*

★★ **Princess Theatre** CITY CENTRE An empty seat is left in the Princess Theatre's dress circle on opening nights for the friendly ghost of Federici, an actor who died of a heart attack after a performance of *Faust* here in 1888. The theatre's elegant cafe is named in his honour. This beautifully restored building—as extravagant inside as it is outside—has been home to many of the world's most successful stage productions, including *The Phantom of the*

The extravagant Princess Theatre.

At the Rooftop Cinema, watch a movie or the twinkling lights of the city skyline.

Opera, *Les Misérables*, *Cats*, *Mamma Mia!*, *The Producers* and *Guys and Dolls*. *163 Spring St. ☎ (03) 9299 9800. www.marrinertheatres.com.au. Ticket prices vary. Train: Parliament. Map p. 107.*

★★ Regent Theatre CITY CENTRE Built in 1929, the Regent fell into disrepair in 1969 and its stage was dark for 25 years. Now, after a $35-million renovation, it's been restored to its gilded former glory. *191 Collins St. ☎ (03) 9299 9500. www.marrinertheatres.com.au. Ticket prices vary. Train: Flinders St. Map p. 107.*

State Theatre SOUTHBANK Seating 2085 people on three levels and with one of the world's largest stages, this is Melbourne's big venue for opera, ballet and musicals. Tip your head back to contemplate the spectacular ceiling, decorated with 75 000 tiny brass domes. *100 St Kilda Rd. ☎ (03) 9281 8000. www.theartscentre.com.au. Ticket prices vary. Train: Flinders St. Map p. 107.* ●

Under the Stars

Melbourne's largest outdoor venue, the Sidney Myer Music Bowl (in the Kings Domain Gardens, off Linlithgow Ave; map p. 107), is run by The Arts Centre. For 50 years, this hugely popular space has been hosting everything from rock concerts to opera, along with Carols by Candlelight and the Melbourne Symphony Orchestra's free **summertime concerts**. It seats more than 2000, with room for another 11 000 people on the lawn.

In the Royal Botanic Gardens, bring a picnic blanket to watch a **Shakespeare in the Park** performance between late December and mid-March (entry from Birdwood Ave; ☎ (03) 8676 7511. **Moonlight Cinema** (map p. 107) also runs in the Botanic Gardens over summer, from November to March. Bring a picnic rug or hire a beanbag (www.moonlight.com.au).

To get closer to the stars, nab a seat in one of the colourfully striped deckchairs at the **Rooftop Cinema** (Curtin House, 252 Swanston St; ☎ (03) 9663 3596; www.rooftopcinema.com.au; map p. 107). The season runs from late November till the end of March.

9 The Best Accommodation

Accommodation **Best Bets**

Best **Art Hotel**
★★★ Tolarno Hotel $
42 Fitzroy St, St Kilda (p. 125)

Best **Backpacker Hotel**
★ YHA Oasis, $ *76 Chapman St, North Melbourne (p. 126)*

Best **Bathtub**
★★★ The Como Melbourne $$$
630 Chapel St, South Yarra (p. 121)

Best **Bed and Breakfast**
★★ Cotterville $$
204 Williams Rd, Toorak (p. 121)

Best **Boutique Hotel**
★★★ Adelphi Hotel $$$
187 Flinders Ln (p. 120)

Best **Day Spa**
★★★ The Lyall Hotel and Spa $$$$$ *14 Murphy St, South Yarra (p. 123)*

Best **High-Roller Hotel**
★★ Crown Towers $$$$
68 Whiteman St (p. 121)

Best **Indoor Pool**
★ Quay West Suites Melbourne $$$ *26 Southgate Ave (p. 124)*

Most **Irreverent Hotel**
★ The Nunnery Guesthouse $
112–120 Nicholson St, Fitzroy (p. 124)

Best **Outdoor Pool**
★★★ Adelphi Hotel $$$
187 Flinders Ln (p. 120)

Most **Romantic Hotel**
★★★ The Hotel Windsor $$$$$
103 Spring St (p. 123)

Best **Room with a View**
★★★ Sofitel Melbourne $$$$
25 Collins St (p. 125)

Previous page: The pool at the Adelphi Hotel (p. 120) is a welcome city oasis.

This page: The Lyall Hotel and Spa (p. 123).

City Centre Accommodation

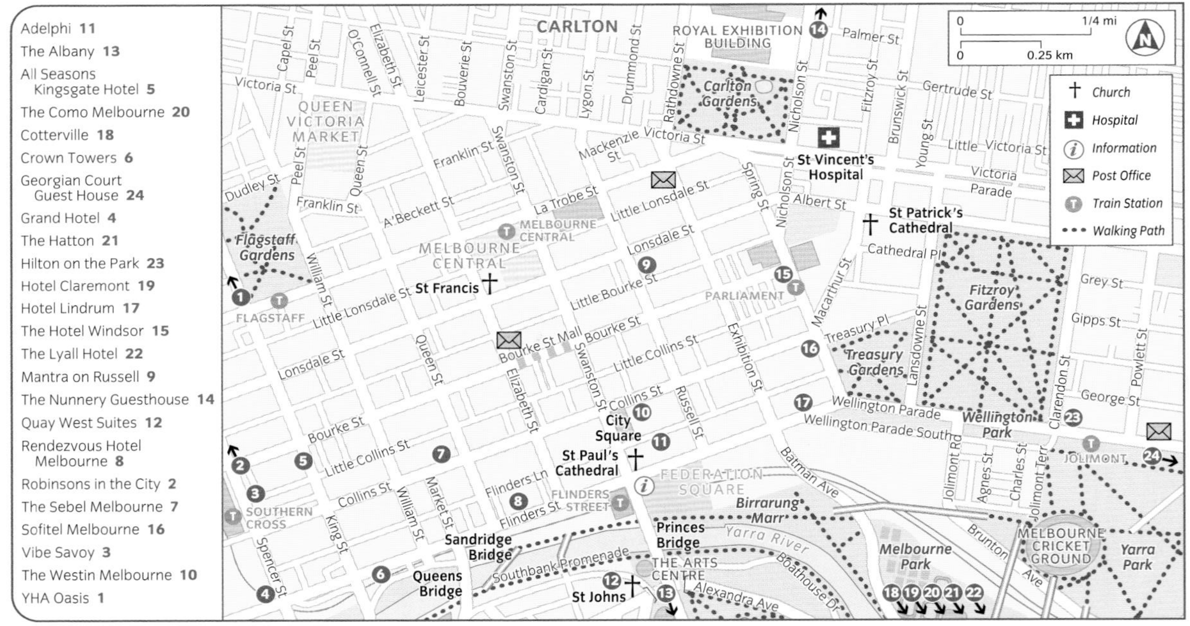

St Kilda Accommodation

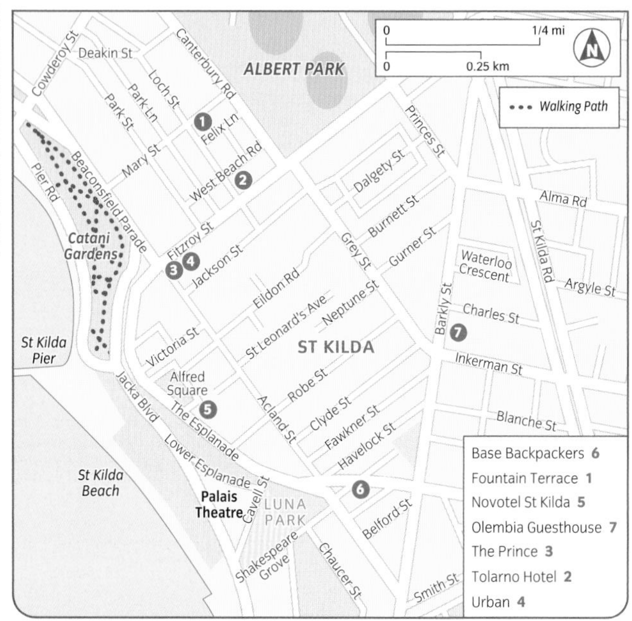

Melbourne Accommodation A to Z

★★★ Adelphi Hotel CITY CENTRE The novelty value of the Adelphi's pool, which juts out over the street, pales into insignificance when you get inside this cool, sophisticated and sexy hotel. Sleek and eclectic decor and lots of special touches. *187 Flinders Ln. ☎ 1800 800 177. www.adelphi.com.au. 34 units. Doubles $255–$590 w/breakfast. AE, DC, MC, V. Train: Flinders St. Map p. 119.*

★★ The Albany SOUTH YARRA Appearances can be deceptive. Don't be fooled by the 1960s 'motel-hotel' exterior here; this is a very cool hotel, incorporating a mansion house next door. Floors are themed: there's fashion, rock'n'roll and trains-planes-automobiles. *Cnr Toorak Rd & Millswyn St. ☎ (03) 9866 4485. www.thealbany.com.au. 83 units. Doubles $145–$225; rock-star penthouse $750. AE, DC, MC, V. Tram: 8. Map p. 119.*

All Seasons Kingsgate Hotel CITY CENTRE The cheapest rooms here have barely enough room to swing a backpack and the bathroom is down the hall, but standard rooms (with ensuite) are more spacious and there are family rooms for four. *131 King St. ☎ 1300 734 171.*

www.kingsgatehotel.com.au. 225 units. Doubles $99–$207. AE, DC, MC, V. Tram: 86, 96. Train: Southern Cross. Map p. 119.

Base Backpackers ST KILDA I'm most impressed by the 'female sanctuary' provided by this hostel, where women guests get a cuppa in bed on weekend mornings and a free glass of champagne each evening. There are mixed dorms, too, and double rooms for couples. A step up from the usual backpacker hostel. *17 Carlisle St. ☎ (03) 8598 6200. www.stayatbase.com. 253 beds. Doubles $99, dorm beds $28–$34. MC, V. Tram: 16, 96. Map p. 120.*

★★★ The Como Melbourne SOUTH YARRA The Como basks in its well-deserved reputation for excellent service and larger-than-usual rooms. Bathrooms have a bath menu and a rubber duck for you to take home. Some suites have a private Japanese garden. *630 Chapel St. ☎ 1800 033 400. www.mirvachotels.com.au. 107 units. Doubles $295–$375. AE, DC, MC, V. Train: Sth Yarra. Map p. 119.*

★★ Cotterville TOORAK You'll love the courtyard gardens and the art and music that surround you in this beautifully restored terrace, and will likely leave fast friends with Cotterville's hosts, Howard and Jeremy. They're experts on the city's arts scene. *204 Williams Rd. ☎ (03) 9826 9105. www.cotterville.com. 2 units. Doubles $160 w/breakfast. MC, V. Train: Hawksburn. Map p. 119.*

★★ Crown Towers SOUTHBANK Glitz and glamour befitting high rollers are the hallmarks of this impressive hotel. For a view, get a room above the 10th floor, for club services choose something above the 28th; you need to go even higher for the luxury tower suites. *8 Whiteman St. ☎ 1800 811 653.*

Cotterville has delightful courtyard gardens.

www.crowntowers.com.au. 482 units. Doubles $395–$1380. AE, DC, MC, V. Tram: 55, 96. Map p. 119.

★ **Fountain Terrace** ST KILDA Classy and comfortable, Fountain Terrace was built in 1880 and has been lovingly restored. This boutique B&B has real character and is a wonderful alternative to a traditional hotel. *28 Mary St. ☎ (03) 9593 8123. www.fountainterrace.com.au. 7 units. Doubles $175–$245 w/breakfast. AE, DC, MC, V. Tram: 96, 16, 112. Map p. 120.*

Georgian Court Guest House CARLTON Modest and comfortable rooms, some with updated ensuites, others with bathrooms down the hall, make this a good budget choice in a great location. The sitting and dining rooms have high ceilings and true old-world atmosphere. *21 George St, East Melbourne. ☎ (03) 9419 6353. www.georgiancourt.com.au. 31 units. Doubles $119–$169 w/breakfast. AE, DC, MC, V. Tram: 48, 75. Map p. 119.*

★★ **Grand Hotel** CITY CENTRE This majestic heritage-listed building, with its Italianate facade, is just as striking inside. Whether you choose a one-bedroom loft or a plush suite, the rooms are whisper-quiet and have all the mod-cons. Some rooms have balconies. Look for the wonderful hidden garden courtyard. *33 Spencer St. ☎ (03) 9611 4567. www.mgallery.com. 103 units. Doubles $215–$518. AE, DC, MC, V. Tram: 48 or 75 from Flinders St. Train: Southern Cross. Map p. 119.*

★★ **The Hatton** SOUTH YARRA This striking Italianate mansion has been restored and stylishly updated into a sophisticated but welcoming boutique hotel. *65 Park St. ☎ (03) 9868 4800. www.hatton.com.au. 20 units. Doubles $195–$220 w/breakfast. AE, DC, MC, V. Tram: 8. Train: Sth Yarra. Map p. 119.*

★ **Hilton on the Park** EAST MELBOURNE The Hilton has a great location just minutes' walk from the Melbourne Park and Olympic Park stadiums. With its smart 2008 renovation, it makes a great city-fringe choice. *192 Wellington Pde. ☎ 1300 301 630. www.hilton.com. 419 units. Doubles $220–$685. AE, DC, MC, V. Tram: 48, 75. Train: Jolimont. Map p. 119.*

The Hotel Windsor is known around town as the 'Duchess of Spring Street'.

Stylish Hotel Lindrum.

Hotel Claremont SOUTH YARRA The high ceilings and the mosaic tiles in the lobby welcome mostly students and budget travellers into this old-world guesthouse. Attractive and comfortable enough, it is a bit sparsely furnished and there's no lift and a lot of stairs. *189 Toorak Rd. ☎ 1300 301 630. www.hotelclaremont.com. 77 units. Doubles $76–$86 w/breakfast. AE, DC, MC, V. Tram: 8. Train: South Yarra. Map p. 119.*

Hotel Ibis Melbourne CITY CENTRE Rooms in this AAA-rated three-star hotel are spacious, immaculate and bright, and apartments have kitchenettes and bathtubs. *15–21 Therry St. ☎ 1300 656 565. www.ibishotels.com.au. 250 units. Doubles $119–$149. AE, DC, MC, V. Tram: 19, 57, 59, 68.*

★★ Hotel Lindrum CITY CENTRE Stylish and contemporary, with larger-than-usual standard rooms, and a great location make this an easy choice. Superior rooms have king-size beds and polished floorboards, and deluxe rooms have large bay windows with views of the Botanic Gardens. The billiard room downstairs is a winner. *26 Flinders St. ☎ (03) 9668 1111. www.hotellindrum.com.au. 59 units. Doubles $425–$475. AE, DC, MC, V. Tram: City Circle. Train: Flinders St. Map p. 119.*

★★★ The Hotel Windsor CITY CENTRE The Windsor oozes class and sophistication, and over its long life has hosted some of the world's notables (think Lauren Bacall and Omar Sharif). A grand dame of a hotel, and no mistake! *103 Spring St. ☎ 1800 033 100. www.thewindsor.com.au. 180 units. Doubles $400–$650. AE, DC, MC, V. Tram: City Circle. Train: Parliament. Map p. 119.*

★★★ The Lyall Hotel and Spa SOUTH YARRA Regular guests—including a few celebrities—describe this contemporary, privately owned hotel as a 'home away from home'. A luxury day spa, mini art galleries on each floor, a champagne bar and a small restaurant complete the picture. *14 Murphy St. ☎ (03) 9868 8222. www.thelyall.com. 40 units. Doubles $525–$945. AE, DC, MC, V. Train: Sth Yarra. Map p. 119.*

★ Mantra on Russell CITY CENTRE Location is everything at this newly renovated apartment hotel, which has spacious studios and one- and two-bedroom suites. It's a stone's throw from Chinatown and several theatres. *222 Russell St. ☎ 1300 557 575. www.mantracityhotels.com.au. 221 units. Doubles $175–$450. AE, DC, MC, V. Train: Flinders St. Map p. 119.*

★★ Novotel St Kilda ST KILDA Spend the small amount extra to get a room with a stunning bay view at this elegant, newly renovated landmark hotel. Some rooms have a corner spa bath, which is also worth asking for. *16 The Esplanade. ☎ 1800 656 565. www.novotelstkilda.com.au. 209 units. Doubles $179–$440. AE, DC, MC, V. Tram: 16, 96. Map p. 120.*

★ The Nunnery Guesthouse FITZROY This informal but welcoming budget hotel, with its mix of dorms and private rooms, plays irreverently on its former life as a convent. The newer adjoining guesthouse offers classier accommodation. *112–120 Nicholson St. ☎ 1800 032 635. www.nunnery.com.au. 30 units. Doubles $26–$125 w/breakfast. MC, V. Tram: 96. Map p. 119.*

Olembia Guesthouse ST KILDA This sprawling Edwardian house is set back from a busy street behind a leafy courtyard. The simply furnished rooms are popular with tourists and families, and there are dorms for budget travellers. Guests share bathrooms. *96 Barkly St. ☎ (03) 9537 1412. www.olembia.com.au. 23 units. Doubles $80. AE, MC, V. Tram: 3, 67. Map p. 120.*

★★★ The Prince ST KILDA An elegant and luxurious foil to the pub behind which it hides, The Prince has hauled in a number of awards for its style and service. No two rooms are the same: some have balconies over Fitzroy St, others a Philippe Starck bathtub. *2 Acland St. ☎ (03) 9536 1111. www.theprince.com.au. 40 units. Doubles $475–$850 w/breakfast & dinner. AE, DC, MC, V. Tram: 16, 96, 112. Map p. 120.*

Beautiful stained-glass windows at The Nunnery Guesthouse.

★ Quay West Suites Melbourne CITY CENTRE Opt for a city river view room, with a spacious balcony looking out to the Yarra and Federation Square. This apartment hotel next to The Arts Centre offers all mod-cons and a terrific indoor lap pool. *26 Southgate Ave. ☎ (03) 9693 6000. www.mirvac.com.au. 97 units. Doubles $269–$435. AE, MC, V. Train: Flinders St. Map p. 119.*

★ Rendezvous Hotel Melbourne CITY CENTRE The Grand Vestibule of this 1913 hotel—one of Melbourne's last remaining truly grand hotels—may well stop you in your tracks. Continue upstairs and you'll find comfortable, newly refurbished rooms. *328 Flinders St. ☎ (03) 9250 1888. www.rendezvoushotels.com. 340 units. Doubles $185–$315 w/breakfast. AE, DC, MC, V. Train: Flinders Street. Map p. 119.*

★ Robinsons in the City CITY CENTRE Artfully sited in what was once Melbourne's first commercial bakery, this comfortable boutique hotel has been tastefully decorated, with lots of personal touches. Colour-coded doors help remind you which bathroom belongs to your room. *405 Spencer St. ☎ (03) 9329 2552. www.robinsonsinthecity.com.au. 6 units. Doubles $185–$315 w/breakfast. AE, DC, MC, V. Train: Southern Cross. Map p. 119.*

★★★ The Sebel Melbourne CITY CENTRE There's no such thing as a 'standard' room here—no two are alike. Go for a room in the heritage wing for high ceilings and

Every room in Tolarno Hotel is filled with quirky artwork.

gorgeous city views. *394 Collins St. ☎ (03) 9211 6600. www.mirvac.com.au. 115 units. Doubles $199–$450 w/breakfast. AE, DC, MC, V. Train: Flinders St. Map p. 119.*

★★★ **Sofitel Melbourne** CITY CENTRE Royalty and celebs stay in this beautiful luxury hotel, where the service is as impressive as everything else. Rooms are large and pleasant, with comfortable king-size beds and all the latest high-tech gizmos. And the city views are quite simply breathtaking, even from the cheapest rooms. *25 Collins St. ☎ (03) 9653 0000. www.sofitelmelbourne.com.au. 363 units. Doubles $350–$430. AE, DC, MC, V. Tram: City Circle. Train: Parliament. Map p. 119.*

★★★ **Tolarno Hotel** ST KILDA Colour your world with the brightest hues and most vivid art at this quirky hotel in a 1950s retro-style building. Rooms vary; the best are those with small balconies overlooking

Serviced Apartments

Serviced apartments are popular with families and business travellers, providing more space than a single hotel room and with the bonus of having cooking facilities for those on a budget or just tired of eating out every night. (For me, the real bonus on a long stay is having a laundry.) Melbourne's apartment inventory is enormous and ranges from luxurious to clean and comfortable, if a little dated. Most apartments can be rented for one night, but there may be a minimum three-night stay in high season.

Medina Serviced Apartments (☎ 1300 633 462; www.medinaapartments.com.au) has five Melbourne properties: three in the city centre and one each in St Kilda and South Yarra. Australia's biggest apartment chain, however, is **Quest Serviced Apartments** (☎ 1800 334 033; www.questapartments.com.au). It has nine properties in the city centre and 34 throughout the suburbs, including ones at St Kilda, South Yarra, Carlton, Brighton, East Melbourne, Richmond, Prahran and Williamstown. A two-bedroom apartment can cost anywhere from around $170 to $720 a night, depending on the location and the season.

The cheeky and groovy Round Room at Urban.

Fitzroy Street. *42 Fitzroy St. ☎ 1800 620 363. www.hoteltolarno.com.au. 31 units. Doubles $145–$265. AE, DC, MC, V. Tram: 16, 96, 112. Map p. 120.*

★ **Urban** ST KILDA Somewhere between retro and ultra-modern, this is a hotel that refuses to conform. Most fun is the Round Room, a circular pad with a bath in the bedroom. It's all a bit cheeky and groovy. *35–37 Fitzroy St. ☎ (03) 8530 8888. www.urbanstkilda.com.au. 80 units. Doubles from $130. AE, DC, MC, V. Tram: 16, 96, 112. Map p. 120.*

★ **Vibe Savoy** CITY CENTRE Behind its lovely heritage facade, the Vibe Savoy Hotel offers sleek contemporary decor and all the usual modern facilities. It's in the thick of the action near Etihad Stadium and the city's laneways. Strange as it sounds, I loved my room's view of the curvy roof of Southern Cross station. *630 Little Collins St. ☎ (03) 9622 8888. www.vibehotels.com.au. 169 units. Doubles $340–$750. AE, DC, MC, V. Train: Southern Cross. Map p. 119.*

★★ **The Westin Melbourne** CITY CENTRE Some guests—including some of my friends—have been known to order their own Westin bed to take home, so comfy are the mattresses here. The hotel also has a fantastic contemporary Australian art collection and you can take a guided tour from Tuesday to Saturday at 6pm, or self-guide at any time. *205 Collins St. ☎ 1800 656 535. www.westin.com.au/melbourne. 262 units. Doubles $309–$1500. AE, DC, MC, V. Train: Flinders St. Map p. 119.*

★ **YHA Oasis** NORTH MELBOURNE A backpacker hostel without bunks or dorms? If you like the sound of that, then this aptly named small hostel is the place to . . . er . . . bunk down. They serve up a pancake breakfast for $2 twice a week, and the leafy location next to Royal Park (near Melbourne Zoo) is only a 12-minute tram ride from the city. *76 Chapman St. ☎ (03) 9328 3595. www.yha.com.au. 56 units. Doubles $68–$76. MC, V. Tram: 55, 57, 59. Train: Southern Cross. Map p. 119.* ●

10 The Best Day Trips & Excursions

Mornington Peninsula

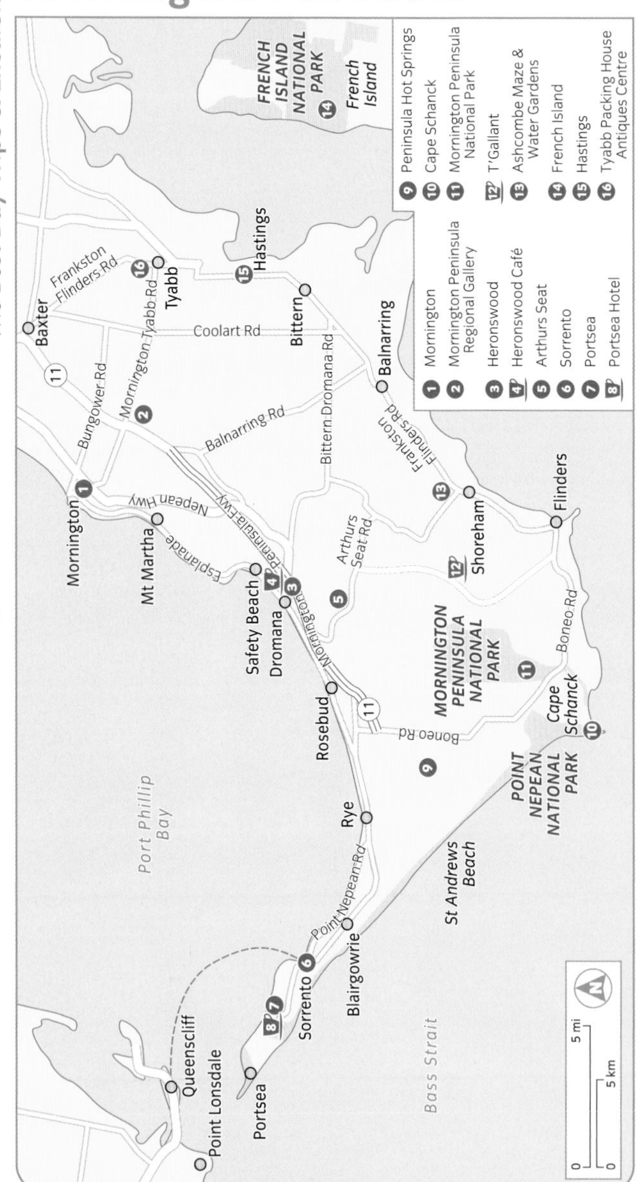

Previous page: The Great Ocean Road (p. 143) is one of Australia's most spectacular drives.

Only an hour's drive from Melbourne, the Mornington Peninsula has long been a favoured holiday spot for Victorians. Its western coastline is dotted with seaside villages, cliff-top mansions, grand gardens, art and antiques galleries, coastal walks, national parks and quiet bays where you can get away from it all.

❶ ★ **Mornington.** The largest town on the peninsula, Mornington is set on a picturesque boat harbour that looks across to the beach with its colourful beach boxes. There's a great range of shops, cafes and restaurants and art galleries to explore, and a coastline with scenic cliff-top walking trails. On Wednesdays, the Main Street Craft Market is the place to pick up local handcrafts. *Mornington Visitor Information Centre, 320 Main St, Mornington.* ☎ *(03) 5975 1644. Mornington Peninsula Visitor Information Centre, 359B Pt Nepean Rd, Dromana.* ☎ *1800 804 009. www.visitmorningtonpeninsula.org.*

❷ ★★ **Mornington Peninsula Regional Gallery.** This peninsula inspired some of the old Heidelberg School artists, and there's also plenty of new blood out there making art. This gallery is where you'll find it on show, in changing and often inspiring exhibitions. 🕘 *30 min. Civic Reserve, Dunns Rd, Mornington.* ☎ *(03) 5975 4395. http://mprg.mornpen.vic.gov.au. Admission $3 adults, $1.50 children. 10am–4.30pm Tues–Fri, 12–4.30pm weekends and holidays.*

❸ ★ **Heronswood.** Wander in these 2ha of historic formal and cottage gardens and admire (from the outside) the two National Trust–classified houses on the property. There's a pocket of rainforest, and Heronswood has a plant nursery and bookshop. 🕘 *30 min. 105 Latrobe Pde, Dromana.* ☎ *(03) 5984 7900. www.diggers.com.au. Admission $8 adults, children free. Daily 9am–5pm.*

A National Trust–classified house and gardens at Heronswood.

Sorrento dolphin swim.

4 **Heronswood Café.** This stylish thatched-roof cafe uses produce straight from Heronswood's kitchen and vegetable parterre gardens. It doesn't get fresher than that! Wash down the Mediterranean-style fare with local wine, organic juice, coffee or herbal tea. ***Heronswood, 105 Latrobe Pde, Dromana.*** ☎ ***(03) 5984 7318. $.***

5 **Arthurs Seat.** At 303m above sea level, Arthurs Seat has the best views on the peninsula. It was named after a similar peak in Scotland by Lieutenant John Murray, during the first exploration of Port Phillip Bay in 1802, and on a clear day, you can see a vast sweep of Victoria. Arthurs Seat State Park also hosts Seawinds Gardens, 34 ha of botanic gardens and bushwalking trails. ***Arthurs Seat Rd, Dromana.***

6 ★★ **Sorrento.** One of Victoria's most popular and fashionable summer destinations, Sorrento's charm stems from its grand old hotels and 19th-century buildings. One of the major attractions is the resident pod of bottlenose dolphins, and dolphin swim tours run regularly. The 'front' beach is great for swimming, while surfers head to the 'back' beach on Bass Strait.

7 ★ **Portsea.** Portsea is another seaside town favoured by the fashionable and famous. Head out to the point for spectacular bay views, or explore the labyrinth of tunnels and fortifications at historic Fort Nepean and the Quarantine Station Museum. The town extends from Port Phillip Bay across a narrow strip of peninsula to the surf beaches on the ocean side.

8 ★★ **Portsea Hotel.** Right on the sands of Portsea front beach, the Portsea pub is a fabulous spot for a beer, a coffee or lunch. Take a table inside or in the beer garden overlooking the ocean, or just flop down on the lawn. ***3746 Point Nepean Rd.*** ☎ ***(03) 5984 2213. www.portseahotel.com.au. $–$$.***

Bathing boxes on Portsea Beach.

The lighthouse looks over the rugged cliffs of Cape Schanck.

9 ★★ Peninsula Hot Springs.

Natural hot mineral springs, discovered on the Mornington Peninsula less than 20 years ago, are now flowing into the public pools and private baths at this hot springs and spa. The public pools are very popular and no more than 70 people are admitted, so it's a good idea to call ahead to see how busy it is if you plan to visit at peak times (Friday to Monday, school holidays and public holidays). For quieter times, try Tuesday to Thursday, particularly before 11am. You can book a private outdoor mineral bath for guaranteed quiet relaxation. Pool temperatures vary from 37 to 43 degrees Celsius. The water contains a range of minerals including sulphur, calcium, magnesium and potassium. *140 Springs Ln, Fingal. ☎ (03) 5950 8777. www.peninsulahotsprings.com. Daily 9am–9pm. Public pools $24–$30 adults (or $15–$20 after 6pm), $16–20 children 5–16, $68–$85 families of 4. No children under 5. Private pools from $77 double for 30 min.*

10 ★★★ Cape Schanck.

Bordered by three bodies of water—Bass Strait, Port Phillip Bay and Western Port Bay—Cape Schanck is wild, rugged and popular with surfers. There are several walking tracks from the lighthouse, but first take the boardwalk down and along to the point. Other walks lead to Bushrangers Bay and Gunnamatta Surf Beach. The Point Nepean National Park stretches along the Bass Strait foreshore, and is home to grey kangaroos, bandicoots, echidnas and lots more wildlife. There's a small museum that runs tours of the lighthouse. *⌚ 2 hr. ☎ 131 963. www.parkweb.vic.gov.au. Tours daily 10am–5pm at 30-minute intervals. Cost $12 adults, $10 children, $33 families of 5. Museum admission $11 adults, $8 children, $27 families.*

Relax in the steaming hot pools at the Peninsula Hot Springs.

A Peninsula Feast

A visit to the Mornington Peninsula can easily become a gourmet feast. The fertile soil, rolling hills and mild climate of this region create ideal conditions for grape-growing—and Melbournians flock to the peninsula with pinot noir, shiraz, pinot grigio and chardonnay on the tasting list. You'll find a cluster of wineries around Red Hill and Main Ridge—names like Main Ridge Estate, Dromana Estate, Willow Creek Vineyard, Hann's Creek Estate, Hickinbotham of Dromana, Lindenderry Vineyard, Red Hill Estate and Stonier's Winery at Merricks, among others. Many of the wineries have great restaurants attached to them, serving up Mediterranean-style platters and dishes that use fresh, local produce. Try cheese-tasting at the Red Hill Cheesery, or if your tastes run to something sweeter, take a sumptuous High Tea at Woodman Estate, sample the strawberry produce at Sunnyridge Strawberry Farm in Main Ridge, or perhaps try lavender tea and scones at historic Nedlands Lavender Farm in Tuerong. Along the roadsides, you will also see signs tempting you to drop in and buy farm-fresh produce—eggs and organic vegetables—and there are also places to pick your own strawberries and cherries.

⑪ **Mornington Peninsula National Park.** Much of what you'll see and visit along the Bass Strait coastline of the peninsula is protected by this park. The 50km of coastline and bushland it covers—around 2680ha—takes in Cape Schanck, Fort Nepean and the beaches of Portsea, Sorrento and Gunnamatta, as well as Arthurs Seat.

12 ★★ **T'Gallant.** Italian-style cuisine, including great wood-fired pizzas, makes this winery a good choice for lunch. Head for the Spuntino Bar rather than the trattoria if you just want something light. Make sure you try T'Gallant's renowned pinot gris! *1385 Mornington Flinders Rd, Main Ridge. ☎ (03) 5989 6565. www.tgallant.com.au. $–$$.*

⑬ ★ kids **Ashcombe Maze & Water Gardens.** Australia's oldest maze is a hit with families. The kids can run wild while you relax or stroll in the lovely woodland gardens. As well as the big hedge maze (yes, you'll get out), there's also a maze made of 1300 rose bushes and a lavender labyrinth. 🕘 *1 hr. Red Hill Rd, Shoreham. ☎ (03) 5989 8387. www.ashcombemaze.com.au. Daily 10am–5pm. Admission $15 adults, $8 children, $40 families of 4.*

T'Gallant is known for its wood-fired pizzas and pinot gris.

Ashcombe Maze is a hit with kids.

⑭ **French Island.** Take a 15-minute ferry ride from Stony Point to French Island, an 11 100ha national park where you can get away from traffic and enjoy peace and tranquillity. French Island National Park is home to a large population of koalas, and you may also see long-nosed potoroos. You can explore by bus, bike or on foot and there are a number of guided tours available. Whole-day, half-day and shorter walks and rides start at Tankerton Foreshore Reserve. The Ranger Station near the jetty has information on all your options. ☎ *(03) 9585 5730 or 131 963. www.parkweb.vic.gov.au.*

⑮ kids **Hastings.** Stroll down the pier to the boat harbour to take a fishing trip or a cruise around Western Port Bay, or just to watch the pelicans. Local families flock to the **Pelican Park Aquatic Centre** near the pier. This is also the finishing point for the Queenscliff to Hastings Ocean Yacht Race, held each September.

⑯ ★ **Tyabb Packing House Antiques Centre.** This complex of more than 45 antique dealers is one of Australia's largest antiques markets. You'll find furniture, crystal, Victorian lace, vintage clothes and more than 40 000 second-hand books. There's also a craft village where working artisans create pottery, china paintings, weavings, iron works, jewellery and folk art. 🕘 ***30 min. 14 Mornington–Tyabb Rd, Tyabb.*** ☎ ***(03) 5977 4414. www.tyabbpackinghouseantiques.com.au. Thurs–Sun & public holidays 10am–5pm.***

Practical Matters: Mornington Peninsula

The easiest way to see the Mornington Peninsula is by car. But for those who don't have their own wheels, there are a couple of public transport options. Trains leave Flinders Street Station regularly every day for Frankston at the northern end of the peninsula. A train also runs from Frankston to Stony Point (Western Port) every two hours or so daily. Peninsula Bus Lines runs public buses throughout the peninsula. From Frankston station, you can get the Portsea Passenger Service bus 788 to Portsea about every 45 minutes on weekdays, every 70 minutes on Saturdays and every two hours from 10am on Sundays. Call ☎ 131-638 or visit www.metlinkmelbourne.com.au for more information.

Ballarat

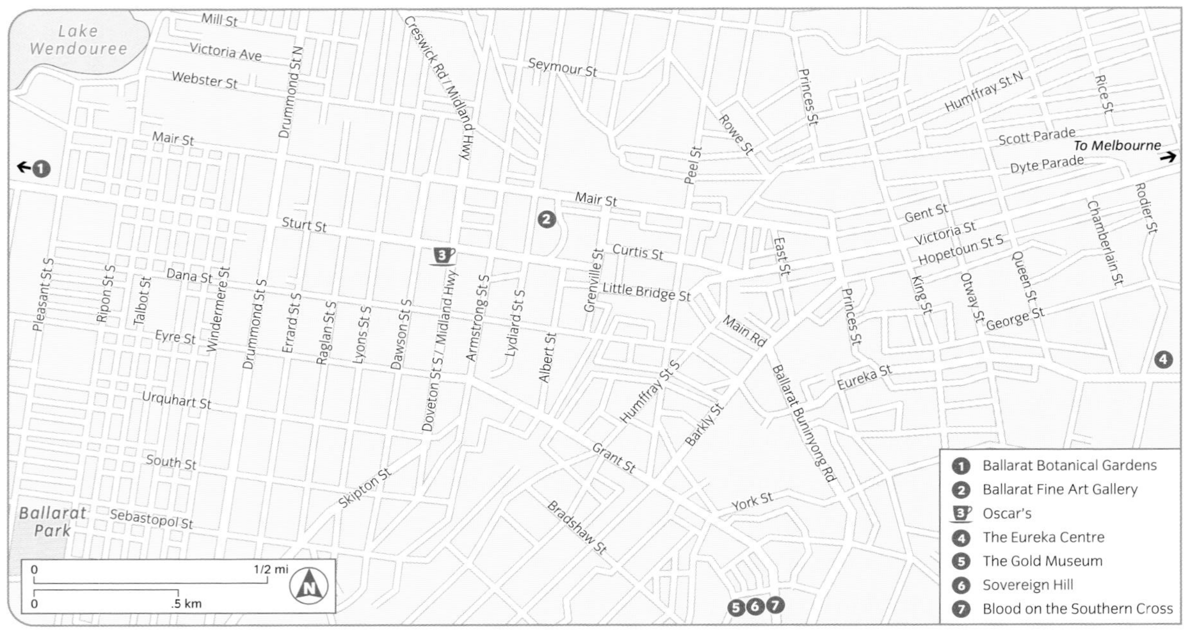
Lake Wendouree
Mill St
Victoria Ave
Webster St
Mair St
Drummond St N
Creswick Rd / Midland Hwy
Seymour St
Princes St
Rowe St
Peel St
Humffray St N
Rice St
Scott Parade
To Melbourne
Dyte Parade
Rodier St
Chamberlain St
Gent St
Victoria St
Hopetoun St S
Queen St
Otway St
King St
George St
Princes St
Eureka St
East St
Mair St
Sturt St
Curtis St
Grenville St
Little Bridge St
Main Rd
Ballarat Buninyong Rd
Humffray St S
Barkly St
Grant St
York St
Bradshaw St
Skipton St
Pleasant St S
Ripon St S
Talbot St
Dana St
Windermere St
Drummond St S
Errard St S
Raglan St S
Lyons St S
Dawson St S
Doveton St S / Midland Hwy
Armstrong St S
Lydiard St S
Albert St
Eyre St
Urquhart St
South St
Sebastopol St
Ballarat Park
0
1/2 mi
0
.5 km
N
1 Ballarat Botanical Gardens
2 Ballarat Fine Art Gallery
3 Oscar's
4 The Eureka Centre
5 The Gold Museum
6 Sovereign Hill
7 Blood on the Southern Cross

Ballarat's impressive colonial buildings are the first evidence you'll see of the wealth from the 1850s gold rush—wealth that built what is now Victoria's largest regional city, about 90 minutes' drive from Melbourne. The impact of the gold rush can't be underestimated, but there's more to Ballarat, and the city makes an interesting day trip—or stay longer if you like.

The Australian Ex-Prisoners of War Memorial at the Ballarat Botanical Gardens.

1 ★★★ Ballarat Botanical Gardens. These delightful gardens are suffering in Australia's drought, but are still well worth visiting. The wealthy philanthropists of Ballarat bestowed magnificent gifts on the gardens from its early days, including a collection of 12 marble statues that now stand in the conservatory, the elegant Statuary Pavilion and its contents—including the wonderful *Flight from Pompeii* by Carlo Benzoni and Charles Francis—and a statue of William Wallace near the gardens' entrance. Other highlights include Prime Ministers Avenue, which is lined with bronze busts of Australia's 25 PMs, and the striking Australian Ex-Prisoners of War Memorial at the south-western end of the gardens. One of the greatest attractions is an avenue of 70 giant redwoods, planted about 130 years ago. ◷ *30 min. Wendouree Pde. ☎ (03) 5320 5135. www.ballarat.vic.gov.au. Admission free. Conservatory open daily 9am–5pm.*

2 ★★★ Ballarat Fine Art Gallery. The highlight of a visit to this excellent gallery—especially after you've learned the story of the Eureka Uprising—is the sight of the original Eureka flag, made from petticoat fabric by the women of the uprising and now enshrined here. This is Australia's oldest regional gallery and houses a fine collection of Australian art, including paintings from the Heidelberg School and a stunning collection of 20th-century modernist works. ◷ *30 min. 40 Lydiard St Nth. ☎ (03) 5320 5858. www.balgal.com. Admission free. Daily 9am–5pm. Guided tours Wed–Sun at 2pm.*

3 Oscar's. This cafe and bar, housed in one of Ballarat's historic old pubs, is in the heart of the town. The gold rush–era hotel has been revamped into an appealing open-plan restaurant with a courtyard and bar. *18 Doveton St Sth. ☎ (03) 5331 1451. www.oscarshotel.com.au. $–$$.*

4 The Eureka Centre. You can't miss this building, with its huge sail signifying the flag of the Southern Cross flying above the original miners' stockade. You can relive the action of the battle through multimedia displays, though it somehow seems slightly sterile for such an impassioned story. ◷ *1 hr.*

Eureka St. ☎ (03) 5333 1854. www.eurekaballarat.com. Admission $8 adults, $4 children, $22 families of 6. Daily 9am–4.30pm (last entry at 4pm).

❺ **The Gold Museum.** This surprisingly interesting museum houses a large collection of gold nuggets found at Ballarat, along with alluvial deposits, gold ornaments and coins. It also has gallery displays relating to the history of goldmining in the area. In 1858, the second-largest chunk of gold discovered in Australia, the Welcome Nugget, was found locally. ⏱ *1 hr. Bradshaw St (opposite Sovereign Hill). ☎ (03) 5337 1107. Admission $8.50 adults, $4.20 children, $23 families of 6. Daily 9.30am–5.20pm.*

❻ ★★★ kids **Sovereign Hill.** Be transported back to the heady days of the 1850s as you wander recreated gold-rush streets and diggings. More than 40 reproduction buildings, including shops and businesses on Main Street, sit on the 25ha former goldmining site. There are also tent camps around the diggings on the lowest part of the site, which would have been the outskirts of the original town. Actors in period costumes go about their daily business and there's a lively atmosphere. You can see see how miners and their families lived, pan for real gold, ride in horse-drawn carriages and watch potters, blacksmiths, wheelwrights and tanners ply their trades. Don't miss the gold pour at the smelting works, or the redcoats as they parade through the streets. The guided tour of a typical underground goldmine takes about 45 minutes. The 'Voyage to Discovery' centre has artifacts from the gold rush, dioramas of mining scenes and interactive computer displays. ⏱ *4 hr. Bradshaw St. ☎ (03) 5331 1944. www.sovereignhill.com.au. Admission (including mine tour & Gold Museum) $35 adults, $16 children 5–15, $90 families of 6. Daily 10am–5pm. Bus: 9 from Curtis St. A free bus, 'The Goldrush Special,' meets the daily 9.08am train (9.28am on Sun) from Melbourne's Southern Cross railway station when it arrives at Ballarat Station, & takes visitors direct to Sovereign Hill. The return service connects with the 4pm train to Melbourne.*

❼ ★★★ **Blood on the Southern Cross.** This breathtaking sound-and-light show recreates the Eureka Uprising, one of the most important events in Australia's history. The uprising was a revolt by goldminers against a government demanding that gold licence fees be paid even by those who came up empty-handed. Corrupt goldfield police instituted a vicious campaign to extract the money, and in 1854, resentment flared. Prospectors demanded

The Eureka Centre tells the story of the Eureka stockade in multimedia.

You'll be transported back to the 1850s at Sovereign Hill.

political reforms such as the right to vote, and the holding of parliamentary elections with secret ballots. When the Eureka Hotel's owner murdered a miner but was set free by the government, the hotel was burned down in revenge. About 20 000 prospectors burned their licences and built a stockade, over which they raised a flag. The troops arrived a month later and attacked at dawn, with 24 miners killed and 30 wounded. However, the uprising succeeded: licences were replaced with 'miners rights' and cheaper fees, and the vote was introduced to Victoria. It's stirring stuff, and the re-enactment does it justice. You'll be outdoors at night, so bring something warm to wear. Bookings are essential.

🕘 90 min. Sovereign Hill, Bradshaw St. ☎ (03) 5337 1199. www.sovereignhill.com.au. Admission $43 adults, $23 children 5–15, $115 families of 4. Package with daytime entry to Sovereign Hill $74 adults, $36 children, $196 families. Package with buffet dinner & stay at Sovereign Hill Lodge $169 adults, $71 children, $443 families. Two shows nightly (times vary seasonally).

Practical Matters: Ballarat

The Ballarat Visitor Information Centre is at The Eureka Centre, Rodier Street (cnr Eureka St; ☎ 1800 446 633; www.visitballarat.com.au). There's also an information centre at the Ballarat Fine Art Gallery. Both are open daily from 9am to 5pm. The **Ballarat Eureka Pass** provides unlimited three-day entry to The Eureka Centre, Sovereign Hill, the Gold Museum and the Fine Art Gallery. It costs $42 for adults, $19 for children 5 to 15 and $107 for families of six. The **Art & Fact Pass** is an all-day pass to The Eureka Centre and the Fine Art Gallery, and costs $9. It's available from the gallery, the Eureka Centre and visitor information centres. The **Gold Pass** covers Sovereign Hill and the Gold Museum as well as a tour of the Red Hill Mine. It costs $35 for adults, $19 for children and $90 for families.

Dandenong Ranges

Melbournians traditionally do a 'day in the Dandenongs' from time to time, winding through the picturesque hills and villages, stopping off for a Devonshire tea and perhaps doing a short bushwalk. Up in the cool high country you'll find native bush, lovely gardens, a vintage steam train and plenty of restaurants. The Dandenong Ranges National Park is one of the state's oldest, set aside in 1882.

1 ★ kids Puffing Billy Railway. For almost a century, Puffing Billy has chugged over a 13km track from Belgrave to Emerald and Lakeside. Passengers ride in open carriages and enjoy the lovely views as the steam train passes through forests and fern gullies and over an old wooden trestle bridge. Trips take around an hour each way. The timetables can be complicated and changeable, so check the website to ensure you have the right information. Special fares that include lunch aboard the train are also available, and on Friday and Saturday nights you can have dinner on board as well. *Belgrave Station, Belgrave. ☎ (03) 9754 6800. www.puffingbilly.com.au. Round-trip fares $20–$47 adults, $11–$22 children 4–16, $68–$94 families of 6. Train: Belgrave.*

2 National Rhododendron Gardens. In spring, thousands of rhododendrons and azaleas burst into bloom in these magnificent gardens. They cover 42ha, with a 3km walking path leading past flowering exotics and native trees. Visitors flock here in summer for the walks, and in autumn to admire the leaves turning red and gold. The tearoom is open every day in the spring and on weekends at other times. ⌚ *1 hr. The Georgian Rd, Olinda.* ☎ *(03) 8627 4699. www.parkweb.vic.gov.au. Admission Sept–Nov $8.25 adults, $3 children 15–17, $20 families; Dec–Aug $6.70 adults, $3 children, $16 families. Children under 15 free. Daily 10am–5pm. Train: Croydon or Belgrave, then bus 688 or 694 respectively.*

The intriguing sculptures of William Ricketts Sanctuary.

3 William Ricketts Sanctuary. This interesting garden, in a forest of mountain ash, features almost 100 clay figures representing the Aboriginal Dreamtime. The sculptures were created by William Ricketts over his lifetime; the inspiration for the sculptures was Ricketts's philosophy that all people need to act as guardians

The exquisite National Rhododendron Gardens.

Yarra Valley Wandering

Any visit to the Dandenongs can be coupled with a swing through the wine region of the Yarra Valley. This lovely region is dotted with villages, historic houses, gardens, craft and antique shops, restaurants and more than 50 wineries. The best way to explore is by car, and you can follow the self-guided **Yarra Valley Wine Touring Guide**—pick up a brochure from the **Yarra Valley Visitor Information Centre**, Harker Street, Healesville (☎ (03) 5962 2600; www.visityarravalley.com.au). If you want to taste and not drive, join one of the many wine tours on offer. **Healesville** and **Marysville** are the best villages to visit. Stop off at the historic and award-winning **Healesville Hotel** (☎ (03) 5962 4002; www.healesvillehotel.com.au) for lunch. And don't miss **Healesville Sanctuary** (see p. 46, bullet 4) for wildlife encounters.

of the natural environment in the same way as Aborigines. Ricketts died in 1993 at the age of 94. The garden encompasses fern gullies and waterfalls spread out over 13ha. 🕘 *1 hr. Mt Dandenong Tourist Rd, Mt Dandenong. ☎ (03) 9751 1300. www.parkweb.vic.gov.au. Admission $6.70 adults, $3 children 15–17, $16 families of 5. Children under 15 free. Daily 10am–4.30pm. Train: Croydon, then bus 688.*

4 **Paperbark Café.** This nursery cafe offers an all-day grazing menu (pizzas, pies, platters and more). For afternoon, try the cakes, savoury muffins or—for something a bit different—the wattleseed scones served with kookaberry jam, macadamia butter and double cream. Try a local coffee or a cup of lemon myrtle tea. *Kuranga Native Nursery, 118 York Rd, Mt Evelyn. www.kuranga.com.au. $.*

If wine is your thing, head to the Yarra Valley.

Try wattleseed scones served with kookaberry jam at Paperbark Café.

❺ **Tesselaar Bulbs.** Tens of thousands of flowers grow in the display gardens here, putting on a flamboyantly colourful show in the spring (mid-September to mid-October), when the company runs the Tesselaar Tulip Festival. Expect to see a dazzling variety of tulips, daffodils, rhododendrons, azaleas, fuchsias and ranunculi. If you arrive on the Saturday or Sunday during the festival, you'll most likely also be treated to a themed mini-festival weekend, featuring food stalls, wine, beer and music. Bulbs are on sale outside tulip festival time. *357 Monbulk Rd, Silvan. 🕘 1 hr. ☎ (03) 9737 9811. www.tulipfestival.com.au. Admission during tulip festival (mid-Sept to mid-Oct) $15 adults, children under 16 free if accompanied by an adult; free for everyone rest of the year. During tulip festival daily 10am–5pm; rest of year Mon–Fri 8am–4.30pm, Sat–Sun 1–5pm. Train: Lilydale, then bus 679.*

❻ **Kokoda Track Memorial Walk.** Only the fit should tackle The Thousand Steps and the Kokoda Track Memorial Walk. This is a challenging rainforest track, starting at the Ferntree Gully picnic ground and climbing One Tree Hill. Along the way are plaques commemorating Australian troops who fought and died in Papua New Guinea in World War II. Other—easier—walks in the area include a 2.5km (1½ mile) stroll from the **Sherbrook Picnic Ground** through the forest.

Practical Matters: Dandenong Ranges

Dandenong Ranges & Knox Visitor Information Centre is located at 1211 Burwood Hwy, Upper Ferntree Gully (☎ 1800 645 505; www.dandenongrangestourism.com.au; daily 9am–5pm).

The Great Ocean Road

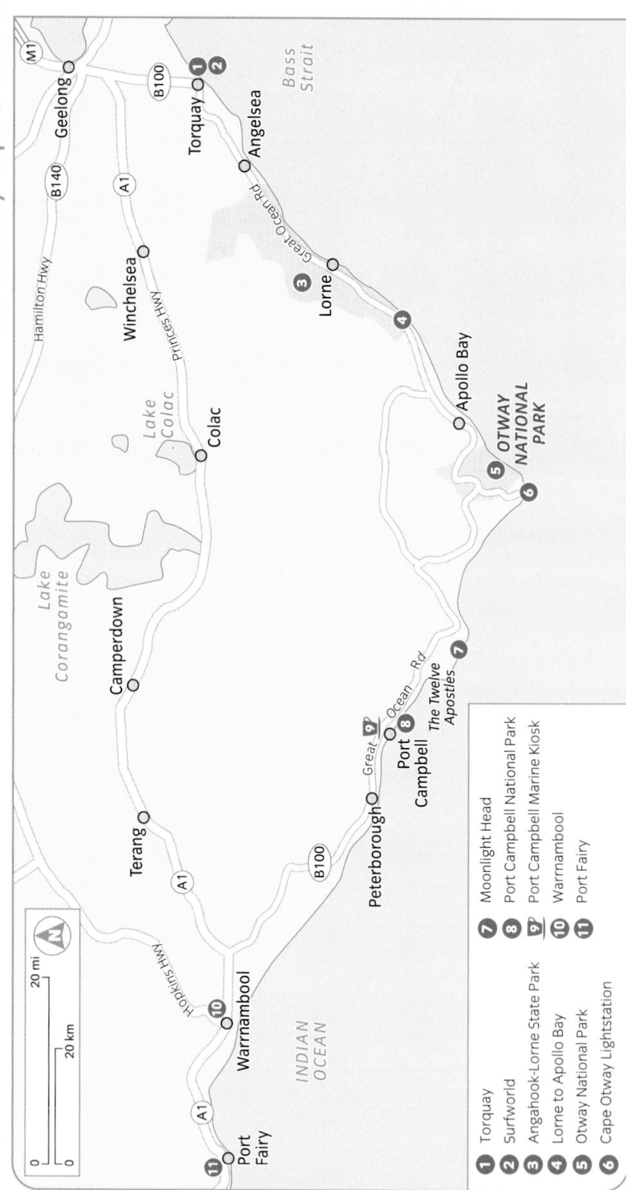

One of Australia's most spectacular drives, the Great Ocean Road hugs the coast for 106km from Torquay to Warrnambool, passing huge cliffs, wild beaches, rainforests and incredible rock formations. The most spectacular section is between Princeton, at the start of Port Campbell National Park, and Peterborough. Make the most of it; don't just drive, get out and feel the wind in your hair.

1 ★ **Torquay**. This town, 95km south-west of Melbourne, is known as the surfing capital of Australia. Here, it's all about surfing, and the main surf beach is much nicer than the one further down the coast in Lorne. Bells Beach, just down the road, is world famous in the surfing world for its perfect waves, and hosts the Rip Curl Pro competition over Easter every year. For those who prefer to keep their feet on the ground, the Surf Coast Walk is a track running about 35km from Jan Juc, near Torquay, to Moggs Creek and past Anglesea. It has great coastal views, forest and heath to walk through and wildlife to spot, including birds and kangaroos. *Torquay Visitor Information Centre, Surf City Plaza, Beach Rd. ☎ (03) 5261 4219. Daily 9am–5pm*.

2 **Surfworld**. A walk-through Kombi Van, surf movies and a 'shaping bay' where you can watch a board-shaper in action are all part of this unique dedicated surfing museum. Find out all about the history of surfing and surfboards in Australia. An 80-seat theatrette shows non-stop historic surfing footage and features an exhibition of surf movie posters. Surfworld is also home to the Australian Surfing Hall of Fame, which details the achievements and lives of famous Australian surfers—the awards mounted on the type of surfboard ridden by each person. The 'Surf Culture' area focuses on art, music and clothing relating to surfing. 🕐 *1 hr. Surfcity Plaza, Beach Rd, West Torquay. ☎ (03) 5261 4606. www.surfworld.org.au. Admission $9 adults, $6 children, $20 families of 5. Daily 9am–5pm.*

Torquay is the surfing capital of Australia.

Great Ocean Walk

lking at least part of Victoria's spectacular west coast really repays the effort. The Great Ocean Walk stretches 91km from Apollo Bay to Glenample Homestead, near the Twelve Apostles, but the trail is designed so walkers can complete short walks or day or overnight hikes as they desire. If you're planning to camp overnight, you must register with **Parks Victoria** (☎ 131 963; www.greatoceanwalk.com.au) and pay a fee of $25 per tent. The walk winds through beautiful and remote areas such as Station Beach and Moonlight Head. It also crosses coastal heaths, dips in and out of the sheltered coastal estuaries of the Aire and Gellibrand rivers, and reveals wet fern and rainforest gullies where huge specimens of the world's tallest flowering tree, the mountain ash, grow. If you like walking but dislike roughing it, various companies offer tours that provide overnight accommodation at plush B&Bs after your day in the wilderness. Visit the website for more information on tours, camping and walking equipment hire and provisioning.

❸ **Angahook-Lorne State Park**. Protecting most of the coastal section of the Otway Ranges, this park has many well-marked rainforest walks and picnic areas at Shelly Beach, Elliot River and Blanket Bay. There's plenty of wildlife around!

❹ ★★ **Lorne to Apollo Bay.** This is one of the most spectacular sections of the route; the road narrows and twists and turns along a cliff edge with the ocean on the other side. Lorne is a popular holiday spot for Melbournians, with a wide beach, a main street dotted with boutiques, cafes and restaurants, and a great pub overlooking the beach. It's also the venue each January for the Lorne Pier to Pub Swim, which attracts around 4000 entrants to race the 1.2km between the two landmarks.

The Great Ocean Walk stretches across Victoria's spectacular west coast.

Whale-watching platforms at Warrnambool's Logan's Beach.

Apollo Bay is a pleasant town that was once a whaling station. It has good sandy beaches and is more low-key than Lorne, which is a bit of a tourist hot spot. *Lorne Visitor Centre, 15 Mountjoy Pde. ☎ 1300 891 152. www.visitsurfcoast.com. Daily 9am–5pm.*

5 ★★ **The Otways.** From the **Great Otway National Park**, head inland towards the old logging town of Beech Forest and turn off to the **Otway Fly Tree Top Walk** (www.otwayfly.com.au). From 25m up in the forest canopy, you can walk through a stand of beech, blackwood and mountain ash, then—if your head for heights is good enough—climb a spiral staircase to a lookout at 45m. Drive back to the Great Ocean Road, and a little further on is **Maits Rest Rainforest Boardwalk**, a lovely spot for a break and a stroll.

Watch Out for Whales

Whale-watching fever takes over on the Great Ocean Road from June to September each year, when you might see (with binoculars) the massive bulk of Southern Right whales as they migrate along the coast. Sightings are sheer luck, but your chances of seeing the passing whales and their calves are usually quite high. Whale-watching platforms have been built along the coast, with the major one at Warrnambool's **Logan's Beach**, where tiered boardwalks in the sand dunes allow great viewing of the frolicking giants of the ocean. Another good spot is Gables Lookout, near Princetown. Later in the year, and slightly further down the coast, near Portland, you may sometimes spot blue whales off Cape Nelson. The Bonney Upwelling just off Cape Nelson is one of only a few known blue whale feeding areas in the world. The whales usually arrive in December and stay until May.

6 ★★ Cape Otway Lightstation. At the end of a 15km unpaved road, the 100m-tall lighthouse stands on a windswept headland. The light was built by convicts in 1848. A guide will greet you at the top of the tower to recount stories of the Cape's traditional owners, shipwrecks, the colourful lighthouse keepers and one of Australia's most famous UFO mysteries. *30 min.* ☎ *(03) 5237 9240; www.lightstation.com. Admission $12 adults, $7 children. Daily 9am–5pm.*

7 ★★ Moonlight Head. This is the start of the Shipwreck Coast, a 120km stretch running to Port Fairy that claimed more than 80 ships in 40 years at the end of the 19th century and the beginning of the 20th. A lonely headstone on the cliffs overlooking Wreck Beach, west of Moonlight Head, pays tribute to those who lost their lives when the *Fiji* ran aground in 1891. From there, climb down the 400 or so steps to Wreck Beach, below the cliffs at the end of Moonlight Head Road. At low tide, if you walk west, you'll come across the rusting anchors of two ships—the *Marie Gabrielle* (which sank in 1869) and the *Fiji*, embedded in the sand a few hundred metres apart. Allow about two hours and only make the walk at low tide, keeping an eye out for sea swells. You can get a trail map from local visitor information centres.

8 ★★★ Port Campbell National Park. With its sheer cliffs and coastal rock sculptures, this is one of Australia's most famous landscapes. The **Twelve Apostles**, a series of rock pillars jutting from the surf just offshore, sadly now number only eight, as nature has reclaimed several in recent years. These ancient limestone stacks rise from the ocean, sculpted by wind and water. You can't see them from the road, so park at the interpretive centre and take the boardwalks to the cliff-tops and lookouts, feeling the elements which have shaped this special place. Other attractions are the Blowhole, which throws up huge sprays of water; the Grotto, a rock formation carved by the water; London Bridge, which looked quite like the real thing until the middle of it collapsed into the sea in 1990; and Loch Ard Gorge.

9 Port Campbell Marine Kiosk may not look like much, but the kiosk-style shop attached to Port Campbell Marine, a marine shop and dive centre, serves up locally handmade Timboon Fine Ice Cream in flavours like plum pudding and Turkish delight. Go down to the beach to eat it. *Port Campbell Marine, 32 Lord St, Port Campbell.* ☎ *(03) 5598 6411.*

The famous and iconic Twelve Apostles.

Visit historic fishing town Port Fairy.

⑩ **Warrnambool.** The largest city on the Great Ocean Road, Warrnambool (pop. 31 000) nevertheless has a relaxed pace, although it can get a bit hectic in summer. The main tourist attraction is Flagstaff Hill, an interactive 1870s maritime village and museum (89 Merri St; ☎ (03) 5559 4600; www.flagstaffhill.com). The precinct contains the heritage-listed Lady Bay Lighthouse and Warrnambool Garrison, as well as a recreated port complete with ships. The museum gives a fascinating insight into the 19th-century life of Warrnambool, and there are many shipwreck relics on display, including a porcelain peacock washed up from the wreck of the ship *Loch Ard* in 1878. At dusk, a sound and light show depicts the story of the ill-fated *Loch Ard*. ***Warrnambool Visitor Information Centre, Flagstaff Hill, 23 Merri St.*** ☎ ***1800 637 725. www.warrnamboolinfo.com.au. Daily 9am–5pm.***

⑪ **Port Fairy.** A lovely fishing town once called Belfast by Irish immigrants, Port Fairy is one of Victoria's most historic towns and has 50 heritage-listed buildings. Stroll across the pedestrian causeway to Griffiths Island, and visit the old bluestone lighthouse at the mouth of the Moyne River at dusk to see the muttonbird colony. The annual Port Fairy Folk Festival in March draws crowds from around the country. ***Port Fairy Visitor Information Centre, Railway Place, Bank St.*** ☎ ***(03) 5568 2682. www.visitportfairy.com.au. Daily 9am–5pm.***

Practical Matters: Great Ocean Road

Most places along the Great Ocean Road have information centres. Among the major ones are the **Geelong & Great Ocean Road Visitors Centre** (Stead Park, Princess Hwy, Corio; ☎ (03) 5275 5797; www.greatoceanrd.org.au), and at the **National Wool Museum** (26 Moorabool St, Geelong; ☎ (03) 5222 2900) and **Port Campbell** (26 Morris St; ☎ (03) 5598 6089). All are open from 9am to 5pm daily. A good website to visit is www.greatoceanroad.org, and www.parkweb.vic.gov.au has information on Port Campbell National Park and Otway National Park.

The **Great Ocean Road Accommodation Centre** (136 Mountjoy Pde, Lorne; ☎ (03) 5289 4233; www.gorac.com.au) rents cottages and units along the route. Other good accommodation websites are www.otwaysaccommodation.com.au and www.shipwreckcoastaccommodation.com.au.

Phillip Island

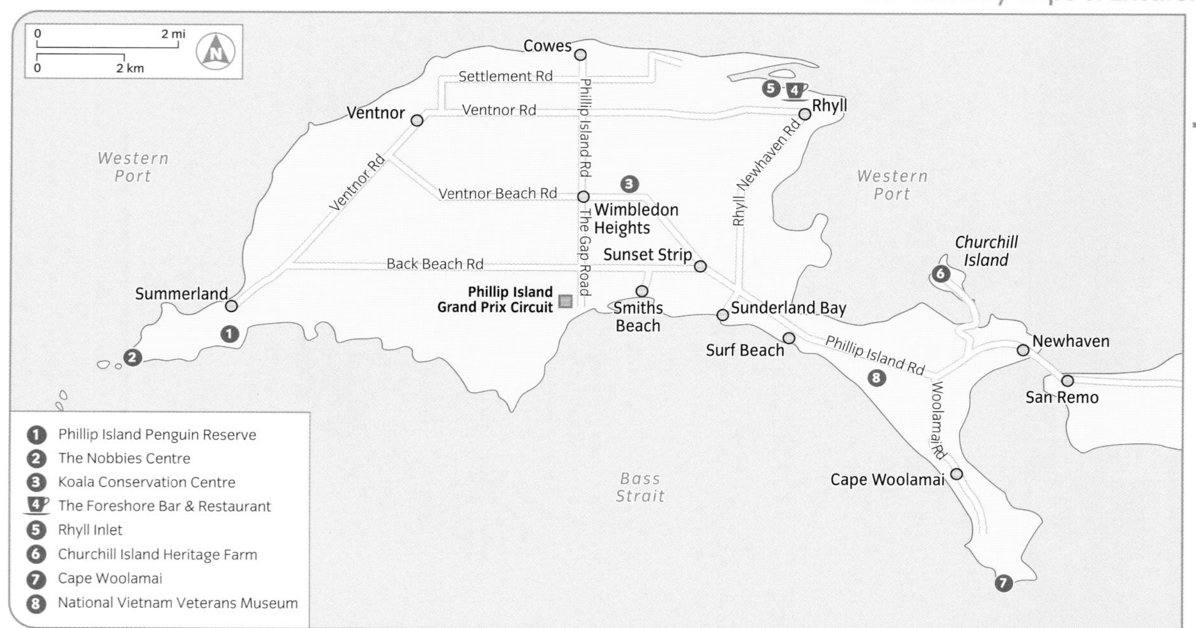

Phillip Island's daily penguin parade is one of Australia's most popular wildlife attractions. The island, 139km south of Melbourne, also has nice beaches, good bushwalking and fishing and a seal colony. If you have the time you could spend two days here or more. It's an easy two-hour trip from Melbourne along the South Gippsland Highway and then the Bass Highway; a bridge connects the island to the mainland.

1 ★ kids **Phillip Island Penguin Reserve.** The Penguin Parade takes place every night at dusk on the south-west coast about 15km (9½ miles) from Cowes. Hundreds of little penguins appear at the water's edge and waddle up the beach towards their burrows in the dunes. Photography, smoking and touching the penguins are all banned. It's very commercial, with busloads of tourists squashing in to get a look; bookings are essential during holiday periods. More exclusive (and expensive) small group tours give you a better view. Penguins Plus allows you to watch the parade from an exclusive boardwalk, while the Penguin Sky Box is an adults-only elevated viewing tower staffed by a ranger. The 'Ultimate Penguin Tour' for groups of only 10 people (no children under 16), takes you to a secluded beach away from the main viewing area to see penguins coming ashore. Another option is a ranger-guided tour, which runs a few hours before the penguins appear and looks at behind-the-scenes research. *Summerland Beach, Phillip Island Tourist Rd, Cowes. ☎ 1300 366 422. www.penguins.org.au. Admission $20 adults, $10 children 4–15, $50 families of 4. Admission to visitor centre only $4 adults, $2 children 4–15, $11 families of 4. Penguins Plus $35 adults, $18 children, $88 families; Penguin Sky Box $50; Ultimate Penguin Tour $70; ranger-guided tour $10 adults, $5 children, $25 families (in addition to visitor centre entry). Visitor centre open in summer daily 9am–6pm; in winter daily 9am–5pm.*

2 ★ **The Nobbies Centre.** The west coast of Phillip Island's Summerland Peninsula ends in an interesting rock formation called The Nobbies, where there's a marine interpretive centre and some spectacular views of the coastline and islands. On the most distant of the two islands live around 12 000 Australian fur seals, the largest colony in Australia. I like the hundreds of nesting silver gulls here, too. *1 hr. Ventnor Rd, Summerlands. ☎ (03) 5951 2816; www.nobbies-centre.org.au. Admission free. Daily 10am (11am in winter) until sunset.*

Hundreds of little penguins waddle up the beach at dusk at the Phillip Island Penguin Reserve.

Phillip Island Grand Prix

Every October, Phillip Island hosts a round of the annual MotoGP World Championship (www.motogp.com.au). The three-day motorcycling event showcases racing in three Grand Prix classes plus national racing categories, and offers other entertainment on and off the track. At any time of year, you can take a guided tour of the circuit, hire a go-kart, visit the History of Motorsport exhibit or strap yourself in for three laps around it with a professional racing car driver—all for a price, of course. The visitor centre (Back Beach Rd; ☎ (03) 5952 9400; http://phillipislandcircuit.com.au) has a cafe, slot car games and a kids' playground.

3 Koala Conservation Centre. Koalas were introduced to Phillip Island in the 1880s and thrived in its predator-free environment. Overpopulation, the introduction of foxes and dogs, and the clearing of land for farms and roads have taken their toll, however, and while you can still sometimes spot koalas in the wild, the best place to find them is at this sanctuary. An elevated boardwalk allows you to get quite close. At around 4pm, the usually sleepy koalas are on the move—but this is also the time when a lot of tour buses arrive, so it can get crowded. ◷ *1 hr. Phillip Island Tourist Rd, Cowes.* ☎ *(03) 5952 1307. Admission $10 adults, $5 children 4–15, $25 families of 4. Daily 10am–5pm.*

4 ★ The Foreshore Bar & Restaurant. Has sandwiches and wraps for lunch, as well as heartier fare like big bowls of mussels or risotto. Large windows and a terrace with outdoor tables make the most of the water views. *11 Beach Rd, Rhyll.* ☎ *(03) 5956 9520. $–$$.*

5 Rhyll Inlet. This inter-tidal mangrove wetland on the north coast of the island is a great place for bird watchers. You'll see wading birds such as spoonbills, oystercatchers, herons, egrets and cormorants, and the rare bar-tailed godwit and whimbrel.

6 kids Churchill Island Heritage Farm. Highland cattle may greet you as you approach this historic working farm. On 57ha, this is the site of the first European attempts at agriculture in Victoria —the farm dates back to the 1850s. There's a restored and furnished farmhouse and cottages, but most kids will want to get among the animals—which include Clydesdale horses. ◷ *1 hr. Off Phillip Island Rd.* ☎ *(03) 5956 7214. www.churchillisland.org.au. Admission $10 adults, $5 children under 16, $25 families of 4. Daily 10am–4pm.*

A sleepy koala at the Koala Conservation Centre.

Cape Woolamai has fabulous coastal views.

7 ★ Cape Woolamai. The island's highest point has fabulous coastal views; walking trails lead through heath and pink granite to the lookout. From September to April, the cape is home to thousands of short-tailed shearwaters (also known as mutton birds).

8 ★★ National Vietnam Veterans Museum. It may seem an unusually remote spot for a national museum, but this one won't disappoint. Its collection of about 6000 artifacts includes the marbles used in the conscription lottery, uniforms, vehicles and weapons. There's also a photo gallery, dioramas depicting aspects of the war, a moving audio-visual exhibit and a display about the Australian-Vietnamese community. The big star is a Bell AH-1G HueyCobra helicopter gunship, one of only three in Australia. A restoration project is also underway on a Canberra Bomber, the sole surviving one of its kind in the world. ⌚ *30 min. Veterans Dve, Newhaven. ☎ (03) 5956 6400. www.vietnamvetsmuseum.org. Admission $5 adults, $2 children under 15, $12 families of 4. Daily 10am–5pm.*

Practical Matters: Philip Island

The Cowes Visitor Information Centre (Thompson Ave, Cowes; ☎ 1300 366 422; www.visitphillipisland.com) is open daily 9am to 5pm.

A **Three Parks Pass** gives discounted entry to the Koala Conservation Centre, the Penguin Parade and Churchill Island Heritage Farm. The pass costs $34 for adults, $17 for children aged 4 to 15 and $85 for families of four. It can be purchased online (www.penguins.org.au) or at any of the attractions.

The charming **Holmwood Guesthouse** (37 Chapel St, Cowes; ☎ (03) 5952 3082; www.holmwoodguesthouse.com.au; doubles $195–$210) is set in lovely cottage gardens, just a short walk from the beach and town centre. You can choose between three slightly old-fashioned rooms in the main house, all with ensuites, or two stylish modern cottages alongside, each with its own courtyard garden.

Several tour companies run day trips. Among them are **Gray Line** (☎ (03) 9663 4455; www.grayline.com), which operates daily 'penguin express' trips that leave Melbourne at 3.15pm (later in summer) and return between 9pm and 11.30pm. Tours cost $109 for adults and $54 for children, and can be booked online in US dollars before arrival.

Macedon Ranges

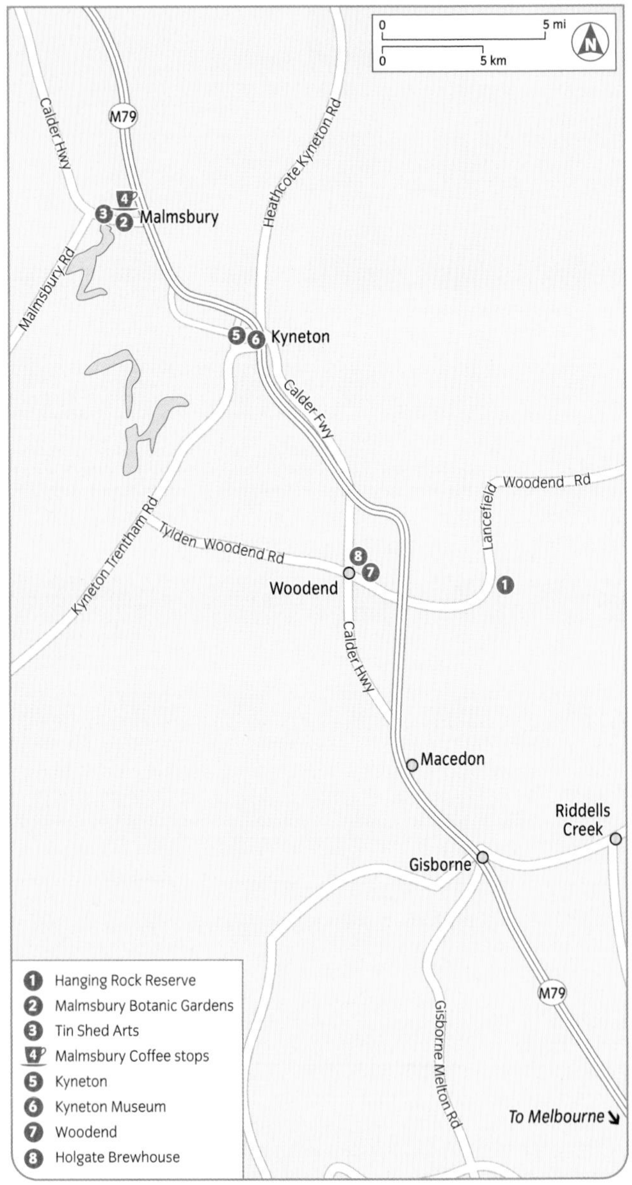

Impressive mansions and some of Victoria's finest gardens sprinkle the hills and valleys of the Macedon Ranges, just an hour from Melbourne. In bygone times, the wealthy swapped the city's heat for the cooler climes of Macedon and Mount Macedon each summer. Their legacy of 'hill station' private gardens is one reason for visiting; another is the region's 40 cool-climate wineries and its gourmet foods.

1 ★★ kids Hanging Rock Reserve. The ghost of Miranda (the ethereal schoolgirl who vanished at Hanging Rock in author Joan Lindsay's 1967 novel *Picnic at Hanging Rock*) is never far away here. Indeed, the visitor centre here fairly thrives on the fiction. Peter Weir's 1975 film of the novel cemented its fame, but the mystery seems unimportant once you see how beautiful this spot is. You can climb the rock, walk the tracks, explore caves with names like 'The Black Hole of Calcutta' and 'The Cathedral' or—yes—picnic. The Hanging Rock Discovery Centre explains the geology and history of the area, and revisits the book and movie. There are guided tours, including night tours during summer, and lots of wildlife: koalas, kangaroos, sugar gliders, echidnas and wallabies. Picnic horse races have also been run here every Australia Day (January 26), New Year's Day and Labour Day for the past 80-plus years. *South Rock Rd, Woodend. ☎ 1800 244 711. www.hangingrock.info. Admission $10 per car or $4 per pedestrian. Daily 8am–6pm.*

A picnic horse race at Hanging Rock.

2 ★ Malmsbury Botanic Gardens. The Malmsbury Botanic Gardens, next to the Malmsbury Town Hall, were designed to take advantage of the Coliban River valley and a billabong, which was transformed into a group of ornamental lakes. Malmsbury's most famous landmark is the bluestone railway viaduct, built by 4000 men in 1859. At 25m high with five 18m spans, it's one of Australia's longest stone bridges and is best viewed from the gardens. The 5ha grounds feature a superb collection of mature trees and are a popular

Gorgeous Gardens

If you want to see fantastic gardens, the best times to visit the Macedon Ranges are April and November, when some of the best are showing their autumn and spring colours. For me, autumn wins! These are Open Garden months (www.opengarden.org.au), but some homestead gardens are open year round, including **Duneira** (☎ (03) 5426 1490) and **Tieve Tara** (☎ (03) 5426 2435) at Mt Macedon, **Bringalbit** (☎ (03) 5423 7223) near Kyneton, and the Edna Walling garden at **Campaspe Country House** (☎ (03) 5427 2273), Woodend. It pays to call ahead to check times and access, and entry fees apply. For keen gardeners, the area also has a number of nurseries, from cottage-garden specialists to native-plant and rare-species retailers.

spot for barbecues and petanque. At Apple Hole, you'll often find kids leaping into the river from a rope swing, but at quiet times, you may be lucky enough to spot a platypus. 🕘 *30 min. Calder Hwy, Malmsbury.*

❸ ★ **Tin Shed Arts**. I've popped in to this spacious gallery several times in the past few years and it always has something interesting and unexpected. It hangs contemporary and traditional art from both local artists and well-known names from around Australia, including paintings, mixed media, sculpture and craftwork. *Calder Hwy, Malmsbury. ☎ (03) 5423 2144. Daily 10am–5pm.*

Piper Street, Kyneton, is the place to come for antiques, crafts and tea rooms.

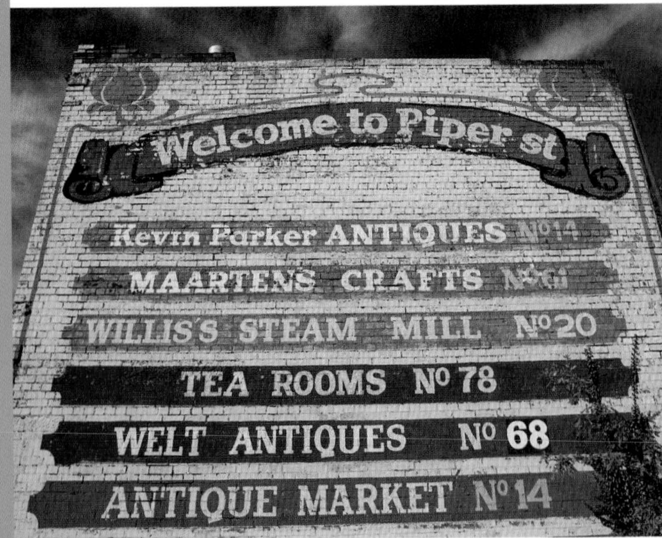

4 There are a couple of good options for coffee stops in Malmsbury. The quaint **Malmsbury Bakery** (77 Mollison St; ☎ (03) 5423 2369) is renowned for its pies, cakes and bread. For something a bit more upmarket, **The Providore** (73 Mollison St; ☎ (03) 5423 2000) offers gourmet goodies from around the country and very good coffee.

A Macedon vineyard.

5 ★ **Kyneton.** Turn down **Piper Street** for antiques, homewares, cafes, providores, a heritage pub and much more. Among the shops to look out for are **Slow Living Organic Whole Food** (54A Piper St; ☎ (03) 5422 3818), **Kyneton Gourmet Foods** (43a Piper St, ☎ (03) 5422 7088), and for homewares, **L'Echoppe** (56 Piper St; ☎ (03) 5422 2600). The **Kyneton Farmers' Market** is held at St Paul's Park, Piper Street, on the second Saturday of the month from 8am to 1pm. Dine at the **Royal George Hotel** (24 Piper St, ☎ (03) 5422 1390; www.royalgeorge.com.au), a great historic pub (circa 1850) where the menu is as imaginative and the food as good as anything you'll find in Melbourne. The wine list is extensive, and includes many local drops. Open Wednesday to Saturday for dinner, Thursday to Sunday for lunch. For cheap eats with style, drop into **Pizza Verde** (62 Piper St; ☎ (03) 5422 7400) for hors d'oeuvres, a glass of wine and terrific pizza made with 100 per cent organic flour and topped with fresh local produce. *Kyneton Visitor Information Centre, 127 High St. ☎ 1800 244 711. www.visitmacedonranges.com. Daily 9am–5pm.*

6 **Kyneton Museum.** Housed in a sturdy 1856 bluestone former Bank of New South Wales building, the Kyneton Museum collection tells the story of the town and district from the 1850s to the 1930s. Changing

Winery Tours

Given there are more than 40 vineyards and 20 cellar doors, wine buffs who want to sample the Macedon region's product should consider taking a tour. Victoria Winery Tours (☎ 1300 946 386; www.winetours.com.au) runs small-group day tours from Melbourne to the Macedon Ranges, visiting four or five wineries for tasting (with a minimum of two people). Among the stops may be Hanging Rock Winery, Mount Macedon Winery, Glen Erin Vineyard Retreat, Granite Hills, Gisborne Peak Winery, Curly Flat Vineyard, Morgan Field, Farrawell, Riddells Creek Winery, Cobaw Ridge, Rowanston on the Track, Longview Creek or Midhill Vineyard. Pick up in Melbourne is at 9am, returning by about 5.30pm, and it costs $142 per person, including morning tea and lunch.

exhibitions often draw on the museum's historical photographs. *30 min. 67 Piper St. ☎ (03) 5422 1228. Fri–Sun 11am–4pm.*

7 ★ **Woodend.** After the gold rush of the 1850s, Woodend became a resort town, with guesthouses, hotels, large private gardens and a racecourse and a golf club. Reminders of those days abound in the historical buildings and clock tower in High Street, and there are plenty of cafes, providores, boutiques and galleries. Check out **Literary Latte** (81 High St) and **Maloa House Gourmet Delights** (95 High St). *Woodend Visitor Centre, 711 High St. ☎ 1800 244 711. www.visitmacedonranges.com. Daily 9am–5pm.*

8 ★★ **Holgate Brewhouse.** Keatings Hotel has stood on the corner of High Street for a century. Today, it's home to this family-owned brewhouse, which busily turns out handcrafted beers for its thirsty patrons. The brewery produces a range of draught beers and you can buy 'tastings' until you decide on your favourite. The beer is brewed traditionally and naturally using just four ingredients—malt, hops, yeast and pure Macedon Ranges water. *30 min. 79 High St, Woodend. ☎ (03) 5427 2510. www.holgatebrewhouse.com. Mon 2pm–late, Tues–Sun noon–late.*

Holgate Brewhouse uses pure Macedon Ranges water in its brews.

Practical Matters: Macedon Ranges

There are two visitor information centres in the region, at Kyneton (see bullet **5**), and at Woodend (see bullet **7**). The website www.visitmacedonranges.com is a good source of information.

The Rectory (61 Ebden St, Kyneton, ☎ (03) 5422 6738; www.triplehillabs.com.au/propertydetails/Rectory) is a romantic bluestone National Trust building converted to a luxury contemporary-style B&B. The rooms look out onto stunning gardens by leading Australian garden designer Paul Bangay, and there's a French provincial–style bathroom. The Ruby Lounge has an open fire. Doubles $180–$190.

Apartment 61A (61A Piper St, Kyneton, ☎ (03) 5422 1211; www.macedonrangesinteriors.com.au) has two fresh, bright bedrooms overlooking Piper Street. All supplies are provided for breakfast, including organic juice, bacon and eggs, cereal, organic muesli and biodynamic lemon myrtle yoghurt. Doubles $160.

Walhalla

Tucked in a lush valley in the Victorian Alps, 180km east of Melbourne, the village of Walhalla is home to only around a dozen people. A century ago, though, it was one of the world's richest goldmining towns; what remains of it has been faithfully preserved and restored. Walhalla was the last town in Victoria to get electricity, as recently as 1999.

1 ★ Long Tunnel Extended Gold Mine. You can take an interesting guided walking tour of the old goldmine, which dates back to 1865 and was once the richest paying mine in Australia, with 13.7 tonnes of gold extracted over 40 years of operation. The mine covered 10ha and had 9km of tunnels to a depth of 1000m. Friendly volunteer guides take you to the huge machinery chamber and past all the original gold workings. It's a fascinating tour that I highly recommend for its insight into the town, as well as the mining process. *50 min. ☎ (03) 5165 6259. Entry $15 adults, $12 children, $36 families. Daily at 1.30pm weekdays, 12pm, 2pm & 3pm weekends & public & school holidays.*

2 ★ Walhalla's Star Hotel. Rebuilt in 1999 just after electricity was connected to the town, Walhalla's Star Hotel has 12 air-conditioned guest rooms, all of a good size, and some with verandas overlooking the street. There's

The quaint historic village of Walhalla.

also a restaurant and bar with wood fires for chilly nights, a cosy guest lounge with tea- and coffee-making facilities, a small library of books and CDs and a guest computer. Guest rooms are named after the old mines, and there's some clever use of corrugated iron in the bar and the guest rooms to give a very Australian look to them. *Main Rd. ☎ (03) 5165 6262. www.starhotel.com.au. Rates $199 double, including breakfast. No children under 12.*

The groovy bar at Walhalla's Star Hotel.

3 ★ Walhalla Goldfields Railway. Ride a steam train through lovely bushland from the historic town railway station to Thomson Station, 20 minutes down the line. The journey takes you across six trestle bridges over the lovely Stringers Creek Gorge, then winds down to cross the Thomson River Bridge. You get about 20 minutes to look around—which is plenty—before the return train departs. *⌚ 2 hr. ☎ (03) 9513 3969. www.walhallarail.com. Round-trip fares $18 adults, $13 children under 16, $40 families of 5. Wed, Sat, Sun & public holidays year-round; daily during summer school holidays. Trains depart Walhalla at 11am, 1pm & 3pm & return from Thomson at 11.40am, 1.40pm & 3.40pm. Last train service for the day does not operate June–Aug.*

The heritage-listed Walhalla Post & Telegraph Office.

4 **GreyHorse Café.** This place sells gourmet pies, pastries, cakes and great coffee. Enjoy the great view of Walhalla from the large deck. *Daily, 10.30am–3pm summer & 11am–2pm winter. $.*

5 **Walhalla Post & Telegraph Office.** The elegant heritage-listed post office, built in early 1886, survived the fire of 1888 that destroyed 30 buildings in the town, and a massive flood in 1891. It served the town until 1963, when the postmistress, Doreen Hannan, made it her home; she lived there until her death in 1988. A major restoration project for the building is being planned, but until it's complete, the building can

The Town Walk

The best way to see everything Walhalla has to offer is simply to step into the street and go for a walk. Mud maps of the town walk are available from the Star Hotel and the museum, and there's plenty to see. The **Freemason's Lodge** (1866), originally a Wesleyan church, is one of Walhalla's oldest buildings. **St John's Church of England** dates from 1918. On the roadside near the store is the old bank vault of the **Bank of Victoria**—it held gold from the mine—which was destroyed by fire in 1945. The **fire station**, straddling Stringer's Creek, is now a museum, with old fire-fighting equipment and photographs of the town's history. Opposite the Star Hotel is the **band rotunda** (c. 1896), once used by the Walhalla Mountaineers' Brass Band. Beyond the hotel and rotunda are several quaint cottages, including a former miner's home known as **Spett's Cottage** (c. 1871). If you have plenty of energy, take the track up the hill to the **Walhalla cricket ground**—the only place the town's cricketers could level off some land, with the advantage that the 30-minute climb up the knoll just before the match was said to ensure a home team victory over opposing teams unused to the added exertion! For a bird's-eye view of the town, take the **Tramline Walkway** from the Long Tunnel Extended Gold Mine and walk the length of the town from high on the hill. You can descend at two points, at about the halfway point near the rotunda or further along, near the General Store. The **General Store** (Main Rd; ☎ (03) 5165 6250) serves as post office, museum and information centre. It's open daily 10am to 4pm and until 5pm on Saturdays.

The gardens of Walhalla burst into colour in spring.

only be admired from the outside. *Main Rd.*

❻ **Walhalla Cemetery.** The graves and ghosts of long-gone miners inhabit a steep hillside at the edge of town. A wander along the terraced paths among the (sometimes ornate) headstones is a good reminder of how harsh life was for goldminers and their families. The cemetery dates back to 1872 and is laid out according to religion.

❼ **Australian Alps Walking Track.** This track runs 650km (403 miles) from Canberra to Walhalla, but the best option for visitors is the two-day guided 40km walk developed by the Star Hotel and the nearby Mt Baw Baw Alpine Resort. The walk starts with a transfer from Walhalla to Mt Baw Baw for dinner and an overnight stay at the resort. One night is spent in a bush camp (sleeping bag and tent provided) and the last night finishes with dinner and a bed at the Star Hotel. The cost is $980 per person twin share, including hotel accommodation and all meals along the way. The bush campsite is fully equipped, so there's no need to carry heavy backpacks. ☎ *(03) 5165 6262. www.greatwalhallaalpinetrail.com.* ●

Practical Matters: Walhalla

The General Store (Main Rd; ☎ (03) 5165 6250 or 1800 621 409) serves as post office, museum and information centre. It's open daily 10am-4pm and until 5pm on Saturdays. The website www.walhalla.org.au is a good source of information, as is www.visitwalhalla.com.au.

The Savvy Traveller

Before You Go

Tourist Offices

Tourism Australia's website, www.australia.com, has more than 10 000 pages of listings of tour operators, hotels, car-rental companies, special travel outfitters, holiday packages, maps, distance charts, suggested itineraries and much more. Sign up for the free e-newsletter and you'll receive regular updates on hot deals and events. You can also order brochures online. Tourism Australia operates a website only, no telephone lines. The **Melbourne Visitor Centre**'s website, www.thatsmelbourne.com.au, and **Tourism Victoria**'s sites, www.visitvictoria.com and www.visitmelbourne.com, are also good sources of planning information.

The Best Time to Go

Melbourne's changeable weather can be difficult to predict at any time of year, but for me the best weather is in spring and summer, from September through to March. Winters can be grey, wet and bleak, and summer can be very hot, though without the humidity that plagues so much of Australia. But even in winter, temperatures rarely dip below freezing, and snow falls only in the Victorian ski fields, not in Melbourne. Peak season is from Christmas Day to the end of January, when schools are on summer holiday.

Festivals & Special Events

Australia Day, on January 26, is a national holiday marking the landing of the First Fleet of convicts at Sydney in 1788.

Over four days in the first or second week of March, Melbourne hosts the first event on the year's international FIA Formula One World Championship circuit. The **Australian Formula One Grand Prix** is battled out at Albert Park; surrounding streets may be closed. For tickets, contact Ticketek ☎ 132 849 or book online at http://cars.grandprix.com.au.

Anzac Day, April 25, is Australia's national day of mourning for servicemen and women who have died in wars and conflict. Melbourne's major commemorative event is the dawn service, held at the Shrine of Remembrance. Thousands turn out. It's followed by a street parade for returned servicemen and women through the city centre. Details of services can be found at www.dva.gov.au/commem/anzac.

On the first Tuesday of every November, Melbourne is home to 'the race that stops the nation'—literally. **Melbourne Cup Day** is a public holiday in the city (but not nationwide). The race is held at Flemington racecourse, and at race time, 3.20pm, the city seems to freeze as everyone focuses on just one thing. For tickets, contact Ticketmaster (☎ 1300 136 122; www.ticketmaster.com.au); for information, visit www.vrc.net.au.

The Weather

Dial ☎ 1196 for recorded weather information, or visit the Bureau of Meteorology website, www.bom.gov.au.

Previous page: Trams on Swanston Street.

MELBOURNE'S AVERAGE TEMPERATURE & RAINFALL

	JAN	FEB	MAR	APR	MAY	JUN
Daily temp (°C)	26	26	24	20	17	14
Daily temp (°F)	79	79	75	68	63	57
Days of Precipitation	5	5	6	6	8	8
	JUL	**AUG**	**SEP**	**OCT**	**NOV**	**DEC**
Daily temp (°C)	13	14	17	19	22	24
Daily temp (°F)	55	57	63	66	70	75
Days of Precipitation	8	10	9	9	8	6

Useful Websites

- CitySearch Melbourne: http://melbourne.citysearch.com.au
- The official City of Melbourne site: www.melbourne.vic.gov.au
- Tourism Victoria's website: www.visitvictoria.com
- The official tourism site for the city: www.visitmelbourne.com
- Also worth a look is the locally run site www.onlymelbourne.com.au
- Parks Victoria's site has information about national parks: www.parkweb.vic.gov.au

Cell Phones (Mobiles)

Cell phones are widely called 'mobiles' in Australia. Most Australians use GSM cell phones (GSM stands for 'Global System for Mobile Communications'), so if yours is on a GSM system you should have no problems. Just call your phone company and ask for international roaming to be activated on your account. If you want to rent a phone, **Vodafone** (☎ 1300 365 360; www.vodarent.com.au) has an outlet at Melbourne Airport. Rental costs $5 to $8 a day, plus call charges and insurance. You can also rent a SIM card for $1 a day or $15 a month.

Visa Requirements

All visitors except those from New Zealand need a visa to enter Australia. Short-term visitors and business travellers can apply online for an Electronic Travel Authority (ETA) at www.eta.immi.gov.au. This is an electronic visa that takes the place of a stamp in your passport. ETAs are free, but there's a $20 service charge for applying online. You can also apply for the visa at Australian embassies, high commissions and consulates. Children travelling on a parent's passport must have their own ETA.

Getting **There**

By Plane

Melbourne Airport's international and domestic terminals (www.melair.com.au) are all under one roof at Tullamarine, 22km from the city. Domestic airlines Qantas and Virgin Blue have their desks and gate lounges here. Low-cost carrier Tiger Airways has a separate terminal next door, distinguished by the tiger-striped water tower landmark outside it. **Qantas** (☎ 131 313; www.qantas.com.au) and **Virgin Blue** (☎ 136 789; www.virginblue.com.au) both fly to Melbourne from all state capitals. Qantas's discount arm, **Jetstar** (☎ 131 538; www.jetstar.com.au), flies to and from Darwin, Townsville, Hamilton Island, the Sunshine and Gold coasts and Hobart. Jetstar also flies between Avalon Airport, about a 50-minute drive outside Melbourne's city centre, and Sydney, Brisbane, Perth and Adelaide. There's a shuttle bus that runs from Avalon to Melbourne. **Tiger Airways** (☎ (03) 9335 3033; www.tigerairways.com.au) has its hub in Melbourne, and from there flies to Adelaide, Alice Springs, Canberra, Perth, Hobart and Launceston in Tasmania, Mackay, Rockhampton, and the Gold and Sunshine coasts in Queensland. Tiger has a travellers' information desk on the ground floor of the international terminal that's open from 6am until the last flight. Baggage carts are free in the international baggage claim hall, but cost $3 in the car park, departure lounge and domestic terminal. The **Hilton Melbourne Airport** (☎ (03) 8336 2000) and **Holiday Inn Melbourne Airport** (☎ 138 388) are both within five minutes' walk of the terminals.

By Car

You can drive from Sydney to Melbourne along the Hume Highway (a straight trip of about 9½ hours), via Goulburn in New South Wales and Wangaratta in Victoria. Alternatively, drive along the coastal Princes Highway, for which you will need a minimum of two days, with stops. For information on all aspects of road travel in Victoria, contact the **Royal Automotive Club of Victoria** (RACV; ☎ 131 329, www.racv.com.au).

By Train

Interstate trains arrive at **Southern Cross Railway Station** on the corner of Spencer and Little Collins streets in the city centre. You'll still hear locals refer to this as Spencer Street Station, as it was only renamed Southern Cross in 2006. Taxis and buses connect with the city.

The Sydney–Melbourne **XPT** (express passenger train) travels between Australia's two largest cities daily; it's an 11-hour trip. Contact Countrylink (☎ 132 232; www.countrylink.info) for details.

The Overland train provides a daylight service between Melbourne and Adelaide three times a week (trip time: just under 11 hours). Contact Great Southern Railways (☎ 132 147; www.gsr.com.au).

V/Line services also connect Melbourne with Adelaide, via train from Melbourne to Bendigo, and then by bus from Bendigo to Adelaide. Total trip time is around 11 hours. The **Canberra Link** connects Melbourne with the nation's capital via train from Melbourne to Albury, and via bus from there to Canberra. The journey takes around 12 hours. Contact V/Line (☎ 136 196; www.vline.com.au).

By Bus

Several bus companies connect Melbourne with other capitals and regional areas of Victoria. One of the biggest is **Greyhound Australia** (☎ 1300 473 946; www.greyhound.com.au). Coaches stop at Melbourne's Transit Centre, 58 Franklin Street, two blocks north of the Southern Cross Railway Station in Spencer Street. Trams and taxis serve the station; **V/Line buses** (☎ 136 196; www.vline.com.au), which travel all over Victoria, depart from the Spencer Street Coach Terminal.

Getting Around

By Tram & Train

The free **City Circle Tram** is the best way to get around the city centre. These burgundy-and-cream trams travel a circular route between all the major central attractions and past shopping malls and arcades. The trams run in both directions every 12 minutes between 10am and 6pm (and until 9pm Thursday to Saturday). The route takes all the major thoroughfares, including Flinders and Spencer streets. Burgundy signs mark the City Circle Tram stops.

Normal trams stop at numbered green-and-gold tram-stop signs, sometimes in the middle of the road (so beware of oncoming traffic!). To get off the tram, press the button near the handrails or pull the cord above your head.

You can buy **Metcard** tickets at ticket machines on trams, at special ticket offices (such as at the tram terminal on Elizabeth Street near the corner of Flinders Street), at most newsagents, and at Metcard vending machines at railway stations. Vending machines on trams only accept coins—but give change—whereas the larger machines at train stations accept coins and notes and give change up to $10. If you plan to pack in the sightseeing, the best buy is a **Zone 1 daily Metcard**, which allows travel on all transport (trams, trains and buses) within the city and inner suburbs for a full day. A Metcard needs to be validated by a machine either on the tram, on the station platform or on the bus before each journey; the only exception to this is when you purchase Metcards from vending machines on trams—they are automatically validated for that journey. You can pick up a free public transport route map from the Melbourne Visitor Centre in Federation Square or the **Met Information Centre**, 103 Elizabeth Street, at the corner of Collins Street (☎ 131 638; www.metlinkmelbourne.com.au), which is open Monday through Friday from 8.30am to 4.30pm, and Saturday from 9am to 1pm.

By Bus

The free **Melbourne City Tourist Shuttle** operates buses that pick up and drop off at 11 stops around the city, including the Melbourne Museum, Queen Victoria Market, Immigration Museum, Southbank Arts Precinct, the Shrine of Remembrance and Botanic Gardens, Chinatown, Flinders Lane, and many other attractions. You can hop on and off during the day. The whole loop takes about an hour non-stop, and there's a commentary. The bus runs every 15 minutes from 9.30am until 4.30pm daily (except Christmas Day and Good Friday). *See p. 16.*

By Taxi

Cabs are plentiful in the city, but it may be difficult to hail one in the city centre late on Friday and Saturday nights. Taxi companies include **Silver Top** (☎ 131 008), **Embassy** (☎ 131 755) and **Yellow Cabs** (☎ 132 227). After 10pm on Friday and Saturday nights you must pay an estimated fare in advance.

By Car

Melbourne's roads can be confusing. With trams to negotiate, there's a rule that you must turn right from the left lane at some major intersections in the city centre—called a 'hook turn'—to leave the right lane free for trams and through traffic. You must always stop behind a tram if it stops, because passengers usually step directly into the road.

On Foot

Many of Melbourne's main attractions are within a comfortable distance of each other in the CBD or close to it. It's a relatively flat city, and easy to walk around.

Fast Facts

APARTMENT RENTALS Several of Australia's major serviced apartment chains have Melbourne accommodation, including **Medina Serviced Apartments** (☎ 1300 633 462; www.medinaapartments.com.au) and **Quest Serviced Apartments** (☎ 1800 334 033; www.questapartments.com.au).

ATMS ATMs are widely available throughout Melbourne. Go to your card's website to find ATM locations. Many banks impose a fee every time you use a card at another bank's ATM. The fee can be up to around $5 for international transactions and is usually $2 for domestic ones.

BANKING HOURS Most banks are open Monday to Thursday from 9.30am to 4pm and until 5pm on Fridays, but some offer extended hours and some are open on Saturday mornings.

B&BS Reasonably priced B&Bs are widely available. A good source is *The Australian Bed & Breakfast Book* (☎ (02) 8208 5959; www.bbbook.com.au), which lists more than 400 B&Bs. The book can be purchased from the website and is widely available in bookshops and at newsagents. What Next? Productions (☎ 0438 600 696; www.beautifulaccommodation.com) publishes a series of *Beautiful Accommodation* guides listing around 500 properties. The book sells for $30 in bookstores or online.

The website of **Bed & Breakfast and Farmstay Australia**, www.australianbedandbreakfast.com.au, has links to all state B&B organisations.

BUSINESS HOURS Shops are usually open Monday to Wednesday and Saturday from 9am to 5.30pm, on Thursday from 9am to 6pm, on Friday from 9am to 9pm, and on Sunday from 10am to 5pm. Large department stores usually stay open a little later: until 7pm on Thursday and until 6pm Monday to Wednesday, Saturday and Sunday.

CONSULATES & EMBASSIES All of the following have consulates in Melbourne: **United States**, Level 6, 553 St Kilda Road (☎ (03) 9526 5900); **United Kingdom**, Level 17, 90 Collins Street (☎ (03) 9652 1600); **New Zealand**, Level 3, 350 Collins Street (☎ (03) 9642 1279); **Ireland**, 295 Queen Street (☎ (03) 9397 8940); and **Canada**, Level 27, 101 Collins Street (☎ (03) 9653 9674).

CREDIT CARDS Visa and MasterCard are universally accepted in Australia; American Express and Diners Club less so. Always carry a little cash, because many traders will not take cards for purchases under $15 or so.

CUSTOMS The duty-free allowance in Australia is $900 or, for those under 18, $450. Anyone over 18 can bring in up to 250 cigarettes or 250g of cigars or other tobacco products, and 2.25L of alcohol. A helpful brochure is Know Before You Go, available from Australian consulates, Customs offices and online. For more information, contact the **Customs Information and Support Centre** (☎ 1300 363 263; www.customs.gov.au).

Australia has strict quarantine regulations. For information on what is and isn't allowed, contact the nearest Australian embassy or consulate, or the **Australian Quarantine and Inspection Service** (☎ (02) 6272 3933; www.affa.gov.au). Its website has a list of restricted or banned foods, animal and plant products and other items.

DENTISTS Call the **Dental Emergency Service** (☎ (03) 9341 1040) for an emergency referral to a local dentist.

DOCTORS The casualty department at the **Royal Melbourne Hospital**, Grattan Street, Parkville (☎ (03) 9342 7000), responds to emergencies. The **Traveller's Medical & Vaccination Centre** (2nd Flr, 393 Little Bourke St; ☎ (03) 9602 5788) offers full vaccination and travel medical services.

ELECTRICITY In Australia, the current is 240 volts AC, 50 hertz. Sockets take two or three flat prongs. North Americans and Europeans will need to buy a converter before leaving home (don't wait until you get to Australia; stores are likely to stock only converters for appliances to fit American and European outlets). Some large hotels have 110V outlets for electric shavers (or dual voltage), and some will lend converters, but don't count on it. Power does not start automatically when you plug in an appliance; you need to flick the switch beside the socket to the 'on' position.

EMERGENCIES Dial ☎ 000 for the police, an ambulance or the fire department.

FAMILY TRAVEL International airlines and domestic airlines in Australia charge 75 per cent of the adult fare for kids under 12. Most charge 10 per cent for infants under 2 not occupying a seat. Australian transport companies, attractions, and tour operators typically charge half-price for kids under 12 or 14 years. Children entering Australia on a parent's passport still need their own visa.

GAY & LESBIAN TRAVELLERS The **Gay & Lesbian Counselling and Community Service** runs a national hotline (☎ 1800 184 527; www.glccs.org.au) every day from 7.30pm to 10pm. **Gay & Lesbian Tourism Australia** (www.galta.com.au) has listings of gay-friendly businesses in each state.

HOLIDAYS The major public holidays—when almost everything shuts down—are New Year's Day (January 1), Good Friday, Easter Sunday and Easter Monday, Christmas Day (December 25) and Boxing Day (December 26). On Anzac Day (April 25, a war veterans' commemorative day), most shops and all government departments are closed, but some tourist attractions reopen at around 1pm. Australia Day (January 26) is a national public holiday. Melbourne Cup Day (on the first Tuesday in November) is a public holiday in Melbourne city only.

INSURANCE Trip-cancellation insurance will help you get your money back if you have to pull out of a trip or depart early, or if your travel supplier goes bankrupt. Trip cancellation traditionally covers such events as sickness, natural disasters and government advisories. The latest news in trip-cancellation insurance is the availability of 'any-reason' cancellation coverage—which costs more but covers cancellations made for any reason. You won't get back 100 per cent of your prepaid trip cost, but you'll be refunded a substantial portion. The cost of travel insurance varies widely, depending on the cost and length of your trip, your age and health and the type of trip you're taking. Read the fine print and ask lots of questions. Travellers and their families who make more than one trip per year may find an annual travel insurance policy works out cheaper.

Travel medical insurance is also a good idea. A brochure is available at airports or through travel agents, listing countries that have reciprocal rights with Australia for Medicare-style services. The Insurance Council of Australia advises travellers to consider three points when choosing a policy. First, look out for exclusions that help keep the premium low, but may affect your ability to claim successfully. Second, ensure the policy meets all your needs and provides the right level of cover. Third, make sure you are provided with an international emergency contact number.

If you're planning to rely on the travel insurance provided by your credit card, you should get written confirmation of exactly what the insurance covers, the period of time you will be covered and what conditions are attached. Don't assume that by having a credit card you're entitled to immediate coverage when you leave the country.

Most US health plans (including Medicare and Medicaid) do not provide international coverage, and the ones that do often require you to pay for services upfront and be reimbursed when you return home. Americans requiring additional medical insurance can try **MEDEX Assistance** (☎ (410) 453 6300; www.medexassist.com) or **Travel Assistance International** (☎ (800) 821 2828; www.travelassistance.com). Canadians should check with their provincial health plan offices or call **Health Canada** (☎ (866) 225-0709; www.hc-sc.gc.ca) to find out the extent of their coverage and what documentation and receipts they must take home if they're treated overseas. Travellers from the UK should carry their European Health Insurance Card (EHIC) as proof of entitlement to free/reduced cost medical treatment abroad (☎ (0845) 606 2030; www.ehic.org.uk). The **Association of British Insurers** (☎ (020) 7600 3333; www.abi.org.uk) gives advice by phone and publishes Holiday Insurance, a free guide to policy provisions and prices.

INTERNET ACCESS There are many internet cafes along Elizabeth Street, around Flinders Lane and in Little Bourke Street in Chinatown. Most are open from early in the morning until well into the night. The State Library in Swanston Street and other public libraries also offer internet access.

LOST PROPERTY Contact the nearest police station or visit Melbourne Town Hall, Swanston Street (☎ (03) 9658 9779), about lost property. If you lose something on a tram, call ☎ 1800 800 166 between 6am and 10pm; on a train, call ☎ (03) 9610 7512 between 9am and 5pm weekdays (including public holidays).

MAIL & POSTAGE The **General Post Office** (GPO) at 250 Elizabeth Street (☎ 131 318) is open Monday to Friday from 8.30am to 5.30pm, Saturday from 9am to 4pm, and Sun from 10am to 4pm. It costs 55¢ to post a letter within Australia.

MONEY The Australian dollar is divided into 100¢. Coins are 5¢, 10¢, 20¢ and 50¢ pieces (silver) and $1 and $2 pieces (gold). Prices often end in a variant of 1¢ and 2¢ (for example, 78¢ or $2.71), a relic from the days before 1¢ and 2¢ pieces were phased out. The total amount of your purchases is rounded to the nearest 5¢. Banknotes come in denominations of $5, $10, $20, $50 and $100.

PARKING Parking in Melbourne's city centre can be difficult and expensive. If you are planning to have a vehicle, check if your hotel has free parking or offers a special deal. There are lots of large commercial car parks, as well as metered parking on the streets. Casual parking fees in parking buildings can be around $13 an hour or $50 a day. Take the tram instead!

PASSES The **See Melbourne & Beyond Smartvisit Card** (☎ 1300 661 711; www.seemelbournecard.com) provides entry to many of the city's major attractions, including the Old Melbourne Gaol, and to a range of Victoria's best regional sights, such as the Phillip Island Penguin Parade and Ballarat's Sovereign Hill. Cards can be purchased for one, two, three or seven consecutive days, starting from $69 for adults and $49 for children between 4 and 15 for one day. A seven-day card costs $205 for adults and $135 for children.

PASSPORTS Visitors from all nations except New Zealand need a visa to enter Australia. Short-term visitors and business travellers can apply for an Electronic Travel Authority (ETA) on the internet at the Australian government site www.eta.immi.gov.au. You can also apply for the visa at Australian embassies, high commissions and consulates. Children travelling on a parent's passport must have their own ETA. US, Canadian, British and Irish citizens aged from 18 to 30 may qualify for a working holiday visa that allows them to stay and work in Australia for a year (with conditions).

PHARMACIES One inner-city pharmacy that has extended hours is **Mulqueeny Pharmacy**, on the corner of Swanston and Collins streets (☎ (03) 9654 8569). Mon–Fri 8am–8pm, Sat 9am–6pm, Sun 11am–6pm.

SAFETY Driving probably poses one of the greatest risks to international visitors to Australia. Australians drive on the left, and by law, drivers and passengers, including taxi passengers, must wear a seatbelt at all times. It's generally risky to walk alone at night, as in most big cities. In particular, the inner-city King Street nightclub precinct has often been the scene of violence in recent years.

SENIOR TRAVELLERS Seniors from other countries don't always qualify for the discounted entry prices to tours, attractions and events that Australian seniors—often called 'pensioners'—enjoy, but it's always worth asking. The best ID to bring is something that shows your date of birth or that marks you as an 'official' senior, like a membership card from AARP.

SMOKING Smoking is banned in most public areas, including airports, museums, cinemas and theatres, as well as in restaurants, pubs and clubs. Some venues have rooftop bars where smokers can puff away in the open air.

TAXES Australia applies a 10 per cent Goods and Services Tax (GST) on most products and services. Through the **Tourist Refund Scheme** (TRS), you can claim a refund of the GST you paid on any purchase of more than $300 from a single outlet within the last 30 days before you leave the country. (You can also claim a refund of a 14.5 per cent wine tax called the 'Wine Equalisation Tax' or 'WET', under the same conditions.) Just present your receipt (aka 'tax invoice') to the TRS booths in the International Terminal departure areas at the airport. Pack the items in your carry-on baggage, because you'll have to show them to Customs. You can use the goods before you leave Australia and still claim the refund, but you can't claim for things you've used up (such as film or food). You cannot claim a refund on alcohol other than wine.

TAXIS Taxi companies include **Silver Top** (☎ 131 008), **Embassy** (☎ 131 755) and **Yellow Cabs** (☎ 132 227).

TELEPHONE The area code for Victoria is (03) and you must use this if you are calling a Victorian number from outside the state. To make international calls, dial 0011 and then the country code, followed by the area code and number. For directory assistance, ☎ 12455 for a number in Australia, and ☎ 1225 for other countries. Australian numbers beginning with 1800 are toll-free, and those starting with 13 or 1300 are charged at the local fee of 30c. The cost of a local call from a payphone is 50c, either in coins or with a phone card. Some phones only take prepaid phone cards, which can be purchased from newsagents.

TICKETS The two major ticketing outlets are **Ticketek** (☎ 132 849; www.ticketek.com.au) and **Ticketmaster** (☎ 136 100; www.ticketmaster.com.au). Cheap tickets for the opera and other arts events can be bought on the day of the performance from the **Half-Tix Desk** (www.halftixmelbourne.com) in the Melbourne Town Hall, Swanston Street. The booth is open on Monday from 10am to 2pm, between Tuesday and Thursday from 11am to 6pm, on Friday from 11am to 6.30pm and on Saturday from 10am to 4pm. Tickets must be purchased in person and paid for with cash.

TIPPING Tipping is not expected in Australia. If you choose to tip, around 10 per cent is the usual percentage, or you can round up to the nearest $10 for a substantial meal in a family restaurant. Some passengers tip in a cab, but it's okay to wait for your change. People sometimes tip hotel porters, but no-one tips bar staff, barbers or hairdressers.

TOURIST INFORMATION The **Melbourne Visitor Centre** in Federation Square (cnr Swanston & Flinders sts; ☎ (03) 9658 9658; www.thatsmelbourne.com.au) is a one-stop shop for information, accommodation and tour bookings, event ticketing, public transport information and ticket sales. It also has an ATM and internet terminals. It's open daily 9am to 6pm. The Melbourne Greeter Service also operates from here, connecting visitors to local volunteers who offer free one-on-one half-day orientation tours of the city, starting at 10am daily. Bookings ☎ (03) 9658 9658. In the city centre look for **Melbourne's City Ambassadors**, who give tourist information and directions. They wear bright red shirts and caps. The official tourism site for the city is www.visitmelbourne.com.

TRAVELLERS WITH DISABILITIES For information on all kinds of facilities and services for people with disabilities, contact **National Information Communication Awareness Network** (☎ 1800 806 769 voice and TTY; www.nican.com.au). This free service can put you in touch with accessible accommodation and attractions, as well as with travel agents and tour operators who understand your needs.

Melbourne: **A Brief History**

1835 Melbourne's Indigenous Kulin people, who had lived here for about 40 000 years, witness the arrival of the first European settlers. John Batman sails up the Yarra and buys 600 000 acres of land from eight Aboriginal leaders. Later that year, the ship *Enterprize*, chartered by John Pascoe Fawkner, lands along the Yarra and establishes the first settlement.

1836 Settlers establish their own de facto government; the town they've called 'Bearbrass' has 13 buildings and a population of 142 males and 35 females.

1837 First allotments of land put up for sale. The new settlement is named after Viscount Melbourne, the British Prime Minister.

1838 Melbourne Cricket Club founded.

1839 Charles Joseph La Trobe arrives as Superintendent of Port Phillip District.

1842 Melbourne is declared a municipality and elections for the first council are held.

1847 Queen Victoria declares Melbourne a city.

1851 Port Phillip District separates from the colony of New South Wales and the colony is renamed Victoria, in honour of the Queen.

1853 University of Melbourne is founded, and Melbourne Cricket Ground (MCG) is proclaimed.

1854 Flinders Street Station building is completed. State Library is founded.

1860 Burke and Wills leave Melbourne on their journey of exploration into Central Australia.

1861 First Melbourne Cup horse race is held at Flemington.

1861 State funeral for Burke and Wills, with a crowd of more than 40 000 attending.

1877 First season of Victorian Football Association.

1879 Electricity is used to light a football match at the MCG.

1880 Melbourne International Exhibition is held in the newly completed Royal Exhibition Building, and bushranger Ned Kelly is hanged at Old Melbourne Gaol.

1885 First cable tram operates between Melbourne and Richmond.

1901 Opening of Federal Parliament in Melbourne at the Royal Exhibition Building. Melbourne remains the seat of Federal Government until 1927.

1905 First Australian Open tennis championships held.

1919 First electric train runs from Flinders Street to Essendon.

1923 Electrification of cable trams.

1927 Canberra replaces Melbourne as the national capital.

1928 Melbourne's population reaches one million.

1956 Olympic Games held in Melbourne. First television transmission.

1964 A civic reception for The Beatles is held in the Town Hall.

1968 Work commences on the West Gate Bridge.

1970 A section of the West Gate Bridge collapses, killing 15 men. Vietnam War protest marches see 70 000 people take to the streets.

1983 On February 8, a massive dust storm sweeps across Victoria, hitting Melbourne and reducing visibility in city streets to 100 metres. Temperatures reach over 43 degrees. It is a precursor to the devastating Ash Wednesday bushfires, which follow a week later. Huge tracts of land are razed across Victoria, with affected areas including the Dandenong Ranges, the Macedon Ranges, and towns along the Great Ocean Road, such as Aireys Inlet, Anglesea and Lorne. Forty-seven people are killed, including 14 fire-fighters, and thousands lose their homes.

1986 A car bombing outside the Russell Street Police Headquarters kills a police officer, injures another 22 people and causes more than $1 million worth of damage to buildings.

1986 The theft of Picasso's *Weeping Woman* from the National Gallery of Victoria makes international headlines. The painting was left in a locker at Spencer Street (now Southern Cross) railway station less than three weeks later. The thieves, a group known as the Australian Cultural Terrorists, threatened to burn the $1.6 million painting, the most expensive the gallery had bought, unless arts funding was increased by 10 per cent over three years and a $25 000 annual art prize called the Picasso Ransom established. The government rejected the demands. The thieves were never caught.

1987 A gunman kills seven and injures 19 in the Hoddle Street Massacre; later in the year eight are killed and five injured in the Queen Street Massacre.

1990 Southbank promenade opens, paving the way for urban renewal in Southbank.

1996 First Formula One Grand Prix is held at Albert Park.

1997 Crown Casino and Entertainment Complex, Melbourne's first gambling centre, opens.

2002 Federation Square opens.

2006 Melbourne hosts the Commonwealth Games.

2006 The Eureka Tower opens, becoming the world's second tallest residential building. It stands 297.3m high, with 91 storeys, one of only six buildings in the world with 90 or more storeys.

Melbourne **on Page & Screen**

The first Australian literature, penned by bush poets AB 'Banjo' Paterson and Henry Lawson, still provides an insight into the country; the best known of their works is Paterson's epic poem 'The Man from Snowy River', which first hit the bestseller list in 1895 and was made into a film in 1982. It's set in Victoria's high country.

The Australian literary scene has always been lively, and you can find many books about Melbourne—both fiction and non-fiction—to deepen your knowledge of the city and of Australia as a whole.

For history buffs, *The Birth of Melbourne* (Text Publishing, 2002) is an anthology of writing from Melbourne's inhabitants—Aboriginal elders, Chinese immigrants, convicts, politicians and more. It's a fascinating read, and was edited by the 2007 Australian of the Year, Melbourne-born Tim Flannery. Also interesting is *Yarra—A Diverting History of Melbourne's Murky River* by Kristin Otto (Text Publishing, 2005). For a wider view of Australia's history, *The Long Farewell* (Penguin Books, 1983) by Don Charlwood—if you can find it—presents firsthand diary accounts of long journeys from Europe to Australia in the last century. A good historical account of Australia's early days is Geoffrey Blainey's *The Tyranny of Distance* (Pan Macmillan, 1977), first published in 1966. Robert Hughes's *The Fatal Shore—The Epic of Australia's Founding* (Vintage Books, 1988) is a best-selling history later adapted into the award-wininng play, *Our Country's Good*.

Perhaps the most famous novel about Melbourne life is Frank Hardy's 1950 book *Power Without Glory*, which caused a sensation when it was released and was the subject of a famous defamation case. A thinly veiled description of the rise to power of real-life figure John Wren, it was originally self-published but was later released by Random House and is still in print. It's considered by many to be one of the most influential novels in Australian history.

Another Australian classic is Joan Lindsay's 1967 mystery *Picnic at Hanging Rock*, first published by FW Cheshire and later made famous by the movie adaptation of the same name by director Peter Weir. The evocative movie, set in the Macedon Ranges (see p. 152), was released in 1975 and gained such status that many believe the story to be true (which it is not).

Contemporary Australian writers worth seeking out include Melbournian Helen Garner, David Malouf, Elizabeth Jolley, Sue Woolfe, Tim Winton and Peter Carey, whose *True History of the Kelly Gang* (Vintage Books, 2001), a fictionalised autobiography of the Victorian outlaw Ned Kelly, won the Booker Prize in 2001. For a non-fiction look at the bushranger, tackle *Ned Kelly—A Short Life*, by Ian Jones (Lothian Books, 2003).

Outsiders who have written about Australia include Bill Bryson, who wrote *Down Under* (Black Swan, 2001; published in the US as *In a Sunburned Country*, Broadway Books, 2001). While not always a favourite with Australians, it may appeal to international readers.

A Year in Melbourne: **Major Events**

JANUARY

Australian Open tennis, Melbourne Park Tennis Centre. Tennis greats—and fans—from around the world converge for this major event on the world circuit. *See p. 42, bullet* ❸.

St Kilda Festival, Fitzroy Street, St Kilda Beach and surrounds. St Kilda jumps for nine days with live bands, entertainment, dining and family activities. The biggest is Festival Day, when streets are closed and thronged with people. *www.stkildafestival.com.au. See p. 51*.

Midsumma, Melbourne's premier gay and lesbian arts and cultural festival, runs from mid-January to early February. *www.midsumma.org.au*.

FEBRUARY

Chinese New Year Festival, Chinatown. Melbourne's Chinese community celebrates with events including dragon parades, cultural performances and food stalls, usually over two days.

MARCH

Australian Formula One Grand Prix held at Albert Park. Rev-heads rejoice at the roar of engines as some of the fastest drivers in the world compete on this street circuit. *www.grandprix.com.au. See p. 43, bullet* ❽.

AFL season starts. Melbournians unleash their passion for 'footy'—and it's a winter-long fixation, leading up to Grand Final weekend in September. *See p. 42, bullet* ❺.

APRIL

Melbourne International Comedy Festival. *www.comedyfestival.com.au. See p. 111*.

ANZAC Day, war commemorations at the Shrine of Remembrance, April 25. *See p. 13, bullet* ❷.

JULY

Melbourne International Film Festival, late July to mid-August. Features a mix of new releases, shorts, and avant-garde movies at venues around the city. *www.melbournefilmfestival.com.au. See p. 111*.

AUGUST

Melbourne Writers Festival runs for 10 days, with a host of international and Australian talent, including some of the big names of the literary world. *www.mwf.com.au*.

SEPTEMBER

AFL Grand Final held on the last Saturday in September at the MCG. *See p. 42, bullet* ❺.

OCTOBER

Melbourne International Arts Festival runs for 17 days, with 600 performances. *www.melbournefestival.com.au. See p. 111*.

Melbourne Fringe Festival runs during the first three weeks of October. *www.melbournefringe.com.au. See p. 111*.

Lygon Street Festa, Carlton. *See p. 59*.

NOVEMBER

The Melbourne Cup runs at Flemington Racecourse on the first Tuesday of the month, as part of the annual Spring Racing Carnival. *www.vrc.net.au. See p. 43, bullet* ❼.

DECEMBER

Melbourne Boxing Day Cricket Test Match starts December 26 at the Melbourne Cricket Ground and runs for three or four days. *www.cricketvictoria.com.au*.

Phone Numbers & Websites

Airlines

AIR CANADA
☎ 1300 655 767 in Australia
☎ 888 247 2262 in the US and Canada
www.aircanada.com

AIR CHINA
☎ (03) 86025555 in Australia
☎ 4008 100 999 in China
☎ 1 718 751 2263 in the US
☎ 44 20 77440800 in the UK
www.airchina.com.cn

AIR NEW ZEALAND
☎ 132 476 in Australia
☎ 800 663 5494 in Canada
☎ 0800 737 000 in New Zealand
☎ 800 262 1234 in the US
www.airnewzealand.com

BRITISH AIRWAYS
☎ 1300 767 177 in Australia
☎ 0870 850 9850 in the UK
☎ 1890 626 747 in Ireland
www.britishairways.com

CATHAY PACIFIC
☎ 131 747 in Australia
☎ 020 8834 8888 in the UK
www.cathaypacific.com

EMIRATES
☎ 1300 303 777 in Australia
☎ 800 777 3999 in the US
www.emirates.com

ETIHAD AIRWAYS
☎ +971 2 6939711
☎ 800 2277 in the United Arab Emirates
www.etihadairways.com

JAPAN AIRLINES
☎ 1300 525 287 in Australia
☎ 0120 25 5971 in Japan
www.jal.com

JETSTAR
☎ 131 538 in Australia
☎ 0800 800 995 in New Zealand
www.jetstar.com.au

MALAYSIA AIRLINES
☎ 132 627 in Australia
☎ 0870 607 9090 in the UK and Ireland
www.malaysiaairlines.com.my

PACIFIC BLUE
☎ 131 645 in Australia
☎ 0800 670 000 in New Zealand
www.pacificblue.com.au

QANTAS
☎ 131 313 in Australia
☎ 800 227 4500 in the US and Canada
☎ 0845 774 7767 in the UK
☎ 1 407 3278 in Ireland
☎ 0800 808 767 in New Zealand
www.qantas.com.au

REX
☎ 131 713
www.rex.com.au

SINGAPORE AIRLINES
☎ 131 011 in Australia
☎ 0844 800 2380 in the UK
www.singaporeair.com

THAI AIRWAYS INTERNATIONAL
☎ 1300 651 960 in Australia
☎ 0870 6060 911 in the UK
www.thaiair.com

TIGER AIRWAYS
☎ (03) 9335 3033
www.tigerairways.com.au

UNITED AIRLINES
☎ 131 777 in Australia
☎ 800 538 2929 in the US and Canada
www.united.com

VIRGIN ATLANTIC
☎ 1300 727 340 in Australia
☎ 1 800 821 5438 in the US
☎ 0870 380 2007 in the UK
www.virgin-atlantic.com

VIRGIN BLUE
☎ 136 789
www.virginblue.com.au

Car Rental Agencies

AVIS
☎ 136 333 in Australia
☎ 800 331 1212 in the US and Canada
☎ 084 4581 8181 in the UK
☎ 0800 655 111 in New Zealand
www.avis.com

BUDGET
☎ 1300 362 848 in Australia
☎ 800 527 0700 in the US
☎ 087 0156 5656 in the UK
☎ 0800 283 438 in New Zealand
www.budget.com

EUROPCAR
☎ 1300 131 390 in Australia
☎ 877 940 6900 in the US and Canada
☎ 0870 607 5000 in the UK
☎ 0800 800 115 in New Zealand
www.europcar.com

HERTZ
☎ 133 039 in Australia
☎ 800 654 3001 in the US
☎ 0870 844 844 in the UK
☎ 0800 654 321 in New Zealand
www.hertz.com

RED SPOT
☎ 1300 668 810
www.redspotrentals.com.au

THRIFTY
☎ 1300 367 227 in Australia
☎ 918 669 2168 in the US
☎ (01494) 751 540 in the UK
☎ 0800 737 070 in New Zealand
www.thrifty.com

Index

See also Accommodation and Restaurant indexes, below.

D

E

L

M

N

O

Y

Z

Accommodation

Restaurants

Photo **Credits**

p. viii: © Richard Jupe; p. 4: © Eureka Skydeck Media Dept; p. 5: © Getty Images/Jack Atley; p. 6 © Richard Jupe; p. 7: © Getty Images/The Image Bank/Andy Caulfield; p. 9: © Richard Jupe; p. 10: © Sabina Hopfer; p. 11, top: © Andrew Lloyd 2007; p. 11, bottom: © Richard Jupe; p. 13: © Getty Images/William West; p. 14: © Richard Jupe; p. 15: © Richard Jupe; p. 16: © The Hotel Windsor; p. 17: © Richard Jupe; p. 20: © Southern Star Observation Wheel ; p. 21: © Richard Jupe; p. 22: © Richard Jupe; p. 23: © Photolibrary.com/Wayne Fogden; p. 25: © Museum Victoria Image Collections; p. 26: © AAP Image/Wildlight/Bill Bachman; p. 27: © Richard Jupe; p. 29: © National Gallery of Victoria; p. 30: © Lee Mylne; p. 31: © Heide Museum of Modern Art; p. 33: © Melbourne Aquarium; p. 34: © Melissa Hobbs; p. 35: © Newspix/News Ltd/Matthew Bouwmeester; p. 37: © Richard Jupe; p. 38: © National Trust of Australia (Vic); p. 39: Richard Jupe; p. 42: © Newspix/Alex Coppel; p. 43: © Melbourne Cricket Club; p. 45, top: © Fairfax Photo Library/Sandy Scheltema; p. 45, bottom: © Newspix/Bruce Magilton; p. 46: © Newspix/Smith Mark; p. 47: © Photolibrary.com/Yoshio Tomii Photo Studio; p. 49: © Sabina Hopfer; p. 50: © Richard Jupe; p. 51: © Veg Out Communications; p. 53: © Richard Jupe; p. 54: © Richard Jupe; p. 55: © Richard Jupe; p. 57: © Photolibrary.com/David Messent; p. 58: © Andrzej Gwizdalski; p. 59: © Richard Jupe; p. 61: © Richard Jupe; p. 62: © Richard Jupe; p. 63: © Richard Jupe; p. 64: © The Johnston Collection; p. 65: © Alice Euphemia; p. 66: © Design a Space; p. 68: © Richard Jupe; p. 69: © Richard Jupe; p. 70: © Richard Jupe; p. 71: © Richard Jupe; p. 72: © Richard Jupe; p. 73: © Fairfax Photo Library/Australian Financial Review/James Davies; p. 74: © Richard Jupe; p. 75: © Getty Images/Axiom Photographic Agency/Andrew Watson; p. 77: © Richard Jupe; p. 78: © Richard Jupe; p. 79: © Richard Jupe; p. 81: © Jason Nixon; p. 82: © Fairfax Photo Library/Sandy Scheltema; p. 83: © Newspix/Steven Crabtree; p. 85: © Richard Jupe; p. 85: © Richard Jupe; p. 86: © Richard Jupe; p. 87: © Vue de Monde; p. 91: © Brunetti; p. 92: © Sumangal Mishra; p. 93: © Chinta Ria Soul; p. 94: © Colonial Tramcar Restaurant; p. 95, top: © MoVida; p. 95, bottom: © Stalactites Restaurant; p. 96: © Richard Jupe; p. 97: © Richard Jupe; p. 100: © Richard Jupe; p. 101: © Double Happiness; p. 102: © Richard Jupe; p. 103: © Richard Jupe; p. 104: © Richard Jupe; p. 105: © Photolibrary.com/Kordcom Kordcom; p. 106: © Newspix/Richard Cisar-Wright; p. 109: © Melbourne Symphony Orchestra; p. 110: © AAP Image/William West; p. 111: Newspix/News Ltd; p. 112: © Richard Jupe; p. 113: © Richard Jupe; p. 114: © Richard Jupe; p. 115: © Richard Jupe; p. 116: © Newspix/David Geraghty; p. 117: © Adelphi ; p. 118: © Lyall Hotel and Spa; p. 121: © Cotterville B&B; p. 122: © Fairfax Photo Library/Marina Oliphant; p. 123: © Hotel Lindrum Melbourne; p. 124: © The Nunnery Guesthouse; p. 125: © Hotel Tolarno; p. 126: © Urban; p. 127: © Photolibrary.com/David Wall; p. 129: © AAP Image/Heronswood Gardens; p. 130, top: © See All Dolphin Swims; p. 130, bottom: © Fairfax Photo Library/James Davies; p. 131, top: © Cape Schanck Lighthouse; p. 131, bottom: © Peninsula Hot Springs; p. 132: © T'Gallant Vineyard, photo courtesy of Fosters Group Ltd; p. 133: © Fairfax Photo Library/Gary Medlicott; p. 135: © Lee Mylne; p. 136: © City of Ballarat; p. 137: © Photolibrary.com/Robin Smith; p. 139, top: © Parks Victoria; p. 139, bottom: © Parks Victoria Image Library; p. 140: © Photolibrary.com/Kevin Judd; p. 141: © Paperbark Café; p. 143: © Newspix/Nick Cubbin; p. 144: © Visions of Victoria; p. 145: © Zulisman Maksom; p. 146: © Photolibrary.com/Kordcom Kordcom; p. 149: © Photolibrary.com/Japan Travel Bureau; p. 150: © Lee Mylne; p. 151: © AAP Image/Phillip Quirk; p. 153: © Fairfax Photo Library/Andrew De la Rue; p. 154: © Tourism Macedon Ranges Inc./David Hannah; p. 155: © Macedon Ranges Tourism; p. 156: © Holgate Brewhouse; p. 158, top: © Lee Mylne; p. 158, bottom: © Lee Mylne; p. 159: © AAP Image/Patrick Horton; p. 160: © Michael Leaney; p. 161: © Newspix/Simon Schluter.